ENTREPRENEURIAL MARKETING

COMPETING BY CHALLENGING CONVENTIONS

D1282069

Ian Chaston

ıshed 2000 by
LLAN PRESS LTD
ıills, Basingstoke, Hampshire RG21 6XS
ındon
ɟanies and representatives
ıghout the world

ɟN 0–333–79298–X
ɟBN 0–333–79299–8

A catalogue record for this book is available
from the British Library.

10 9 8 7 6 5 4 3 2 1
09 08 07 06 05 04 03 02 01 00

Printed in Great Britain by
Creative Print & Design (Wales), Ebbw Vale

CONTENTS

PREFACE

The history of the twentieth century has been dominated by the emergence of the US as a global economic and subsequently a socio-political global leader. The American economic model is rooted in the proven strengths associated with the exploitation of mass production and mass marketing management philosophies, demonstrated by corporations such as Ford, General Motors, Procter & Gamble, Coca-Cola and McDonald's. The operations of such organisations have provided the foundations upon which the American business schools construct their approach to teaching. This teaching revolves around a central core hub which has subsequently become known as the classicist philosophy of strategic marketing management.

During the 1970s and 1980s, the appearance on the world stage of the new Pacific Rim 'Tiger' nations such as Japan and Taiwan had a dramatic impact on the performance of both the European and the American multinationals. Their reaction, ably aided by the guidance offered by academics and management gurus, was to carefully study the new enemy. From these activities they learned that new concepts such as Total Quality Management, Just In Time, employee empowerment, downsizing and process re-engineering were all required if the large Western corporations were ever to recover their share of lost sales in global markets.

Another stark reality which became apparent in the 1980s, however, was that the Western model of large firms providing the major source of jobs within countries was probably gone for ever. As this juncture, many of these nations began to realise that the small firms sector would have an increasingly important role in the provision of employment of future generations within these countries. Governments began to invest significant sums in the provision of small firm support services and universities began to expand their teaching programmes to assist the increasing number of small firm owner/managers who were becoming their most important source of students seeking relevant vocational education.

For a number of reasons, many academics found that it was quite difficult retaining the respect of their colleagues if they described their new teaching and research activities as being concerned with small firms. The apparent solution has been to create professorial chairs and open new departments committed to the subject of entrepreneurship. As a result, most of the available texts on the subject of entrepreneurial marketing are mainly concerned with the practices associated with delivering customer satisfaction in the small business sector.

The unfortunate side effect of this trend is that it possibly ignores the fact that many small businesses are essentially non-entrepreneurial (such as hotels and nursing homes). Additionally, many major large firms are beginning to add the concept of entrepreneurial marketing to their business vision in recognition of the importance of innovation to their competitiveness in rapidly changing world markets. Thus, when these large organisations send their managers along to business schools to gain new insights on entrepreneurial marketing, what they frequently receive is guidance on the management process within smaller firms.

In view of the importance of adopting an entrepreneurial marketing orientation in both the small and large firm sector, the aim of this text is to present some basic conceptual tools concerning entrepreneurial marketing which (a) relate to the actual management of process and (b) can be applied by organisations large or small to exploit the classical philosophy as a path by which to enhance future performance.

To develop this text, the author has had to confront an apparent oxymoron; namely, entrepreneurial management. The classic image of the successful inventor or the intuitive entrepreneur, such as Bill Gates or Anita Roddick, is that their ventures were founded without too many concerns about applying structured analytical tools to plan and guide the marketing operation. It is necessary to appreciate, however, that most individuals lack the creative, intuitive brilliance exhibited by such individuals. Nevertheless, there is a need for many managers in both the small and large firm sectors to expand their organisation's level of entrepreneurial marketing skills. Hence the purpose of this text is to provide some structured tools and techniques for use by the rational entrepreneur.

Chapter 1 presents an alternative definition of entrepreneurship, describing the activity as the challenging of convention. The chapter then goes on to describe the type of conventions which exist in industrial sectors. Most firms can be expected to continue to apply conventional marketing strategies to sustain performance. As the entrepreneurial marketer needs to understand the mind of the 'enemy', Chapter 2 examines how most organisations continue to use modifications to conventional strategies as the basis for further improving performance.

Chapter 3 presents a possible marketing planning model for use by the individual and/or the organisation seeking to identify new entrepreneurial opportunities, determine capability, fix performance goals and select an appropriate strategy. Outstanding entrepreneurship is often associated with visioning beyond current markets, and the implications of this type of activity are also described in this chapter.

Chapter 4 covers the issue of entrepreneurial promotion, while Chapters 5 and 6 are concerned with utilising entrepreneurial changes in marketing mix to enhance performance. Chapter 5 discusses pricing and distribution, and Chapter 6 moves on to cover the issues associated with the development and launch of entrepreneurial new products. A major proportion of Chapter 6 draws upon existing writings concerning the issue of innovation management.

New technologies, especially those associated with information technology, have had a dramatic impact on the processes used by organisations to generate outputs that are supplied to customers. Additionally, in recent years, firms in the forefront of innovation have demonstrated the critical importance of minimising 'time to market'. Chapter 7 thus covers the issues associated with entrepreneurial approaches to changing process technologies and minimising new product development cycles.

The size of the organisation creates very different operational conditions and obstacles for managers who wish to instigate change based upon heightened entrepreneurial marketing behaviour. Chapter 8 therefore covers the issues concerned with entrepreneurship in large firms. This is followed in Chapter 9 by a similar discussion concerning the management of the smaller firm.

In recent years, two sectors of the economy have exhibited major growth. These are service industries and the public sector, both of which have had a significant impact upon gross national product and employment, and Chapters 10 and 11 examine the managerial processes associated with implementing increased entrepreneurial marketing behaviour in these two sectors.

Research by individuals such as Seth in the US and Pedler in the UK have shown that change is crucially influenced by the learning styles exhibited by individuals, teams and entire organisations. In Chapter 12, a review is presented concerning the implications that the application of organisational learning theory may have for the level of entrepreneurial marketing exhibited by organisations.

ENTREPRENEURSHIP AND MARKET CONVENTIONS

INTRODUCTION

In the early nineteenth century, the French economist J.B. Say defined the entrepreneur as an individual who shifts economic resources from an area of low productivity into an area of higher productivity and greater yield. As this specification could probably be applied to the activities of any manager, it seems doubtful that in today's world we would consider Say's definition to provide an accurate description of the activities of those individuals we perceive as entrepreneurs.

Joseph Schumpeter, another famous economist, also concerned himself with the role of the entrepreneur in an economy. He perceived entrepreneurship (that is, the practice of the entrepreneur) to be a meta-economic event typically associated with the impact of a major change such as the introduction of a new technology into an industrial sector. Thus, in the Schumpeterian model of economics, managers continue to use traditional conventional approaches in those situations where demand is stable and perceived customer needs are clearly understood. In contrast, entrepreneurship is the process most likely to prevail in those circumstances where markets are in disequilibrium and customers have needs which are not being fulfilled by existing suppliers.

Since World War II, a somewhat broader view of entrepreneurship has emerged among management theorists. Miller (1983), for example, proposed that the entrepreneurial orientation of a firm is demonstrated by the extent to which top managers take risks, favour change and exploit innovation in order to obtain a proactive competitive advantage over other firms. This definition is also echoed in an article by Hills and LaForge (1992) who, on the basis of a review of research published to date, concluded that successful entrepreneurship requires the presence of four attributes; namely, creation of a new organisation, innovation, uniqueness and growth. In both cases these writers have associated the outcome of entrepreneurial activity with changes in the marketing processes being utilised within an industrial sector.

A major stimulus to research on entrepreneurship has been that many Western universities are now establishing professorial posts in the field and opening new departments dedicated to the teaching of the subject. When one examines many of these initiatives, however, they often appear to be strongly orientated towards the issues associated with the creation and operation of small businesses. Justifications frequently offered to explain this trend are (a) that small businesses now represent the greatest source of new employment opportunities in many Western economies, and (b) that the management of small firms should be considered as a distinct business discipline because these types of trading entity face operationally specific constraints which set them apart from larger organisations.

Birley (1982), for example, has suggested that the constraints confronting smaller firms include (a) goals not based on analysis of opportunity, but determined by the actions which appeal to the owner/manager, and (b) a lack of resources and/or knowledge which preclude decision making based on the classic strategic marketing approach of analysing markets, selecting a long-term growth strategy and optimally managing a detailed business plan. Carson (1985) subsequently proposed that the lack of general management expertise and the limited number of customers will also influence the management processes employed by smaller firms.

In accepting the widely espoused view that entrepreneurial behaviour is a characteristic of the smaller firm, it is nevertheless important not to fall into the trap of assuming that all small firms are entrepreneurial and that all large firms adopt somewhat more traditional management philosophies. As Drucker (1985) has noted, some large firms utilise a strategic philosophy grounded in the delivery of superior satisfaction by continually seeking to exploit new, innovative product opportunities (for example, the 3M corporation – founders of the Post-It market). Drucker posits that the reason researchers tend to associate entrepreneurial behaviour with the smaller firm is that the smaller organisation is structurally and culturally more able to respond rapidly to changing market opportunities. As Drucker points out, however, once an emerging opportunity is more clearly understood, existing large firms can also be innovative and respond by launching products capable of exploiting a newly identified customer trend (for example, IBM's entry into the personal computer (PC) market following recognition of the success enjoyed by the Apple corporation).

Conversely, it is also important to recognise that not all small firms are entrepreneurial. Many, in fact, merely duplicate that which has been done before (such as the husband and wife team opening their own hairdressing salon or establishing a new restaurant). Clearly, such individuals will benefit from attending courses at their local further education facility on topics such as starting a new business, selecting suitable premises, cash flow planning and marketing. What is very important, however, is to ensure that the academics delivering the teaching do not to fall into the trap of believing that such businesses must always be managed as entrepreneurial entities. Instead, individuals engaged in the delivery of small business management training programmes should focus on communicating that in many circumstances (for example, a highly transactional, standard goods market in which customers are not interested in building a close relationship with suppliers), small to medium enterprises (SMEs) might find the utilisation of a classicist management approach across functional areas such as marketing and manufacturing to be a very effective path by which to deliver customer satisfaction. An example of this, consider the bottom end of the domestic replacement window market. In this case, given that most customers' purchase decisions will be determined primarily by price, a newly established window installation company planning to operate in this sector of the market would probably be well advised to create an extremely cost effective business capable of offering a standard product at very competitive prices.

MARKETING MANAGEMENT STYLE

As the dominant trading nation for most of the twentieth century, it is understandable that over the last 100 years, the US has become the primary source of many of the new theories of management. The initial success of the US in world markets was based upon the principle of exploiting the scale benefits of mass production to supply competitively priced, standardised goods, such as automobiles, refrigerators and televisions.

Alfred Sloan, who rescued General Motors during the 1920s recession, held the view that the secret of successful management is grounded in the concept of applying rational planning to achieve the single-minded goal of maximising profits. To assist in the formalisation of this theory, Sloan and his supporters from within the academic community, such as Chandler and Ansoff, have drawn upon the conceptual rules of business established by the economist Adam Smith (author of *The Wealth of Nations*) and the militaristic principles of the Greek and Roman empires. Described as a 'classicist' approach to business, the principles of rational planning models as a path by which to optimise organisational performance have subsequently become the foundation stone for the syllabi of many business schools around the world (Whittington 1993).

Understandably, Western business schools produce graduates who are well grounded in the advantages of adopting a standard rational problem solving approach for exploiting new opportunities and/or responding to market change. Contained within this philosophy are the well established rules: one uses market data to examine scenarios and, having evolved a new or different approach, undertakes further research to minimise risk by ensuring that one has selected the most suitable solution. The steps associated with this process are shown in Figure 1.1.

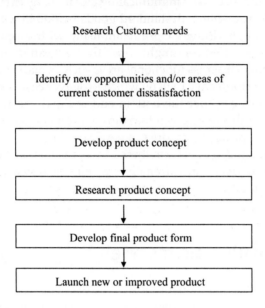

┌─────────────────────────────────┐
│   Research Customer needs   │
└─────────────────────────────────┘

┌─────────────────────────────────┐
│ Identify new opportunities and/or areas of │
│   current customer dissatisfaction   │
└─────────────────────────────────┘

┌─────────────────────────────────┐
│   Develop product concept   │
└─────────────────────────────────┘

┌─────────────────────────────────┐
│   Research product concept   │
└─────────────────────────────────┘

┌─────────────────────────────────┐
│   Develop final product form   │
└─────────────────────────────────┘

┌─────────────────────────────────┐
│   Launch new or improved product   │
└─────────────────────────────────┘

Figure 1.1   Classic structured approach to product development

Thus, for example, the introduction of automated washing machines in the UK during the 1970s caused Procter & Gamble to research customer attitudes concerning the effectiveness of its existing detergent brands in these new machines. The company identified the problem that existing products generated too many bubbles which were impairing the wash cycle and that, over the long term, these bubbles had the potential to damage the washing machine. Proctor & Gamble's solution was to develop a 'low suds' detergent. After careful market testing of its new formulation, the product was launched into the UK market under the Bold brand name. The brand immediately achieved leadership in this segment of the detergent market.

More recently, its competitors, Uniliver, having carefully studied the utilisation of washing powder in UK automatic washing machines, found that consumers were encountering problems because they were not carefully measuring the amount of detergent they were putting into their machines. This resulted in both a build-up of unused powder in the detergent dispenser and too much detergent being added to the wash cycle. Unilever's very logical, rational response to this situation was to introduce a solid tablet version, product line extension of Persil, its most successful detergent brand.

One way to compare and contrast this type of rational problem solving management style with the approach typically used by an entrepreneur is to examine the activities of successful entrepreneurs. Take the case of Trevor Bayliss, the individual who asked himself the apparently eccentric question, 'Why do radios have to run on electricity?' From this unconventional thought emerged the clockwork radio which is suitable for use in remote villages in developing nations which do not have access to electricity. Having had the idea rejected by Marconi and Philips, Bayliss set up his own company to manufacture the radio, which now sells across the world. The clockwork radio is both a practical solution for rural populations with no access to electricity, and a fashion good in developed nations.

Another example of entrepreneurial behaviour is provided by James Dyson of vacuum cleaner fame. He observed that as the collection bag in traditional vacuum cleaners becomes full, the machine loses suction. His solution was to develop the 'bagless cleaner'. This was launched in 1993 and by 1997 had become UK market leader, stealing sales from well known names such as Hoover and Electrolux.

In these two examples, the entrepreneurs apparently entered the problem solving process without bothering to undertake extensive research because they based their actions upon personal observation and intuitive reasoning.

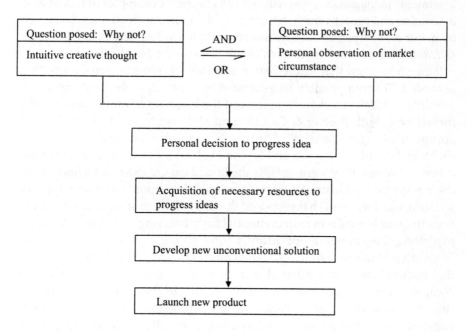

Figure 1.2 Entrepreneurial approach to product development

They ignored the conventional marketing management approach of seeking to improve on existing solutions and instead posed the question, 'Why Not?' This then led them to develop a radically different solution which was subsequently launched without any detailed research about the potential market reaction to the new proposition. The elements of this entrepreneurial marketing process are summarised in Figure 1.2.

REVISITING THE DEFINITION OF ENTREPRENEURSHIP

One of the few attempts to quantitatively research entrepreneurial versus traditional management style was undertaken by Covin and Slevin (1988). They based their measurement of entrepreneurship on the earlier Miller definition that entrepreneurial firms exhibit the behavioural dimensions of risk taking, innovation and proactive response. The six-item scale that they developed has since become possibly the most widely validated tool for assessing the degree to which firms exhibit entrepreneurial behaviour.

A potential drawback with the tool is the implicit assumption that non-entrepreneurial firms do not take risks, are not innovative and/or are not proactive. By merely observing large firms perceived as adopting a classicist approach to strategic management, one will rapidly encounter examples of risk taking, innovation and proactiveness (for example, the radical technologies developed by major oil companies such as Exxon or BP to exploit new fields in hostile environments such as the Alaskan North Slope or the North Sea).

It therefore seems that an alternative definition of entrepreneurial marketing is needed. This can possibly be generated by contrasting the Bold and Persil examples with the clockwork radio and the bagless vacuum cleaner. In the former case, both Procter & Gamble and Unilever applied the traditional approach of logical, analytical thinking to resolve an identified market problem. In contrast, Bayliss and Dyson evolved solutions which were very different because they went outside the boundaries of existing technology in their respective industrial sectors. Commenting upon this latter type of scenario, Gardner (1991) has proposed that the influence of unsatisfied market need frequently results in entrepreneurial firms breaking with convention and exploiting this emerging opportunity through the provision of new, more innovative solutions. Similarly, Hamel and Prahalad (1994) have concluded that major changes in industrial sectors have typically occurred because a company 'has changed the rules of the game'. In their view, 'to create the future, a company must (1) change in some fundamental way the rules of engagement, (2) redraw the boundaries between industries and/or (3) create entirely new industries'.

Thus, on the basis of such perspectives, it is proposed that an alternative definition of entrepreneurial marketing is:

The behaviour exhibited by an individual and/or organisation which adopts a philosophy of challenging established market conventions during the process of developing new solutions.

An important attribute of this definition is that it provides a simple method of assessing whether any observed market innovation can be classified as entrepreneurial or non-entrepreneurial. If the observed change is based upon a logical extension of current, well established practices such as those utilised to develop Bold detergent, then the outcome can be classified as conventional innovation. If the change clearly breaks convention(s), then the observed outcome can be diagnosed as entrepreneurial.

A very useful secondary advantage offered by the proposed alternative definition is that it also permits the classification of entrepreneurial versus non-entrepreneurial marketing activities at any level within the organisation (for example, a new approach to decision making within a department), between organisations, between industrial sectors and between different countries, because within any of these comparisons, one is merely testing whether the solution is an extension of existing industry practices or whether it breaks with convention. In addition, the definition accommodates the fact that in the real world, marketing style is rarely a black or white process because one will encounter mixed models where certain activities within an organisation or industrial sector might be conventional, whereas other aspects may be unconventional and therefore clearly entrepreneurial.

An example of a mixed management model is provided by the Häagen-Dazs ice cream company. This organisation adopted a conventional marketing strategy of competing against other brands by offering a superior quality product at a premium price. Where the firm departed from convention, however, and therefore can be considered to be an entrepreneurial marketer, was in its approach to advertising. The company positioned its product as a provider of added eroticism within adult male/female relationships. This positioning, which is overtly different from the convention of promoting ice cream as an enjoyable eating experience for children and families, is considered by many industry observers to be the primary reason for Häagen-Dazs's success in various markets around the world.

RATIONAL ENTREPRENEURIAL MARKETING

Various researchers over the years have observed the behaviour of outstanding entrepreneurs. The conclusion often reached in such studies is that the majority of highly successful entrepreneurs have made little use of formalised management theories such as strategic planning or selection of an appropriate market position. Rather, their approach to management very much follows Henry Mintzberg's (1987) philosophy of 'management by crafting'. Actions do not appear to flow from extensive detailed reasoning, but instead reflect an intuitive selection of appropriate action centred on a deep commitment and understanding of the business of which they are part. An example of this type of entrepreneurial behaviour offered by Mintzberg et al. (1998) is Steinberg's, a Canadian retail chain. In 1933, one of the stores hit a trading problem. Sam Steinberg's solution was to close the store on a Friday night and to reopen the outlet as a 'cut price' self-service operation. He employed a similar managerial approach when moving into the shopping centre business in the 1950s. It is also interesting to note that after his death, the company was sold to a conventional company known for their financial management expertise, and the Steinburg operation subsequently went bankrupt.

Unfortunately for colleges offering courses in entrepreneurship, there is probably no way that traditional educational approaches can assist the Baylisses and Dysons of this world to become more effective entrepreneurial marketers. Additionally, it is probably the case that the academic cannot provide any form of input which might enhance the mental maps that management craftspersons appear to utilise while creating their vision of market circumstance from which their next successful entrepreneurial ideas then flow.

Nevertheless, most organisations, large or small, are staffed by people who are not intuitive entrepreneurs but who could benefit from further developing their entrepreneurial marketing skills. Thus, because intuitive entrepreneurship cannot be taught, the approach that is adopted within this text is the same as the approach that is followed in most management writings; namely, to present a series of rational, analytical models which can offer the reader who is not an intuitive entrepreneurial marketer, a series of systematic, logical steps that can be used to plan and implement management processes which contain a higher degree of more innovative ways of thinking about business problems.

The rational entrepreneurship model presented in Figure 1.3 is based upon the posited definition that entrepreneurial marketing is concerned with the challenging of conventions. As can be seen, the entry point is that of first determining conventions. Furthermore, as most managers and/or organisations are more comfortable with further enhancing existing processes known to influence performance, it is suggested that the first action is to assess whether sustaining current market conventions can deliver the future performance goals which have been specified. Only in those cases where this appears not to be feasible is it suggested that an individual consider adopting an entrepreneurial marketing orientation and begin to evaluate the implications of influencing future performance by challenging existing operational conventions within an industrial sector.

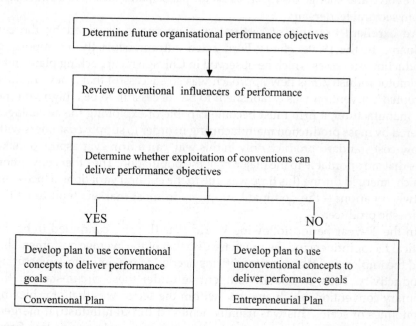

Figure 1.3 Entrepreneurial versus non-entrepreneurial planning pathway

Central to a rational management approach to entrepreneurial marketing is the systematic analysis of situations, the evaluation of alternative actions and the definition of appropriate action rules. However, three important guidelines need to be remembered throughout this process. First, the analysis should not be so extensive that the volume of generated data over-complicates the activity to the point that a definitive decision cannot be reached. Second, knowledge gained through experience should become the basis for the manager to learn how to become an even more effective decision maker in the future. Third, in those cases where the individual does not feel comfortable with the solution generated by rational analysis, the person should be willing to rely upon intuition to determine appropriate next actions.

SECTORAL CONVENTIONS

Sectoral conventions are the strategic rules which guide the marketing operations of the majority of firms in a sector of industry. The conventional organisation would be well advised to adopt these if it hopes to remain successful in the future. It should be noted, however, that these conventions will evolve and change over time as sector participants jockey to achieve and retain sectoral leadership.

An excellent example of sectoral conventions is provided by the car industry. In the 1920s, Henry Ford acted entrepreneurially by importing production processes which he observed in Chicago meat packing plants into the motor industry. His new approach was so successful that a new, rapidly accepted convention was established: to be successful, to be a high-volume car manufacturer, a firm must become capable of exploiting the advantages offered by mass production manufacturing in order to supply customers with a low-cost standard product; only in this way can a firm ever aspire to make cars that are affordable to the majority of the population. The other convention which emerged during this time was due to the cultural variations which exist between nations – the dominant suppliers in most markets tend to be the domestic producers.

In the 20-year period following World War II, price continued to be the critical factor influencing the purchase decision of the average customer. This had the implication that successful firms needed to maximise manufacturing productivity. Thus, to remain competitive under these circumstances, the primary convention which emerged within the sector was that of achieving economies of scale. This was usually achieved through industrial mergers between domestic producers, eventually leading to only one or two firms dominating each Western home market (for example, Ford and General Motors in the US; British Leyland (subsequently Rover Group) in the UK, Volkswagen in Germany; Fiat in Italy; and Renault and Citroën in France). As these firms gained experience in manufacturing technology, the next convention to emerge was a design convergence – in order to further optimise productivity – which led to the standard, volume car specification being based upon front-wheel drive and four- or six-cylinder engines.

The OPEC (Organisation of Petroleum Exporting Countries) oil crisis in the 1970s sparked much higher customer interest in fuel economy. This event offered both European and Japanese producers the convention disruption opportunity to break into the largest car market in the world, the US. While the American car makers were struggling with the joint problems of learning how to make smaller cars and how to manage in what had become a highly unionised production environment, the Japanese were left to experiment with unconventional concepts such as robotics plus Just In Time (JIT) to further enhance productivity and Total Quality Management (TQM) to improve 'build quality'. Their success in these areas enabled them to become global players in the world car market. Furthermore, their new approaches to manufacturing soon became the sector convention that other major firms have to adopt if they wish to remain significant high-volume producers.

It is important to note that many of the Japanese advances in manufacturing which took firms such as Toyota and Honda to market leadership were often achieved by their willingness to challenge industrial conventions. As such, therefore, these firms were acting entrepreneurially. Furthermore, as if often the case, once an entrepreneurial idea is recognised as being superior to existing conventions, the new idea is rapidly adopted by other organisations and becomes the new convention within a sector. Thus, in the car industry, using robots on the assembly line and basing operations around TQM and JIT manufacturing philosophies is now the accepted convention.

For those car manufacturers who have felt unable to follow the conventions required to become a global high-volume marketer, the alternative has been to find a sector of the market in which they could survive without having to build massive car plants. Hence the alternative convention is to select a segment of the market where one is able to out-compete the volume players. Examples of this alternative approach include specialisms such as luxury cars (Mercedes-Benz), performance cars (Ferrari), safety/reliability (Volvo) or the very low price sector (Skoda).

It is important to recognise that sectoral conventions influencing market behaviour are not just restricted to the private sector. For example, in the UK, the National Health Service (NHS), was established on the basis of a new 'delivery of care' convention that simple every-day medical problems are handled by general practitioners (GPs), while a patient requiring complex treatment or surgery will be admitted to a hospital. In the early years of the NHS, there existed a mix of large and small hospitals. The latter were usually located in every small town. In the case of these latter institutions, their more complex medical cases were redirected to the larger hospitals located in larger towns and cities.

In the 1970s and 1980s, however, as technological advances drove up medical costs and high inflation crippled welfare state spending, the new convention which emerged was to concentrate more and more medical care in the very large hospitals and concurrently close down the smaller medical units based in small towns. By the late 1980s, as funding problems continued to worsen in the NHS two new conventions had emerged: the introduction of non-stay surgery in hospitals, and some minor surgery being undertaken by GPs at their practices.

PERFORMANCE CONVENTIONS

In the private sector, managers are charged by financial stakeholders with generating profits from operations sufficient to ensure an adequate return on the assets of the organisation. This financial requirement is usually met through average or above-average performance in areas such as total revenue, gross margin, total value added per employee, working capital employed and/or return on investment in fixed assets.

The minimum required performance standard is usually set by the 'best in class' firms within an industrial sector; it is their market achievements which provide the basis financial conventions against which they and their competitors are judged. Similar to strategic conventions, these performance conventions will change over time. For example, in Europe at one time the high employee productivity and optimal utilisation of available production capacity meant that the German car manufacturers were the ones which set the productivity standards against which both managers and investors assessed the financial performance of the car companies in other European countries.

During the 1970s, the level of industrial unrest and high rate of inflation meant that the UK car industry was seen as the most inefficient, highest cost producer in Europe. Over the last 20 years, however, actions such as legislation to limit the power of the unions, major changes in working practices (such as delayering and multi-skilling) and the refusal to accept certain aspects of the European Union (EU) Social Charter has permitted the UK car industry to become the productivity standard to which other European producers, including the Germans, now aspire. In recent years, this achievement has been reflected in the improved performance in both domestic and international markets of brands such as Land Rover and Jaguar.

During the 1950s, the Japanese had another unconventional idea, that of visiting thousands of companies around the world to (a) observe practices which might be incorporated back into their industries at home, and (b) identify techniques or technologies in one area which could be transferred to another sector of manufacturing. Their approach, which is a fundamental element within the philosophy of continuous improvement, or *kaizen*, has subsequently become recognised as a driving force for change in Japanese industry because it is founded on the premise that every aspect of process should be assigned a target performance standard which should be achieved and eventually exceeded if possible.

Although many Western managers initially perceived the infinite curiosity of the Japanese as an activity designed to permit them to 'steal ideas' from competitors, as their own firms began rapidly to lose sales to Pacific Rim producers in both overseas and domestic markets, they soon came to realise that the philosophy of assessing one's own manufacturing processes against intra- and intersectoral standards is an extremely powerful tool in the ongoing war of share in world markets.

One of the first firms to wake up to this Pacific Rim hazard was the photocopier giant, Xerox. The company realised that in order to respond to the fact that the new competitors were able to sell equivalent products more cheaply, it would need to commence assessing its internal operational processes against the performance standards now being set by firms such as Canon. The Xerox solution was to instigate a project known as 'Best Practice Benchmarking' which resulted in an eventual recovery of the ability to survive in the world's photocopier markets. Other Western firms rapidly saw the sense in the Xerox approach, and performance comparison, or 'benchmarking', has now become a standard practice within the marketing operations of virtually all of the world's major corporations (Bendell et al. 1993).

One of the organisations which has embraced benchmarking is IBM. There were two very influential stages in their adoption of the philosophy. The first was in the late 1970s, when a corporate edict was issued which required that all new hardware and software products must have superior performance over both their IBM precursor and the best of competition. The second critical event was the corporation's decision that in order to actually deliver an excellent level of customer service it was necessary to adopt the service standards specified in the American Malcolm Baldridge National Quality award as the basis for defining minimum achievement both for products and for all operational processes within the organisation. This now means that at IBM, business areas such as product quality, customer satisfaction, internal operations and supplier performance are continuously assessed against the performance conventions set either by competitors or by lead organisations in another sector of industry who excel at one or more business functions such as customer response, work-in-progress levels and/or order–delivery cycles.

More recently, Western governments have begun to recognise the benefits of introducing the philosophy of benchmarking into public sector organisations to assess organisational performance more effectively. Typically, these initiatives have been greeted with severe resistance by public sector unions who perceive such actions as a restriction of the members' freedom of action in the workplace. Over time, such resistance has gradually been worn down and in the UK, for example, league tables are now published annually describing the performance of schools in national examinations and the ability of hospitals to minimise the 'wait time for surgery' being endured by their patients. Additionally in the UK, the National Audit Office carries out in-depth examinations of the financial performance of various areas of the public sector and where possible makes comparisons with the cost of such operations within equivalent private sector operations.

CUSTOMER CONVENTIONS

Ultimately, all organisations are in the business of seeking to satisfy the needs of their customers. Such needs are rooted in the customer's requirement for a product or service to deliver required benefits (for example, toothpaste for cleaning teeth; a bank to provide interest on savings). Through both the experience gained by the customer during the processes of purchase and consumption, coupled with the service behaviour of suppliers (such as supermarket chains altering shopping habits by being willing to open 24 hours a day), the average customer over time acquires expectations concerning the minimum standard of performance which should be delivered by every product or service that he or she purchases. These expectations form the conventions against which the market performance of each supplier is then judged. Furthermore, if a supplier breaches conventions deemed critical by the purchaser, the customer may subsequently switch his or her allegiance to an alternative supplier (for example, if an airline overbooks a flight and is then unwilling to offer free overnight accommodation, many of the affected passengers will vow never to fly with the carrier again).

Buyer behaviour is an extremely complex subject which has engaged the minds of numerous academics over the years. In the context of defining market conventions for a specific product or service, one would need to carry out highly detailed research in order to identify which factors across every aspect of the organisation may have influence over customer product and services perceptions. Figure 1.4 provides a description of the more common generic factors known to influence conventions in any market.

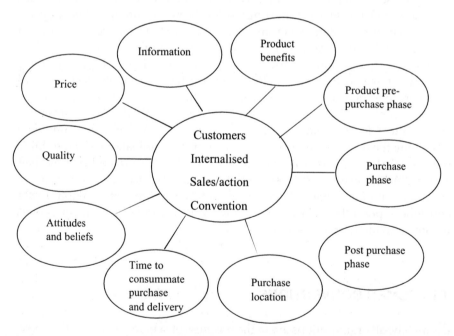

Figure 1.4 Factors influencing customers' expectations over purchase satisfaction

Again, similar to the case for strategic and performance conventions, customer conventions can be expected to change over time due to the effect of experiences generated during earlier purchases and/or changing industrial sector circumstances (for example, most people buying a replacement PC after a gap of some two or three years would now expect, if paying the same price as their last purchase, to receive a much more powerful machine. Alternatively, if they are seeking the same specification as their last machine, they would expect now to pay a much lower price). It is important to note, however, that the ten factors described in Figure 1.4 should not to interpreted as a complete, total definition of variables known to influence customer conventions. In real life, some other factors may need to be added (in the case of consulting firms bidding on a major government contract, for example, the existing reputation of these firms have established while previously undertaking similar types of projects is another influential factor). Conversely, in a very simple purchase scenario such as buying a box of matches, some of the factors in Figure 1.4 may be deemed redundant to process. Additionally, it is necessary to note that the relative importance of factors may change over time. For example, in periods of recession, supermarket customers may consider relative price as the most important factor, whereas in times of economic up-turn, issues such as product quality and speed of service might become more important than lowest possible price.

CONVENTIONS DEFINING CRITICAL MARKET SUCCESS FACTORS

In most industrial sectors, managers can usually describe those factors which are known to be critical in terms of deciding market success or failure. If an organisation can achieve a high rating for fulfilling the requirements for those factors known to be critical to market success, then it can probably be expected to outperform competitors who lack certain key competences.

It is proposed in Figure 1.5 that the three sources of influence determining critical market success factors are the conventions specified by strategy, sector performance and customers. If the non-entrepreneurial firm wishes to outperform competition it must therefore be able to meet these conventions; thereby fulfilling the critical market success factors which exist in the sector of industry of which it is a part. To illustrate this concept, a simplified application of the model is provided for the volume car sector in Figure 1.6. Most of the major players, such as Ford or Toyota, strive daily to excel in fulfilling these well established factors in this market sector.

The alternative, however, is for one or more firms to decide that competing on the basis of matching the behaviour of others may be less impactful than

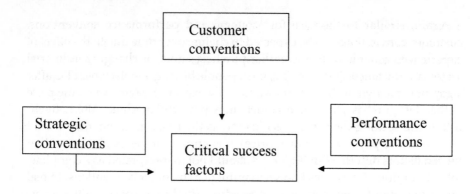

Figure 1.5 Sources of conventions impacting on critical success factors

adopting the entrepreneurial approach of breaking with one or more known existing conventions. Thus, for example, it is the convention in the UK car market for the major car companies to distribute the bulk of their output through independently owned 'main dealerships'. Upon entering the UK market, the Korean car company Daewoo adopted the unconventional approach of not appointing dealers but instead establishing its own outlets to sell the vehicles direct to the final customer. Daewoo's perspective, which is essentially an entrepreneurial approach, was that effective communication of its claims concerning superiority in areas such as build quality, value for

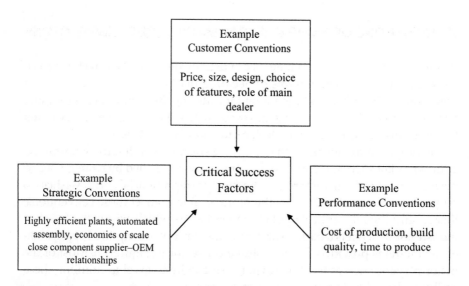

Figure 1.6 An example of some of the conventions influencing critical success factors in the volume sector of the car industry

money and post-purchase vehicle maintenance would be best met by retaining absolute control over available distribution channels. On the basis of its achieved market share in the first few years after initial market entry, it can probably be concluded that Daewoo's break with convention has been an extremely wise move.

A SERIAL CONVENTION BREAKER

An example of a firm which continually seems to break market conventions and succeeds is the Justice Technology corporation (Freedman 1998). It was founded by David Glickman who saw the opportunity offered by 'callback' telephone services. Essentially, how callback works is that if you are living outside the US, you can dial a US callback number; by hanging up while the telephone number is still ringing and then picking up the telephone again, you get a US dialling tone. Dial your international party and you will be connected. You will owe the callback service for the cost of the switch call to you and your call from the US to the international party. The savings from avoiding having to go through your own country's telephone service are typically in the region of 50–75 per cent.

Glickman started his first operation in Argentina and soon he had money pouring in from customers such as United Parcel Service (UPS) and British Airways. His next unconventional idea was to pose the question, 'Why should I pay US callback providers?' So he then flew to America and persuaded IDB Worldcom to handle all his switching business in return for 60 per cent of the profits. Then one day the callback service ceased to work because a US telephone company developed a programme that detected the overseas incoming dialling tones and automatically disconnected the call. Glickman's solution was to develop a device that transmitted the outgoing switch not as a touch-tone dial phone, but as computer data.

Having proved his case in Argentina, Glickman moved back to the US and opened Justice Technology which is now a multinational business. Then in 1994, the new owners of IDB Worldcom informed Justice Technology of their intention of pulling out of the switching business in six weeks' time. So Glickman set up his own telephone switching operation in just 90 days! He is aware, however, that callback services have a finite life, so now Justice owns its own switches in several countries and has also gone into the direct-dial business. To succeed in this latter arena, Glickman has bought capacity from the international phone service providers and, because of his unconventional negotiating approach to the industry, has been able obtain deals at less than 50 per cent of the prices that the major carriers pay for the equivalent routes. To optimise call efficiency, Justice then spent $2 million developing Pipeline, which is its own proprietary, complex network analyser software tool which monitors call costs and identifies re-routing strategies that can further reduce transmission costs. This has been so successful that Glickman's latest unconventional idea is to sell back his low-cost excess international capacity to his competitors.

REFERENCES

Bendell, T., Boulter, L. and Kelly, J. (1993), *Benchmarking for Competitive Advantage*, Financial Times, Pitman Publications, London.

Birley, S. (1982), 'Corporate strategy and the small firm', *Journal of General Management*, Vol. 8, No. 2, pp. 82–6.

Carson, D.J. (1985), 'The evolution of marketing in small firms, *European Journal of Marketing*, Vol. 19, No. 5, pp. 7–16.

Covin, J.G. and Slevin, D.P. (1988), 'The influence of organisational structure on the utility of an entrepreneurial top management style', *Journal of Management Studies*, Vol. 25, pp. 217–37.

Drucker, P.F. (1985), *Innovation and Entrepreneurship*, Butterworth-Heinemann, London.

Freedman, D.H. (1998), 'Chaos theory', *Inc. Online*, Goldhirsh Group, Boston, MA, pp. 50.

Gardner, D. (1991), 'Exploring the marketing/entrepreneurship interface', in Hills, G.E. and LaForge, R.W. (eds), *Research at the Marketing/Entrepreneurship Interface*, Joint UIC/AMA Conference, University of Illinois at Chicago, pp. 43–52.

Hamel, G. and Prahalad, C.K. (1994), *Competing for the Future*, Harvard Business School Press, Boston, MA.

Hills, G.E. and LaForge, R.W. (1992), 'Research at the marketing interface to advance entrepreneurship theory', *Entrepreneurship Theory and Practice*, Spring, pp. 33–59.

Miller, D. (1983), 'The correlates of entrepreneurship in three types of firm', *Management Science*, Vol. 29, pp. 770–91.

Mintzberg, H., Ahlstrand, B. and Lampel, J. (1998), *Strategy Safari*, Free Press, New York.

Mintzberg, H. (1987), 'Crafting strategies', *Harvard Business Review*, July–August, pp. 70–81.

Whittington, R. (1993), *What is Strategy and Does it Matter?*, Thomson Business Press, London.

2 UNDERSTANDING THE CONVENTIONAL COMPETITOR

INTRODUCTION

Military leaders down through the ages have learnt the importance of gaining a detailed insight into the enemy's strategies and tactics prior to launching a new offensive. The rational entrepreneur would be wise to follow the same advice when planning to challenge conventional firms. These latter organisations have usually acquired extensive experience of responding to new market threats. Furthermore, they can be expected to have access to a more than adequate level of financial reserves to fund a strong response to any threat from what they would perceive as an 'entrepreneurial interloper'.

In most cases, one of the few operational advantages available to entrepreneurs is that they can expect conventionally managed enemies to base their response around existing business strategies. Entrepreneurs, on the other hand, frequently have the option of selecting a strategy which offers the most effective route through which to steal market share. Thus, early into finalising their campaign to steal sales from competition, entrepreneurs should make a detailed study of the strategies being used by their conventional foes.

CONVENTIONAL STRATEGIES

The success of the American economy for the majority of the twentieth century is founded upon the outstanding abilities of the US to mould together the two concepts of mass production and mass marketing. Richard Tedlow (1990), a business historian at Harvard Business School, has analysed the life histories of a number of well known American companies in the automobile, electrical goods, retailing and soft drinks sectors. From his research on company behaviour both before and after World War II, he has formulated some generic guidelines concerning effective strategies for establishing successful mass market firms, which include the following.

1. Exploiting the economies of scale associated with mass production to generate high absolute profits by selling large volumes of standard goods.
2. Re-investing generated profits in high levels of promotional activity as mechanism through which to shape and mould market demand.
3. Creating of a vertical system in which raw materials are sourced, production operations are managed and products are delivered to the final consumer. This vertical system usually involves integration within the firm of the key steps within the production process (for example, car companies owning assembly and component manufacturing plants) accompanied by contractual relationships for other elements within the distribution system (such as the move by Coca-Cola to reduce costs by supplying concentrate syrups to bottling companies who manage production and distribution in a specified market area).
4. Having achieved market dominance through being the first company to exploit a strategy of high volume/high absolute profits, to then create economies of scale barriers to ward off attacks from competition (as, for example, the major international airlines such as United Airlines and British Airways have done).

Tedlow has proposed that during the twentieth century, long-term survival of the leading mass market companies necessitated a convention change from a 'profit through volume' strategy towards a new operating philosophy based on segmenting the market and offering a variety of goods to the now more sophisticated and experienced customer. The higher costs associated with expanding product line variety are not a problem because (a) many market segments are quite large (thereby permitting some degree of ongoing economies of scale) and (b) even more importantly, the supplier now had the freedom to 'price in accord with the special value that a particular market segment places on the product, independent of the costs of production'.

The basic theories of conventional marketing strategy management were initially evolved by academics through a study of the battles for market share between major American firms in the North American tangible goods markets. However, researchers seeking to validate the benefits of classicist theories of marketing in other sectors and countries have often encountered severe diffi- culties in locating evidence that these management concepts are widely accepted as 'conventional wisdom' by managers within the industrial sectors being studied.

Initially, the apparent absence of a strategic marketing orientation was often attributed to the inadequacies of managers who failed to appreciate the benefits of a structured, formalised approach to the management of markets. In the Nordic countries, however, a 'grounded theory' approach of avoiding preconceived hypotheses of management process, of observing actual events and of seeking convergence in practice, has led to identification of alternative management models. Pioneering work by the Industrial Marketing and Procurement (IMP) group proved that firms in many industrial markets, instead of seeking to build market share through emphasis on intense competition with other brands, are often orientated towards the concept of interfirm cooperation as a path by which to build long-term relationships based upon trust and commitment.

Writers such as Nystrom (1990) posit that the classicist school of mass production and marketing is based upon the economic theory of the firm in which well defined products are made available in a market where both supplier and customer are fully informed about the relative merits of competing offerings. He further argues that classicist marketing thinking is founded on the assumption that access to information permits the customers to make a rational choice based upon a comparison of benefits offered by competing firms. However, he also feels that classicist strategic thinking incorrectly assumes that buyers are passive, reactive users who are not interested in any form of interaction with the supplier.

Studies of the marketing process in service sectors such as finance and retailing have revealed situations where customers do not exhibit a strong, transactionally orientated buying behaviour. Instead, supplier firms act to exploit opportunities for building long-term relationships based on working in close partnership with purchasers. Similarly, in manufacturing environments, the stress on a move towards closer customer–supplier relationships has been given added weight by the managerial philosophies of TQM and JIT.

The outcome has been that some management theorists have concluded that many firms who place emphasis on single transactions should in fact be attempting to build long-term relationships with customers. A strong impetus to this alternative management convention was provided by Reichfeld and Sasser (1990) who demonstrated that a transaction orientation could result in focusing excessive resources on attracting new customers when in fact the real benefits of marketing come from programmes directed at retaining existing customers (or, in their terminology, ensuring achievement of 'zero defections').

A new school of conventional strategic thought has now emerged which believes that firms can orchestrate internal resources and processes to create and sustain customer loyalty. Collectively, this new orientation, which has both American (Berry 1982) and Nordic (Gummesson 1987) roots, is known as relationship management. Supporters of this new management convention argue that in order to survive in markets which have become more competitive and more turbulent, organisations must move away from managing transactions and instead focus on building long-lasting customer relationships (Webster 1992).

Advocates of relationship management will typically support their views through a comparison of process of the type shown in Table 2.1.

Table 2.1 Contrasting management conventions

Transactional management	Relationship management
Orientation towards single purchase	Orientation towards repeat sales
Limited direct customer–supplier contact	Close, frequent customer–supplier contact
Focus on product benefits	Focus on value to customer
Emphasis on short-term performance	Emphasis on long-term performance
Limited level of customer service	High level of customer service
Goal of customer satisfaction	Goal of 'delighting the customer'
Quality a manufacturing responsibility	Quality a total organisation

In most markets, however, there are two groups of customer for whom product needs are unlikely to be totally satisfied by conventional firms who excel at delivering either transactional or relationship orientated strategies. For one of these two unconventional customer groups, the key purchase driver is their desire to have access to products which provide a level of benefit performance well in excess of that available from standard goods producers. For example, Western intelligence agencies involved in both the encryption and the breaking of codes require computers which have a processing power much greater than that offered by even the largest IBM mainframe. In most cases they will turn to an unconventional organisation, the Cray corporation, which specialises in breaking the accepted rules of technology and building hardware capable of processing data at speeds well in excess of what is considered technically feasible by others members of its industry.

At the other extreme of the market spectrum are those customers for whom variables such as ease of purchase, service quality and on-time delivery are considered as secondary issues. What they seek primarily are prices which are so low that the conventional firms usually decide that they cannot serve this sector of market and remain profitable. What often happens in such circumstances is that an entrepreneurial firm develops a new, unconventional organisational philosophy to serve this sector of the market. One recent example of this scenario is Staples, which ignored the convention that office supplies should be sold through small independent distributors, and instead established its own office products superstores.

Another attribute of price orientated customers is that in many cases they accept that they cannot afford the latest technology. Hence, one should ignore the convention of always seeking to improve products and instead find ways of making basic specification products available. These can frequently be manufactured using what the conventional firms would consider to be obsolete, prior-generation technology (an example would be a small business purchasing a bottom-of-the-range PC with limited memory because all it wishes to do is to run a very basic suite of word processing and spreadsheet packages).

STRATEGIC MARKETING BEHAVIOUR

By taking the four dimensions of transaction, relationship, product and price, it is possible to construct a Strategic Pathway Grid of the type shown in Figure 2.1. Once the entrepreneur has identified the position of conventionally managed competitors within the grid, he or she can then expect 'the enemy' to exhibit one of the following four types of strategic marketing behaviour.

1. *Transactional excellence*
   - A price/quality/value product combination superior to that of the competition
   - Standardised products
   - Excellence in managing conventional production and distribution logistics processes
   - An information system designed to rapidly identify manufacturing and/or logistic errors
2. *Relationship excellence*
   - A product/service combination which delivers a complete customer specific solution
   - A product solution based on conventional specifications appropriate for the industrial sector
   - Employee obsession with finding even more effective conventional solutions to customer problems
   - An information system which rapidly identifies errors in solution provision
   - A culture in which all employees are committed to working closely with counterparts within the customer organisation
3. *Product performance excellence*
   - A product offering outstanding superior performance versus competition
   - Orientation towards always seeking to extend the performance boundaries of existing products
   - Excellence across the entire workforce in understanding how the latest advances in technology might be incorporated into products and/or production processes

- A culture in which employees are always striving to apply conventional approaches to finding new market opportunities for exploiting identified product performance improvements
4. *Price performance excellence*
   - Product prices that are significantly lower than the rest of the market
   - Skill in the production of 'no frills' products
   - Excellence in acquiring prior-generation technology and capital equipment at at either zero or low cost
   - An information system designed to rapidly identify adverse cost variance trends across the areas of procurement, manufacturing and distribution
   - A culture in which employees are always striving to find ways of applying conventional thinking to further reducing operating and/or overhead costs.

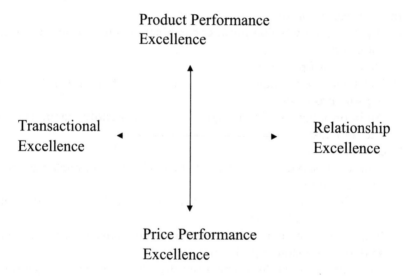

Figure 2.1   A Strategic Pathway Grid

IMPLEMENTING CONVENTIONAL MARKETING STRATEGIES

Abernathy et al. (1983), in their work to develop managerial typologies, have suggested that strategic direction can be described using the two dimensions of market and production processes. Although an adequate model, strict application may result in non-market issues inadvertently being missed by the analyst (for example, external variables such as the role of suppliers in providing access to new technologies; internal organisational issues such as the inability to hire a sufficient number of skilled operatives). Thus, as shown in Figure 2.2, it is proposed that the two dimensions be expanded by using the terminology of external and internal strategies.

		Adequate	Inadequate
EXTERNAL STRATEGIES	Inadequate	Change in External Strategy Expected	Change in Both Internal and External Strategies Expected
	Adequate	No Strategic Change Expected	Change in Internal Strategy Expected

INTERNAL STRATEGIES

Figure 2.2   A Strategic Change Matrix

The Strategic Change Matrix in Figure 2.2 offers four different alternatives. One alternative is that all aspects of performance are considered adequate and therefore the organisation will continue to use the same strategy in the future. Another possibility is emerging evidence of a need to make internal changes in order to sustain future performance (for example, moving from manual to automated production in order to stabilise operating costs). If a need is identified to respond to events outside the company, but internal strategies are perceived as remaining adequate, then the expected action will be a change in external strategy (for example, a decision to form a research and development (R&D) partnership with a supplier to permit the development of a range of new products). Finally, the organisation may identify that both internal and external changes are required in order to implement an integrated performance upgrade strategy (for example, by adopting a flexible manufacturing policy the firm can expand the product line, thereby permitting entry into new segments of the organisation's end user market).

CONVENTIONAL BEHAVIOUR CAN BE HAZARDOUS

During the early years of the post-war recovery of German industry, BMW produced bubble cars and somewhat unstylish limousines. In 1959, Herbert Quandt acquired a dominant shareholder position and steered the company in a more entrepreneurial direction. In 1962, the firm entered the quality production saloon market by positioning its 1500 model halfway between the mass production car segment and the craftsmen-built output of the luxury producers (Moores 1999).

Over the next two decades the firm established the BMW brand as a distinctive marque in the global car industry. Then, in the 1980s, the firm appeared to fall into the trap of believing that it should seek to follow the car industry's convention about size and scale of operation being critical to sustaining success as a global player. To deliver this new strategy, BMW purchased the UK Rover brand and has subsequently struggled to reposition this loss-making operation as a more upmarket producer. Following the recent resignation of BMW's Chief Executive, the question remains as to whether BMW will continue to chase the convention of seeking size and scale or will return to its more entrepreneurial roots of being an entrepreneurial leader in the supply of innovative, technically superior production saloons.

THE EXTERNAL DIMENSION TO STRATEGY IMPLEMENTATION

A highly effective tool for analysing circumstances external to the organisation, which can be used by both conventional firms and entrepreneurial marketers seeking to understand their conventional enemy, is to construct a business system map (Kotler 1997) of the type shown in Figure 2.3. The map shown in Figure 2.3 is of a generalised nature and in a real life situation it can usually be expected to be significantly more complex. Essentially, however, the user of the map can determine the sectoral conventions which exist in relation to the flow of goods and services through a market system. For the entrepreneur, an assessment of these conventions will permit identification of possible opportunities for introducing new management philosophies into the system and a determination as to whether emerging trends within the system might eventually lead to competitors being forced to revise their operational strategies. Any user of the map will also need to take note of the variables surrounding the core of the system, such as economic conditions or legislation, because these also act as a source of conventions and/or provide catalysts for strategic change.

An end user market contains both actual and potential customers. One way of visualising an end user market is to adopt the two-level model of the type

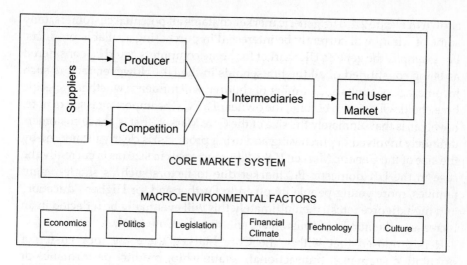

Figure 2.3 A business system model

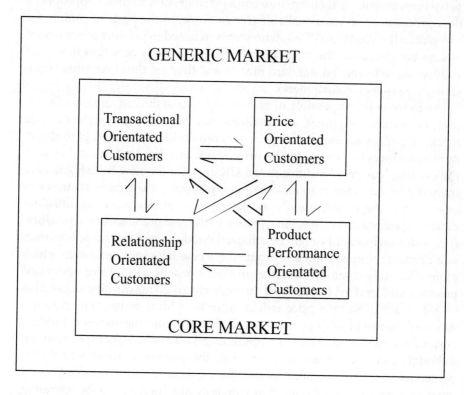

Figure 2.4 A two-level end user market

shown in Figure 2.4. The generic market contains all potential customers, only some of whom will currently be interested in purchasing available products. For example, the generic UK market for home computers could be considered as being constituted of all the households in the UK. However, factors such income, age of adults and number of children will influence whether a specific household will wish to become the owner of a PC. The important issue to note, however, is that ultimately the size of the Core Market (that is, those customers definitely involved in purchasing and using products) is clearly influenced by the size of the Generic Market. If the latter increases in size (as is currently the case in the UK domestic PC market due to factors such as single-parent families, more young people involved in Further and/or Higher Education, and high divorce rates), then ultimately this will eventually be reflected in an increase in the number of customers entering the Core Market.

It is proposed that within the Core Market, there are four customer orientation segments: transactional, relationship, product performance or price. This is an important opportunity for the entrepreneur to recognise ahead of the conventional strategist when customers are beginning to switch between segments as their circumstances change, and to make appropriate new products or services available (for example, in the past, customers for video cassette recorders (VCRs) who were interested in product performance always bought top of the range brands; however, many now find that most features are available on standard brands and they are thus becoming transactionally orientated customers).

The factor which is possibly of greatest concern to the conventional firm is that within each segment, competitors may be altering aspects of their marketing mix, such as product, price and promotion, in an attempt to attract more customers (for example, the price war which has broken out between the existing 'cut price' airlines in the UK and Go, the new British Airways economy brand). Hence, to ensure ongoing success, the strategist strives to ensure that the organisation's marketing mix is perceived as fulfilling customer needs within a specific segment. In the case of transactional products such as frozen foods this might be achieved through conventional actions such as a product reformulation or introducing a new television campaign which more effectively communicates the product's benefit claim. Price orientated products will tend to be supported through a focus on maximising value. This might be achieved by a price reduction or by adding more value through running a series of sales promotions. Companies offering superior product performance will tend to focus on upgrading the actual product specification, although it may also feasible to augment the product in some way that is perceived as a genuine enhancement (for example, a software house might open a website offering free guidance on how modifications to the operating code for a product would permit users to increase the processing speed on their computer). In the case of relationship orientated organisations, their actions are typically focused around new ways of moving closer to the customer. Thus an overnight courier service might offer free software to its customers which permits them to request the collection of a parcel electronically without having to make a telephone call to the courier's offices.

In those systems where they are present, the primary role of intermediaries is to improve logistics efficiency within an industrial sector and thereby lower the costs of linking the producer to the end user. Thus, in reviewing distribution systems, similar to the situation described for end user markets, the conventional strategist will seek ways of using available distribution systems to enhance the primary strategic positioning which is being used to attract customers to the product or service. Transactional firms will tend to focus on ways of servicing customer needs for standard goods more efficiently (for example, a pump manufacturer persuading distributors to carry a more extensive range of spare parts). Price orientated organisations will favour new ways of reducing costs to the final customer (a carpet manufacturer might seek to gain distribution through out-of-town discount furniture outlets, for example). Superior performance firms will often seek to work with intermediaries who can assist in the communication of their product claims (for example, a manufacturer of scientifically balanced diet formulation cat food distributing the product via veterinary practices). In contrast, the relationship orientated producer will favour a distribution channel that can enhance its relationship with customers (an up-market wallpaper manufacturer distributing their products through small, exclusive furniture boutiques which offer the customers a decorating advisory service, for example).

The conventional strategist always has to be concerned about the nature of competition, the potential threat they may represent, and the development of appropriate response strategies. Possibly the most widely known source of theories on the effective management of competitors is Michael Porter, the Harvard Business School professor, whose first major text (Porter 1980) has subsequently been followed by a whole series of writings on this critically important issue. Porter has proposed that competitive threats can be classified into five major types:

1. The threat of other producer firms already operating within the market sector seeking to increase market share (for example, the ongoing battle between brands such as Heineken versus Fosters lager around the world).
2. The threat of customers moving upstream to also become producers and/or using their purchasing power to dominate terms and conditions of purchase (for example, a telephone company starting to manufacture its own telephones; a car manufacturer which might use its purchasing

power to demand price reductions from its component manufacturers during periods when world car sales are falling).

3.   The threat of a supplier moving downstream to become a producer and/or using its control over critical resources to dominate terms and conditions of sale (for example, lumber companies entering the furniture manufacturing business. A natural gas producer seeking to increase prices to electricity generators using gas-fired firms' power stations during a period of very cold weather has created an increase in world energy prices).

4.   The threat of substitute goods entering the market (for example, a new cancer drug which vitiates the need for a piece of specialist medical equipment used by clinicians who have traditionally treated the cancer by carrying out major surgery on their patients).

5.   The threat of a new entrant that was not previously a major player in the market (such as the impact on Kodak of Sony's entry into the digital camera market).

In the past, conventional strategists have tended to focus their attention on monitoring the downstream components within their market system. The risk of this somewhat myopic approach was clearly demonstrated by the oil crisis in the 1970s when the OPEC countries sought to gain greater control over the pricing and consumption of crude oil. Many Western products, such as plastics, automobiles and electrical goods, made affordable by using low-cost hydrocarbon feedstocks as inputs in high volume/low unit manufacturing operation (such as nylon shirts) and/or during consumption, required that the customer have access to low-cost energy sources (V6-engined cars, for example).

The impact of the OPEC restriction of supplies and its concurrent demand for higher crude oil prices was to trigger a global recession which caused strategists, possibly for the first time, to carefully assess the impact of scarce resources on the future positioning of products in their respective markets (for example, the need for American automobile manufacturers to begin offering their customers smaller cars; the requirement of construction firms to improve insulation levels in new houses in order to reduce occupants' energy bills).

More recently, some firms have begun also to realise that suppliers, as well as possibly being able to constrain input resources, can also be a major source of new opportunities. For example, most of the recent advances in the modern computer's data processing capability have come not from the laboratories of the computer manufacturer, but from the entrepreneurial behaviour of its suppliers (examples being Intel's ongoing efforts to create a new computer chip that is even more powerful than its world-beating Pentium product, and the diverse range of Windows products developed by Microsoft).

Over the last few years, the growing recognition of the importance of working closely with key suppliers has caused many conventional original equipment manufacturers (OEMs) to move from the traditional, conflict-based negotiation style of using purchasing power to drive down input prices, towards scenarios based on achieving mutual benefits from their supplier–customer relationships. This change in management practice is often described as 'building stronger supplier–customer chains'. It usually involves firms mutually determining how to optimise responsibilities for the various stages of the value added processes associated with the production and delivery of goods to end user markets (Storey 1994).

Transactional organisations seeking to improve the quality of products may thus open negotiations with key suppliers to adopt a TQM operating philosophy. Price orientated producers might discuss with suppliers the benefits of JIT to reduce work progress costs. Superior product performance organisations might suggest the creation of a joint venture R&D laboratory to incorporate new component technologies more rapidly into their product. The relationship orientated organisation might move to create electronic data interchange (EDI) links with its suppliers in order that this would then improve its ability to advise customers on the probable delivery time for products or services which might be delayed due to late inbound shipments from suppliers.

THE MACRO-ENVIRONMENT AND STRATEGIC RESPONSE

In an increasingly turbulent and rapidly changing world, neither the conventional strategist nor the entrepreneurial marketer can afford to ignore the potential influence of factors contained within the macro-environment. For example, no matter what the strategic positioning of the firm, in 1998/99 no firm would be wise to assume that the global economic turmoil created by the collapse of the new Tiger nations such as Malaysia, Thailand and Korea will have no impact on the performance of their organisations. As we enter the new millennium, and as firms based within the Pacific Rim seek to rebuild exports to generate hard currency, Western transactional and price orientated firms can expect to face a greater intensity of competition in relation to both standard and bottom-of-the-market goods being offered at extremely competitive prices.

The influence of politics is created because politicians often utilise changes in economic policy to deliver the manifesto that they feel will appeal to their electorates and thereby guarantee re-election in the future. For example, in the next few years Western Europe can be expected to be strongly affected by the political aims of countries such as France, Germany, Italy and Holland seeking to make a success of their move to achieve European Monetary Union through the establishment of a single currency. Thus the performance of conventional firms elsewhere in the world, no matter the nature of their strategic positioning, will undoubtedly be critically influenced by the relationship between the value of their currency and the European Monetary Unit, or EMU.

As illustrated by the above examples on economic and political trends, the conventional strategist clearly needs carefully to analyse which factors within the macro-environment can be expected to impact performance, and to plan accordingly. The entrepreneur should remain alert to the fact that these factors often provide just the opportunity he or she has been waiting for to enter new markets. For example, in the mid-1980s, we saw the emergence of a cultural trend in both the US and Western Europe towards the middle classes being increasingly concerned about 'healthy living'. Many of the large, conventional food manufacturers ignored this change, presumably in the belief that it was merely a passing 'fad'. However, smaller firms, such as those involved in the growing and processing of organic foods, rapidly realised that the healthy living trend offered new opportunities to expand rapidly into new markets. As a result, these smaller firms were suddenly able to negotiate contracts with national supermarket chains who were desperate to add organic items to their range of in-store products, but found they were unable to source the items from the larger firms who had traditionally supplied the bulk of their purchases.

THE INTERNAL DIMENSION TO STRATEGY IMPLEMENTATION

Possibly one of the most useful tools for assisting the conventional selection of areas within the organisation which might provide an opportunity for change which will contribute to enhanced delivery of strategy is Porter's (1985) 'value chain' concept. This model, as shown in Figure 2.5, proposes that an opportunity for adding value comes from (a) the five core processes of inbound logistics, process operations, outbound logistics, marketing and customer service, and (b) the four support competencies of management capability, human resource management (HRM) practices, exploitation of technology and procurement.

For transactionally excellent firms, assessment of the value chain will tend to concentrate on analysing internal value added activities to determine potential sources of competitive advantage based around finding new ways to enhance the price/quality/value product combination to be offered to customers. In recent years a major impetus for Western firms to upgrade

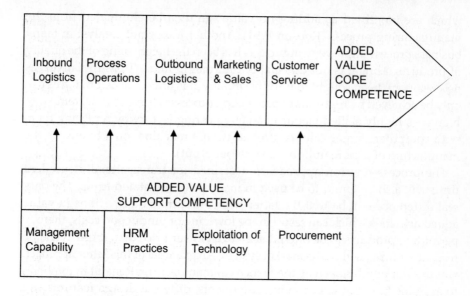

Figure 2.5 A value chain model

existing value added process activities was the evidence from Japan which clearly demonstrated that by concentrating on continuously seeking to improve manufacturing processes, firms in industries such as electronics, automobiles and ship building were able to market standard goods offering a performance/quality/price mix clearly superior to those being offered by other suppliers in global markets.

Recognition of the new standards the Japanese were setting for the overall total product performance of standard goods sparked off a massive re-interest among major Western corporations in how to re-acquire the leadership in manufacturing competence which these corporations had initially acquired during the early years of the Industrial Revolution in the nineteenth century (Harrington 1991). This aim has resulted in widespread acceptance of a whole range of different techniques for upgrading current processes. One example is activity based costing (ABC) which is designed to use management accounting systems as a means of identifying more clearly the nature of the resources required to serve the needs of particular customer groups. Knowledge generated from ABC permits the firm to determine more clearly the nature and impact of real costs on value added activities (for example, time lost in machine set-ups due to excessive product diversity) and then to instigate appropriate remedial actions (Cooper and Kaplan 1991).

An approach known as process value analysis (which originated in the 1950s but only really became popular in the 1980s) involves documenting the time and expense for each activity within the production process. Activities which are identified as adding no value can then be eliminated from the manufacturing process (Robson 1991). Another important catalyst in many business process improvement projects has been the heightening of the quality of products. Thus it is not unusual to find that in many TQM initiatives, as new ways are been sought to improve quality, it is often realised that this can only be achieved by revisions of production processes (for example, removing high cost, highly skilled labour in an engineering factory by replacing them with computer numerically controlled (CNC) machine tools to ensure the manufacture of a more uniform quality of output).

The process revision approaches described for transactionally excellent firms will also be found to be used in many price orientated firms. The only real difference will be that the latter will concentrate on revisions in value added activities which can result in the lowering of production costs, thereby permitting products to be offered at an even lower price than those available from other firms within the market system. An example of this latter approach was the work undertaken by the French car manufacturer Renault in the 1990s to examine how the selection of components, different design features and automation of assembly could be combined to reduce car assembly costs. The outcome in 1998 has been the launch of the new Renault Clio which is several hundred pounds cheaper than economy model hatchbacks being offered by other European producers.

For the superior product performance firm, examination of internal process activities, although often containing an element of concern about sustaining efficiency and lowering costs, tends to be focused primarily on ways of optimising the internal processes associated with development of new and/or improved products. For example, in the pharmaceutical industry, side effect tragedies such as those caused by the drug thalidomide have caused government regulatory bodies (for example, the Food and Drug Administration (FDA) in the US) to place much greater onus on the industry to ensure that new formulations do not have a hazardous impact on patients. Gaining government approval for new drugs is now a major hurdle in seeking to minimise the time from product discovery to market launch. Over the last ten years major players in the industry have thus moved away from minimising contact with the outside word as a mechanism to enforce strict commercial confidentiality for the longest possible length of time. Instead, they have adopted a less adversarial, more cooperative operating culture followed by revisions in development processes, such as working in partnership with the regulatory authorities from day one of the R&D programme and bringing in outside specialist testing laboratories to undertake a major proportion of the clinical trials work.

In the case of delivering a relationship orientated strategy, a firm will tend to examine how internal processes can be streamlined and improved to achieve further improvement in the quality of service offered to customers. As service quality perceptions are heightened, this tends to be accompanied by a further deepening of the relationship between suppliers and their markets. This type of firm will thus often focus on the strategic change issues, such as revising employee job roles and exploiting advances in information technology (IT) to further upgrade the quality and speed of information management across the organisation.

For this reason, many service firms are now moving away from using a hierarchical structure linked to tightly defined job roles, and towards introducing flatter structures centred around self-managed teams with the expectation that these changes will result in these organisations becoming more flexible in their response to serving market needs (Chaston 1998). Similar benefits can also be expected for firms who introduce interactive databases for monitoring process flows through all stages of the service generation and delivery process. This latter type of approach is now common within most major insurance companies which, when contacted by a client concerned about the status of his or her claim, can now use an integrated database system to identify within minutes the stage that has been reached in the claim approval process and accurately to estimate when the customer can expect to receive a decision from the firm. In the late 1990s, many of the larger insurance companies are going beyond using information engineering to manage basic administrative transactions and are now increasingly using IT to manage post-claim approval activities. For example, Direct Line in the UK is now capable of assuming total responsibility for obtaining quotes for a car repair, of evaluating these and then of selecting the garage which will be instructed to undertake the work.

ADDING A DASH OF ENTREPRENEURSHIP

Over the last ten years, the procurement philosophies of the major car manufacturers have undergone fundamental shift. Gone are the days of a muliplicity of suppliers, each producing large volumes of a specific component, with contracts being awarded on the basis of price. In order both to stabilise costs and to improve 'build quality', the car companies are forming closer relationships with a much smaller number of approved suppliers who are expected to manufacture a much broader range of components. Furthermore, these suppliers can no longer survive just by delivering standard parts. They are now expected to undertake the responsibility of designing, testing prototypes, assembling sub-assemblies and completing all aspects of the quality assurance role.

The conventional strategy for any supplier wishing to remain in business has been to diversify its operations through joint ventures, the opening of new plants located nearer to their customers, and the acquisition of other component manufacturers. A good example of this philosophy is provided by the Saturn corporation (Welles 1996) based in Detroit in the US. Originally a single plant operation, over recent years this company has formed joint ventures in China and Europe; has purchased an electromechanical switches producer, Beta Manufacturing, to acquire new plants in Mississippi and Mexico; has expanded into plastic housings by buying MCAM Products, and then broadened the product portfolio by merging with MacoTech Controls.

However, Saturn has realised that although these conventional strategies permit the firm to survive, continued pressure on suppliers from the car companies to reduce prices further will erode profit margins over time. Saturn's solution has been to recognise that it had to become more entrepreneurial. To achieve this goal it have begun to invest in developing new products it knows to be on its customers' 'wish list', but which are not yet available in the marketplace. The advantage of this approach is that these new products are based upon technology over which Saturn can retain proprietary ownership, thereby permitting it to obtain higher prices from its customers. One example is its recent development of an automated rear window opener for minivans which is a third of the weight of any competitor's product, can be produced at half the cost and is easier to install. The entrepreneurial dimension to this product is that it took two years to develop, with no guarantee that customers would buy the product. To close the sale, Saturn developed a computerised sound mapping system which tests the part for quietness, thereby demonstrating to potential customers that the component operates a noise threshold well below that of any other similar component which might be available from other suppliers.

REFERENCES

Abernathy, W., Clark, K. and Kantrow, A. (1983), *Industrial Renaissance*, Basic Books, New York.

Berry, L.L. (1982), 'Relationship marketing', in Berry, L.L., Shostack, G.L. and Upah, G.D. (eds), *Emerging Perspectives on Service Marketing*, American Marketing Association, Chicago, pp. 25–8.

Chaston, I. (1998), 'Self-managed teams: assessing the benefits for small service sector firms', *British Journal of Management*, Vol. 9, pp. 1–12.

Cooper, R. and Kaplan, S. (1991), *The Design of Cost Management Systems*, Prentice-Hall, New York.

Gummesson, E. (1987), 'The new marketing – developing long-term interactive relationships', *Long Range Planning*, Vol. 20, No. 4, pp. 10 – 20.

Harrington, H.J. (1991), *Business Process Improvement: The Breakthrough Strategy for Total Quality, Productivity and Competitiveness*, McGraw-Hill, New York.

Kotler, P. (1997), *Marketing Management: Analysis, Planning, Implementation and Control*, ninth edn. Prentice Hall, Upper Saddle River, New Jersey.

Moores, P. (1999), 'Technology and management', *Financial Times*, 18 February.

Nystrom, H. (1990), *Technological and Market Innovation: Strategy for Product and Company Development*, Wily & Sons, Chichester.

Porter, M.E. (1980), *Competitive Strategy: Techniques for Analysing Industries and Competition*, The Free Press, New York.

Porter, M. (1985), *Competitive Advantage: Creating and Sustaining Superior Performance*, The Free Press, San Francisco.

Reichfeld, F.F. and Sasser, W. (1990), 'Zero defections: quality comes to services', *Harvard Business Review*, September–October, pp. 301–7.

Robson, G.D. (1991), *Continuous Process Improvement*, The Free Press, New York.

Storey, J. (ed.) (1994), *New Wave Manufacturing Strategies: Organisational and Human Resource Management Dimensions*, Paul Champion Publishing, London.

Tedlow, R.S. (1990), *New and Improved: The Story of Mass Marketing in America*, Heinemann, Oxford.

Webster, F.E. (1992), The changing role of marketing in the corporation, 'Journal of Marketing', Vol. 56, October, pp. 1–17.

Welles, E. (1996), 'This year's model', *Inc. Online*, Goldhirsh Group, Boston, MA, p. 28.

MAPPING THE FUTURE

INTRODUCTION

Virtually every major text on management provides extensive coverage of the processes and techniques associated with the development of strategic marketing plans. The roots of this approach are grounded in the principles of Frederick Taylor's theory of scientific management and the classicist school of management thinking. A number of justifications for the benefits of adopting a strategic marketing planning orientation have subsequently been tabled by various authors.

Porter (1980), for example, argued that planning is a process which ensures that the policies of departments are coordinated and directed towards the achievement of a common set of goals. Hax and Majluf (1984) feel that planning provides a mechanism with which to assess systematically a firm's thinking about its long-term future. Wildavsky (1973) supports the view that planning is a superior form of management because it generates policy proposals that 'are systematic, efficient, co-ordinated, consistent and rational ... The virtue of planning is that it embodies universal norms of rational choice.'

Similar views concerning the planning process were also expressed by Jelinek (1979) in her writings concerning the system known as Objectives, Strategy and Tactics (OST) developed in the early 1960s by Texas Instruments. Unusually for a strategic planning approach, one of the primary reasons for the development of OST was to improve the organisation's innovation management capabilities. This was achieved by evolving procedures to improve the way that employees acquire and share the new knowledge that is a requisite for successful new product development.

Published evidence does appear to support the view that under certain conditions, organisations can gain benefits from creating a strategic marketing plan to guide their operations. One of these conditions is that of business stability. Fredickson (1984) found that the comprehensiveness of decision processes was positively related to performance in stable business environments and negatively related in unstable situations. It would also appear that when an industrial sector enters maturity, a dominant technology prevails and market growth is minimal, firms can benefit from using detailed marketing plans to guide future operations.

Additionally, firms which need to make heavy capital investments to achieve specified revenue goals (for example, a coal company planning to sink a new mine shaft in order to provide the output needed to support a planned major expansion into overseas markets) would probably be advised to undertake a detailed evaluation of the financial implications associated with the implementation of future plans. Given the irreversibility of major investments in new fixed asset commitments and the high costs of exiting the sector, it is likely that neither management nor external stakeholders would approve any large-scale project unless the proposal were underpinned by a detailed plan (Woodward 1965) Similarly, the directors of a highly division-alised firm operating across numerous locations would probably not be very comfortable if they were not provided with detailed business plans when being asked to approve decisions about the allocation of scarce resources or when assessing performance variance across a diversity of business portfolios.

Writings on the factors influencing the success and failure of small businesses often tend to conclude that it is critical for owner/managers to adopt a structured approach to marketing planning. Thus it is perhaps not surprising to find that most texts on small business management stress the importance of developing a detailed plan both to identify opportunities and to define how various elements of the organisation will contribute to achieving the firm's specified performance goals (see, for example, Fry 1992). This philosophy is also reflected in many of the training programmes offered to SME firms. In the South West of the UK, for example, within a five-day training scheme funded by the government for individuals interested in starting a new small business, over 50 per cent of the course content is concerned with constructing a marketing plan.

IS MARKETING PLANNING REALLY NECESSARY?

Despite the extensive support which marketing planning as a business process has received over the years in both large and small firms' academic literature, Mintzberg (1994) has very eloquently argued that research based upon observation of actual managerial practices across both differing sectors and sizes of firm has produced only limited evidence to demonstrate convincingly that structured planning is fundamental to the success of organisations. Furthermore, in an earlier study specifically concerned with the behaviour of entrepreneurs, Mintzberg and Waters (1982) concluded that in the case of the Canadian supermarket chain Steinberg Inc., this highly entrepreneurial corporation was directed from inception by Sam Steinberg without any apparent recourse to a formalised business planning process. However, when the company decided that the future lay in the construction of shopping centres, it was necessary for the firm to go to the capital markets to raise additional equity. At this juncture the company found that potential investors were not prepared to back the new initiative unless they were provided with a detailed plan. It was thus necessary for the company to adopt an apparently planning orientated culture, although in reality this behaviour was exhibited only in order to satisfy the desires of potential new stakeholders.

Venture capitalists from as far afield as London, England; Silicon Valley, California; and Auckland, New Zealand, confirm that many of the intuitive entrepreneurs they meet have rarely prepared any detailed information about their new business proposition prior to commencing their search for external funds. Hence the usual opening move in the funding application negotiations is to arrange for the preparation of a detailed marketing plan. Furthermore, the experience of these venture capitalists is that although their organisations will use these plans to monitor the subsequent performance of their investment, they also find that their entrepreneurial partners can rarely be convinced of the benefit of using these plans to assist them in the day-to-day management of their businesses.

Another source of information on the very limited appeal of marketing planning among entrepreneurs is the materials documenting the development and launch of many of the world's most innovative projects. Thomas Edison appears to have had minimal awareness of the need for planning while developing the electric light bulb. Frank Whittle, when working on his jet engine in the 1930s and 1940s, clearly had little interest in quantifying the commercial implications of his radical new approach to aircraft propulsion. Similarly, it seems that Steven Job had few concerns about the need to develop detailed proposals for the future market opportunities of PCs while working on the first Apple computer in his garage at his home in California.

When trying to persuade entrepreneurs of the advantage of having well documented marketing plans, one might mention the possible benefits, including the following.

- It forces an assessment of the external environment
- It forces an assessment of the organisation's internal competences
- It quantifies the expected performance goals for the new venture
- It identifies the scale of required resources and the degree to which these will have to be met through the attraction of external funds
- It creates a 'road map' which can be used to monitor actual performance versus plan upon launch of the venture.

Although such arguments will be accepted without question by a graduate from any business school, the reader should not be surprised to find that it will often be almost impossible to convince most inventors, intuitively entrepreneurial owner/managers and scientists/technologists working in laboratories, of the merits of diverting themselves away from working on their 'big idea' to spend time writing a marketing plan. Nevertheless, on the basis of the author's experience, one can probably hope to gain acceptance for the merits of planning more easily in the following situations.

1. Where an inventor is at the stage in the lifecycle of his or her enterprise where further progress is blocked without being able to attract significant external borrowings and/or equity capital.
2. Where an existing small firm has grown rapidly, managerial staff have been recruited (or employees have been promoted to managerial positions) and the entrepreneurial owner/manager wishes to delegate the firm's 'future visioning' activities increasingly downwards.
3. Where an owner/manager is engaged in succession planning and wishes to ensure that his or her nominated replacement is capable of sustaining the firm's entrepreneurial behaviour.
4. Where a large firm has established a 'new ventures centre' to stimulate all employees to consider developing new entrepreneurial ideas, and needs to ensure that individuals who are generating ideas are capable of presenting a detailed proposal to assist the venture centre staff in evaluating the merits of the proposition.
5. Where a large organisation faces a rapidly changing external environment and, in order to survive, needs to move from an operating philosophy based upon incremental improvements in current strategic practices towards a new philosophy which promotes a higher level of entrepreneurial thinking from all employees.
6. Where a diversified conglomerate with a mix of entrepreneurial and conservative operating divisions is seeking to determine how best to allocate financial resources to the activities associated with new project initiation, project launch and ongoing project operations.

THE PROCESS MAPPING MODEL

Most of the writings on entrepreneurial business planning (for example, Rich and Gumpert 1985) adopt the standard classicist ten-phase process model of

1. undertaking external and internal market analysis
2. developing SWOT

3. summarising key issues
4. specifying performance objectives
5. defining strategy/strategic mix
6. defining strategic tactics
7. describing the action plan
8. presenting financial forecasts
9. specifying control systems
10. examining contingency implications.

Unfortunately, the potential risk of this approach is that it fails to emphasise the importance of determining whether really entrepreneurial solutions exist which can permit the organisation to succeed through the effective challenging of conventions. Additionally, given the apparent adverse reaction the phrase 'marketing planning' seems to evoke among most entrepreneurs, it is probably advisable to use alternative terminology such as 'mapping the future'. Thus, in an attempt to overcome this potential obstacle, an alternative process mapping model is presented in Figure 3.1.

It is important to recognise that although the process model has a linear, sequential appearance, as users progress through the phases of the decision determination process they must expect to encounter new information which necessitates reassessing the validity of earlier decisions (for example, capability assessment may reveal that the organisation lacks certain critical competences, in which case it will be necessary to return to the entrepreneurial opportunity assessment stage to generate alternative ideas that are more compatible with identified capabilities). To underline the likely outcome that model users will have to undertake process reiteration, Figure 3.1 contains a feedback loop as a means of communicating to the reader the importance of not becoming locked into a linear, sequential mindset when developing entrepreneurial plans. Additionally, it is also proposed that where limited

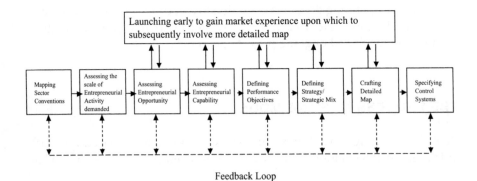

Figure 3.1   A model for mapping the future

information exists and/or there is the need to acquire a higher level of market experience prior to finalising a detailed map, then the firm may decide to implement a small-scale market entry in order to acquire a greater understanding of the actual opportunity which exists from exploiting its new entrepreneurial idea.

The proposed entry point into the process model is first to gain a detailed understanding of the conventions of the type described in Chapter 1 which exist within the industrial sector(s) of which the organisation is member. For most organisations, there is significantly less risk in achieving ongoing performance growth through incremental improvements to current policies or revising conventional strategies, than in adopting a more entrepreneurial operating philosophy. Thus the second step in the model, as shown in Figure 3.2, is to assess the performance gap that exists between aspirations concerning future performance and the level of performance which can be achieved through extrapolation of current strategies versus the alternative of implementing a new unconventional strategy.

Assuming that the scale of the performance gap is of a magnitude that makes an entrepreneurial solution appear to be the best way forward, then the next step is to examine the nature of the opportunities which might exist. Intuitive entrepreneurs can probably immediately vision some extremely creative ideas. Unfortunately, intuitive entrepreneurs are somewhat rare animals in the world of business. Thus, for the majority of managers – who tend to be biased towards a somewhat more logical, analytical approach – one tool which they may wish to consider using is the Opportunity Mapping Matrix of the type shown in Figure 3.3.

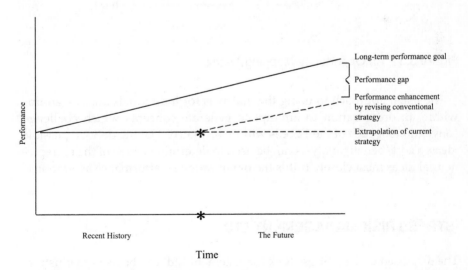

Figure 3.2   Performance gap assessment

Essentially, the matrix in Figure 3.3 suggests that there are two dimensions to entrepreneurial change – internal process change and market change. Furthermore, in both cases the degree of business risk increases the further the idea generation moves away from current practice. Thus, in the case of internal processes, modifying current process is a lower-risk proposition than the introduction of a completely new process. Similarly, along the market dimension, modifying the marketing mix for the current product represents a much lower risk than developing a new product or entering a new market with a new product.

Increasing Risk →

Market Management		Current Process	Revised Process	New Process
	New Market/ New Product	(10) Current Process/ Unconventional New Product in New Market	(11) Unconventional Process Revision and New Product in New Market	(12) Unconventional New Product and New Process in New Market
	New Product/ Current Market	(7) Current Process/ Unconventional New Product	(8) Unconventional New Product and Process Revision	(9) Unconventional New Product and New Process Introduction
	Revised Marketing Mix/Current Product	(4) Current Process & Product/ Unconventional Marketing Mix Activity	(5) Current Product/ Unconventional Mix and Activity Process Revision	(6) Current Product/ Unconventional Mix Activity and New Process Introduction
	Current Market Activities	(1) Current Conventional Behaviour	(2) Current Conventional Market Activity/ Unconventional Process Revision	(3) Current Conventional Market Activity/ Unconventional New Process Introduction

Process Management

(Increasing Risk ↑)

Figure 3.3   An Opportunity Mapping Matrix

The usual approach to using the matrix is for individuals and/or groups within an organisation to attempt to generate concepts which challenge convention for each of the 12 cells within the matrix. Having defined possible ideas, a cost/benefit analysis can be used to determine which of the entrepreneurial ideas most closely fulfils the organisation's performance aspirations.

STRESS RISK MANAGEMENT LTD

The disguised case of 'Stress Risk Management Ltd' can be used to illustrate an application of the Opportunity Mapping Matrix approach. In the early

1990s it became extremely apparent that factors such as work pressures, downsizing, changing work practices and declining job security were combining to raise stress levels in the workplace. Furthermore, in the UK a landmark case brought by a social worker against his employer established the legal precedent that employers can be liable for massive damages if it can be proved that they failed to operate a policy of 'due care and responsibility' for all of their employees.

Stress management is now a rapidly expanding sector of the consultancy and management training scene in the Western world. Most service providers within this market sector focus on identifying stress and then delivering stress management training. The founders of Stress Risk Management, an organisational psychologist and a business lawyer, decided that the core market of delivering stress management courses would rapidly become highly competitive. They therefore adopted the entrepreneurial approach of offering a service to employers that (a) assesses the level of stress within the workplace and (b) provides guidance on whether the level of stress creates a potential legal risk for their client.

In only five years the business grew from nothing to an annual turnover in excess of £5 million. In the mid-1990s, however, the firm realised that a number of competitors were now entering its market segment: unless the firm introduced a radical change in its operations, it was increasingly unlikely that it would achieve its performance goal of exceeding an annual turnover of £10 million two or three years into the next millennium. At one of the organisation's 'weekend retreats', following participation in guidance on sector conventions, brainstorming and lateral thinking, employees were placed into small groups with the requirement that they generate ideas that 'challenge convention' that could be entered into an Opportunity Mapping Matrix. The event facilitators consolidated all the inputs from each of the groups, from which they selected what appeared to them to represent the best ideas. The outcome of this latter activity is shown in Figure 3.4.

As can be seen on the internal process dimension, the two unconventional activities are to (i) introduce self-diagnosis tests which employees can enter onto a computer-based, automated analysis system (currently the company collects data using trained observers), and (ii) combine data inputs from video recordings and environmental sensors for stress scenario analysis using Artificial Intelligence (AI) software.

In the market dimension relating to the current process/product situation, the entrepreneurial marketing mix idea involves forming an alliance with a major business travel agency to launch a free magazine offering guidance on avoiding stress in the workplace and when travelling. However, the groups were unable to generate unconventional ideas for a new product either in the

		Current Process	Revised Process	New Process
Market Management	New Market	(10) No unconventional idea identified	(11) Take self-diagnostic tools into high-stress environments such as law & order, security, fire and medical sectors	(12) Use video and sensors to monitor stress in cockpits of military aircraft
	New Product	(7) No unconventional idea identified	(8) Self-diagnostic tools developed for self-monitoring by employees at risk	(9) Use videos and sensors to create 'total company' stress AI-based evaluation system
	Revised Mix	(4) Launch a free trade magazine with a leading travel firm concerning stress at work and when travelling	(5) Selected self-diagnostic tools made available on company website	(6) Videos and sensors linked to AI system for monitoring employees at risk
	Current Activities	(1) Current Activities	(2) Introduce self-diagnostic computer tools into assessment process	(3) Use video materials environmental sensors to undertake assessment using Artificial Intelligence (AI)

Process Management

Figure 3.4 An Opportunity Mapping Matrix for Stress Risk Management Ltd

existing market or in a new market based around the continued use of the firm's current output generation process.

Revising process to incorporate self-diagnostic analysis tools sparked entrepreneurial ideas for all cells in the market dimension. Similarly, the move to introduce a new process based around AI generated ideas for revising marketing mix, developing a new product for the current market (a totally automated analyser and liability reduction guidance generator capable of monitoring work conditions across an entire organisation) and entering a new market sector. The latter idea was to install the AI system in the cockpits of military aircraft to provide commanders on the ground with a 'real time' assessment of whether situations are beginning to develop in which increasing pilot stress might begin to impair the pilot's judgement in high-risk situations such as combat or attempting to land in worsening weather situations.

Subsequent cost/benefit analysis revealed that all four cells based around the self-diagnostic tools offered greater returns than new actions associated with seeking to expand the business through further investment in marketing the firm's existing conventional process activities. Further investigation of the new process based on exploiting AI revealed that although this was a very exciting idea offering tremendous revenue opportunities, the R&D capabilities and required financial investment were well in excess of the firm's current technical competences and resource base. Additionally, at this early stage in the lifecycle of the new technology, there could be no real guarantee that a viable, fault-free system would be developed. Thus, on the basis of this cost/benefit analysis, Stress Risk Management Ltd decided to centre progress in its planning activities upon exploiting the entrepreneurial opportunities offered by the self-diagnostic stress assessment systems. It was also determined, however, that the firm should seek to form an alliance with a software firm with extensive experience of AI software as the basis for entering this new market segment sometime within the foreseeable future.

TWO APPARENTLY VERY DIFFERENT SOLUTION MAPS

The company Levi Strauss was born in the aftermath of the California gold rush by exploiting the entrepreneurial idea of using denim as the raw material to manufacture extremely durable work clothing. After World War II, the company then initiated the highly entrepreneurial idea of repositioning the product as a fashion good. By the 1970s the firm had become a global player in the clothing industry and sustained market position through very creative advertising campaigns.

Over time, however, the entrepreneurial spirit at Levi Strauss seems to have waned. Attention has increasingly been focused on expanding manufacturing output by opening new plants. Unfortunately, the firm appears to have ignored the emergence of two different threats: being unable to compete on price against producers based offshore in low labour-cost areas of the world and the erosion of their upmarket position by designer brands such as Calvin Klein. In the US between 1990 and 1998, brand share fell from 48 per cent to 25 per cent. The firm's apparent 'solution map' to these problems has been to adopt the conventional mass production solution to uncompetitive production costs by announcing the closure of 22 American plants and cutting 5,900 jobs (Jones and Grant 1999). Presumably, this will be followed by moving virtually all of its manufacturing operations offshore. Given the world-wide recognition of the Levi's brand name it is probable that the company will survive. However, the organisation's apparently current conventional mindset of focusing on lowering operating costs and being unwilling to experiment with the type of entrepreneurial ideas which were the source of past global success, must raise questions over whether remaining a conventionalist will permit the brand ever to regain a significant proportion of lost sales.

Some years ago, similar concerns were being expressed about the computer giant IBM. Having acted as an entrepreneur in the age of the mainframe, the firm positioned as the leading producer of hardware faced massive inroads into its business following the launch of low-cost PC clones in the 1980s. The company's initial response was to cut jobs and close plants. Then, at the beginning of the 1990s, under the leadership of Louis Gerstner, the company adopted a new solution map by repositioning itself from being a 'box manufacturer' to becoming the leading provider of solutions to complex IT problems. A new entrepreneurial spirit has emerged within the company. One recent example of this new orientation is the firm's decision to licence the Java software language owned by IBM's long-time rival, the Sun corporation (Zuckerman 1997). To promote acceptance of Java, IBM has dropped its traditional behaviour of not being willing to share knowledge with others. Instead, it has initiated actions such as sponsoring a Java world tour, preaching the benefits of the technology of the language to software developers around the globe, and participating in a $100 million venture capital fund to finance Java-related start-up companies. Another example is the company's massive promotional investment in seeking to persuade potential customers in the small firms sector that IBM is the leading provider of assistance to organisations seeking to enter the world of the Internet and electronic commerce.

CAPABILITY ASSESSMENT

As demonstrated by the Stress Management case, there is no point in pursuing an opportunity unless an organisation has the competences required to successfully exploit a defined business scenario. One possible approach for the rational entrepreneur wishing to undertake an organisational capability assessment is to draw upon the idea presented in Chapter 2; that to succeed, organisations must have the competences to manage both external and internal environments.

The first step in such an evaluation process is to determine those variables that are important contributors to the effective implementation of external and internal activities. It is important to note that the specific nature and number of variables will probably vary both between organisations within an industrial sector and between industrial sectors. Illustrative examples of factors influencing ability to control external events might include:

1. the entrepreneurial skills of the organisation's marketing team
2. the entrepreneurial skills of the organisation's sales force
3. the effectiveness of the organisation's advertising campaigns
4. the organisation's effectiveness in product/service distribution
5. the effectiveness of the marketing operations executed by the organisation's key competitors.

To generate some form of quantitative assessment, a simple scoring scheme could be used ranging from 1 to 10. A possible rating scale might be 'extremely poor' through to 'extremely strong'. In the case of factors 1 to 4, the stronger the organisation is in an area of capability, the nearer to 10 the allocated score will be. In the case of factor 5, the more effective the competitors, the lower the assigned score will be. An overall mean score for external event management effectiveness can be generated by dividing the total score for factors 1 to 5 by the number of factors.

Illustrative examples of factors influencing ability to control internal events might include:

1. the organisation's effectiveness in undertaking entrepreneurial processes associated with generating the outputs required by customers
2. the level of quality achieved across all aspects of the organisation's activities
3. employee productivity
4. the level of the workforce's entrepreneurial skills
5. the effectiveness of the organisation's management information systems to monitor activities and diagnose causes of performance variance.

A simple scoring scheme ranging from 1 to 10 could again be used to assess internal capability. A possible scale might be 'extremely poor' through to 'extremely strong.' In the case of factors 1 to 5, the better the organisation, the nearer to 10 the allocated scores will be. An overall mean score for internal event management effectiveness can be generated by dividing the total score for factors 1 to 5 by the number of factors.

The next stage is to create a Directional Mapping Matrix of the type illustrated in Figure 3.5. This matrix has two dimensions: capability to manage external activities, and capability to manage internal activities. To permit entry into the matrix of the scores generated during the analysis of factors influencing performance, each dimension is divided into the sub-groups of poor (mean factor score between 1 and 3), average (factor score between >3 and 7) and high (factor score between >7 and 10). As can be seen from the matrix in Figure 3.5, where the mean scores for external and internal mean management effectiveness analysis are entered on the matrix will determine the recommended action for implementing the type of marketing action to exploit most effectively any newly identified entrepreneurial opportunities.

The strategic options offered within the matrix in Figure 3.5 are as follows.

Cell 1 The organisation has low internal and external entrepreneurial management capability. It would then be inadvisable to progress any entrepreneurial ideas until these weaknesses have been overcome.

Cell 2   The organisation has average external entrepreneurial management capability but low internal entrepreneurial activity capability. Under these circumstances only an entrepreneurial idea concerned with minor revisions to marketing programmes should be considered.

Cell 3   The organisation has high external entrepreneurial activity management capability but low internal entrepreneurial activity capability. The focus of action should be on an entrepreneurial idea founded upon fundamental changes in marketing programmes (for example, creating a new distribution channel; introducing a radical, new promotional philosophy).

Cell 4   The organisation has average internal entrepreneurial management capability but low external entrepreneurial activity capability. Under these circumstances only an entrepreneurial idea concerned with minor revisions to output generation processes should be considered.

Cell 5   The organisation has average entrepreneurial internal and external management capabilities. An entrepreneurial idea concerned with significant changes in marketing programmes and significant modifications to existing output generation processes should thus be progressed.

Capability to Manage Entrepreneurial External Activities

(1)	(2)	(3) 0
Terminate entrepreneurial planning due to lack of appropriate capabilities	Only progress plan involving minor revision in marketing programmes	Concentrate on plan concerned only with fundamental changes in marketing programmes
		3
(4)	(5)	(6) >3
Only progress plan involving minor revision in process activities	Progress plan involving changes in marketing programmes and revisions to process activity	Concentrate on plan to change marketing programmes and implement major upgrade in process activities 7
(7)	(8)	(9) >7
Concentrate on plan concerned with significant revision in process activity	Concentrate on plan to modify marketing programmes and introduce radical new process activities	Concentrate on plan to retain leadership through ongoing upgrades to marketing programmes and process activities
0 3	>3 7	>7 10

Capability To Manage Entrepreneurial Internal Activities (row label at left)

Figure 3.5   A Directional Mapping Matrix

Cell 6 The organisation has high external entrepreneurial activity management capability but only average internal entrepreneurial activity capability. The focus of action should be on an entrepreneurial idea founded upon fundamental change in marketing prgrammes coupled with major revisions to current output generation processes.

Cell 7 The organisation has high internal entrepreneurial activity management capability but low external entrepreneurial activity capability. Any entrepreneurial idea should be founded upon significant revision to current output generation processes (for example, replacing manual processes with IT-based decision tools; introducing new technologies into certain assembly processes).

Cell 8 The organisation has high internal entrepreneurial activity management capability and average external entrepreneurial activity capability. The focus of action should be on an entrepreneurial idea founded upon the introduction of a radical new output generation process linked to significant modification to marketing programmes.

Cell 9 The organisation has high entrepreneurial external and internal activity management capabilities, and therefore is probably already a market leader. To retain this leadership position, the focus of action should be upon fundamental ongoing changes in marketing programmes coupled with the development of a radical new output generation process.

PERFORMANCE GOALS AND STRATEGY

Earlier process model work on gap analysis already provides the organisation with a preliminary definition of long-term performance goals in relation to variables such as total sales and/or profitability. Having completed the detailed idea generation and capability assessment activities, it is usually necessary to revisit these earlier preliminary forecasts to determine whether they remain realistic or may require modification.

Most organisations would be well advised to retain the strategic philosophy which has permitted them to achieve their performance aims to date. As proposed in Chapter 2, the strategic options available which apply to both conservative and entrepreneurial organisations are the four alternative pathways of *product performance excellence, price performance excellence, transactional excellence* and *relationship excellence*. Assuming that the organisation decides to retain its existing strategic philosophy when implementing the entrepreneurial change idea defined in the opportunity and capability assessments, then the next step would be to build a detailed plan based around the relevant strategic behaviours described in Chapter 2 which are associated with successful delivery of the chosen strategic pathway.

VISIONING UNSEEN FUTURES

The process model presented earlier in Figure 3.1 assumes that an organisation's new vision is usually built upon the emergence of new ways of challenging convention as a means of generating new solutions to old problems. In today's world it is frequently the case that new solutions are based upon the application of new technologies (for example, the AI solution in the Stress Risk Management case). Such approaches are therefore most likely to appeal to the entrepreneurial organisation which likes to vision by extrapolating from reasonably well documented existing scenarios.

For the 'big dream' entrepreneur, however, such situations would be perceived as constraining the boundaries of opportunity. Although much rarer, such individuals are those whose visions lead to the creation of completely new industries and/or industrial sector operating philosophies (examples in the past are the founders of Bayer, DuPont, Ford, the GE corporation and IBM; more recent examples include Intel and Virgin).

Researchers of globally successful firms, Hamel and Prahalad (1994), have concluded that permanent market leadership can only come from 'seeing the future' and ensuring ownership of this future ahead of competition. They propose that in existing markets this is probably achieved by seeing the future and then, through entrepreneurial activities, establishing new conventions (for example, the founder of Microsoft, Bill Gates, realised that software would replace hardware as the critical basis for gaining competitive advantage). The alternative is to see the future and invent new markets (Xerox's launch of the photocopier is one example).

Hamel and Prahalad believe that successful global players tend to exhibit the following characteristics:

- infinite curiosity and being prepared to take on apparently impossible challenges
- never being satisfied with their achievements, and reinvesting profits into new products and/or process innovation
- always being open-minded and willing to learn from any source.

Once an organisation has acquired these characteristics, then it would be well advised to use materials, such as those provided in the New Zealand Export Board's research study of expected trends for the new millennium, as the basis for constructing a picture of the future (Tradenz 1997). Tradenz has recognised that firms seeking to be 'world class' will need to comprehend and effectively respond to the environments likely to prevail in world markets as we enter the new millennium.*

The Tradenz view of the world is that the forces of openness which have created a borderless world mean that opportunities for growth from expanded global marketing activities are almost infinite. Tradenz highlight, for example, the opportunities available as China moves to establish a developed nation economy, and from India's recent moves to create a more outward-looking economy. They point to the 'flying geese' pattern of industrial development in which developing nations move from labour-intensive production towards the creation of automated, capital-intensive industries. It is argued that for the existing developed nations, by acting to assist these 'flying geese', they will find major new market opportunities for their knowledge-based industries such as computing and automated manufacturing tools.

The study also highlights the importance not just of relying on carefully crafted plans based upon detailed research, but also of being willing to respond rapidly to unforecastable, unexpected 'wild card' events. This philosophy is illustrated by the highly entrepreneurial New Zealand Carter Holt Harvey roofing company when, during a bush fire in California, the only homes in the fire zone which survived were the ones that had a roof made from the company's fire-resistant Decra tile. By exploiting the dramatic evidence provided by aerial photographs of this and other natural disasters, the firm has been able to gain global awareness of the ability of its product to protect homes during events such as forest fires and fires following earthquakes.

Another aspect of the study was to note that the actual manufacturing of goods and/or the production of core services is becoming an increasingly smaller component of the total overall product cost. This is especially the case if globalisation permits the standardisation of the output generation process. The leisure goods producer Nike is cited as an example of an entrepreneurial firm that created what is now increasingly being seen as a new convention: designing the products in the US, subcontracting the manufacturing to Pacific Rim countries, and then marketing the output as a global brand.

Additionally, the advent of modern process technologies permits producers to experiment concurrently with adding value by customising output to suit individual customer needs. Linked to this picture of new millennium markets is the need to 'think global, but respond locally' by exploiting the power of computerised databases to rapidly identify newly emerging micro-market niches and to respond with appropriately tailored products or services (for example, an entrepreneurial producer of yacht sails analysing weather char-

* For those readers who wish to obtain more information on this study, it can be accessed on the Tradenz website at http://www.tradenz.govt.nz

acteristics around the globe and offering customised designs most suited to local climatic wind conditions).

As we enter the new millennium, the entrepreneur will have to be increasingly vigilant about changing power bases within his or her marketing channels. Traditional end user outlets may be replaced by new market entrants (for example, retailers moving into the world of consumer banking and offering an alternative source of financial services). Component suppliers may find that the horizons of their OEM customer base have to be widened to encompass the new manufacturers in countries such as India and Brazil.

The final issue covered in the Tradenz report is the impact of what Tradenz termed 'electronic connectedness', which demands that firms recognise the growing importance of technologies such as EDI, the Internet and video conferencing for communicating with others in their sector's supplier–customer chain. In an electronically interlinked borderless world, firms that resist adopting innovations such as home page sites with 'hot buttons' – for the use of customers seeking more information, comparing offerings, placing orders and/or seeking post-purchase services from their suppliers – are likely to sink into oblivion.

During the process of gaining greater understanding of trends in the next millennium as the basis for the subsequent 'visioning of unseen futures', it is also critical to recognise that few customers exhibit sufficient foresight to be able to describe their future needs (for example, it is doubtful that the average consumer 15 years ago could have accurately described a world in which the

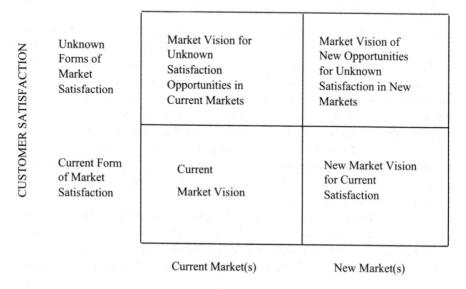

Figure 3.6   Alternative directions for future visions

telephone moved from a being a static device to one which delivers a diverse, mobile communications system). The first step in any entrepreneurial visioning is thus to recognise that a firm's current view of its markets usually represents only the tip of the demand iceberg. Imagine the vast new range of opportunities available if, as suggested in Figure 3.7, the entrepreneurial marketer does not limit thinking merely to extending known satisfaction into new markets, but is prepared to probe the issue of what forms of satisfaction have not yet even been recognised by the customer.

A sample application of the concept of visioning the future can be provided by examining the future opportunities for digital VCRs. Recently introduced into the American market, the digital VCR consists of some integrated circuits, a power supply and a multi-gigabyte hard drive. By connecting the system to your television you are provided with a much more powerful recording system which is expected to render obsolete the traditional tape-based VCR. The reason for this outcome is that the new system is much easier to programme: simply type in the names of the shows you want to tape, or your favourite actor, and the machine will monitor all channels, downloading those programmes that fit your viewing requests.

As summarised in Figure 3.7, this new digital VCR has the capability to open up a whole series of new market visions. For example, in the current market/unknown satisfaction box, it will likely be possible to provide the

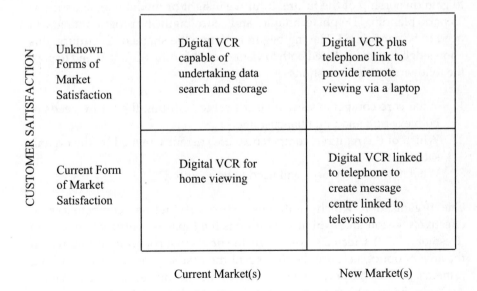

Figure 3.7 Example of directions for future visions

system with key words and phrases against which the system will then search the airwaves for relevant programmes over a specified period of time. Thus, if the children are doing a school project, the system will obtain relevant data to assist them. Furthermore, the visual data can be downloaded for incorporation into the children's project.

In the new market/current satisfaction box, it should be possible to link the system to the user's telephone, e-mail system and/or video conferencing system. This would then create a total message centre which means the customer can now sit comfortably in his or her living room, managing all his or her electronic messages via the television set. Finally, in the new market/unknown satisfaction box, having linked the digital VCR to the telephone system, the user can then dial in from a remote location via a laptop computer and watch his or her favourite programme without having to wait until he or she returns home.

CANON'S APPROACH TO VISIONING

Whatever scale of future vision is adopted by the organisation, it is apparent that in the search for as yet undefined customer satisfaction opportunities, the entrepreneurial organisation will need to go beyond standard research techniques, such as customer surveys or usage and attitude studies, in order to gain ownership of the future. Intuitive insight or methodologies, such as scenario planning, Delphi techniques and neurolinguisitic programming, will need to be considered. Having begun to define the shape of the future, this knowledge can then be used both to vision possible future markets and to pose the following critical questions.

1. What core competences will be critical to fulfilling the future needs of both existing and potential customers?
2. Which of the required competences are currently owned by the organisation?
3. What new competences will need to be acquired?

One organisation which continues to exploit internal competences to effectively vision and exploit the future is the Japanese corporation, Canon (Desmond 1998). Created 60 years ago, the firm's first core competence was in the area of optics, because the firm spent the first 30 years of its life making cameras. In 1962, the decision was made to enter the office equipment market. As Xerox held patents on photocopying technology and would not grant licences, Canon drew upon both existing and newly acquired competences to develop new photocopying technology which did not infringe the Xerox patents. Launched in 1970, their first product, the NP-1100, had a number of entrepreneurial features, including the first-ever toner cartridge which vitiated the need for service calls.

Having become world leader in photocopying machines, the firm then utilised existing competences and some more newly acquired competences to enter the desktop printer market. Their rationale for entering this new market was based on a simple but highly relevant vision: photocopiers would eventually become obsolete because, as computer costs decline, people would increasingly send information via e-mail, which would be downloaded to an adjacent printer. Although Hewlett-Packard beat Canon in terms of launching the first low-cost ink-jet printer (as reflected by Hewlett-Packard currently holding a 52 per cent share of the world market, compared with Canon's 22 per cent share), Canon has continued to sustain its vision concerning opportunities in electronic printing, and is currently concentrating on two areas of opportunity. The first is in adapting ink-jet technology for printing directly on to fabrics. Canon is now the market leader in supplying massive printing machines to the clothing and textile industry. The second, and potentially even larger, opportunity, is to create a digital camera that can be linked to a printer without the need for the intervention of a computer. Consumers could then produce their own photographs without having to own a computer or buy film for their camera. This latest vision clearly links together Canon's competences across the areas of optics, cameras, digital data transmission, print reproduction and specialist inks, and will undoubtedly allow the organisation to sustain its strategy of acting entrepreneurially to further develop and expand its increasingly extensive line of innovative products.

REFERENCES

Fredickson, M.J. (1984), 'Decision making and environments', *Management Science*, Vol. 30, pp. 683–771.

Fry, F.L. (1992), *Entrepreneurship: A Planning Approach*, West Publishing, Minneapolis.

Desmond, E.W. (1998), 'Can Canon keep clicking?', *Fortune Magazine*, 2 February, pp. 58–64.

Hamel, G. and Prahalad, C.K. (1994), *Competing for the Future: Breakthrough Strategies for Seizing Control of your Industry and Creating the Markets of Tomorrow*, Harvard Business School Press, Boston, MA.

Hax, A.C. and Majiluf, N.S. (1984), *Strategic Management: An Integrative Approach*, Prentice Hall, Englewood Cliffs, NJ.

Jelinek, M. (1979), *Institutionalizing Innovation*, Praeger, New York.

Jones, D. and Grant, L. (1999), 'What caused Levi's blues?', *USA Today*, 23 February.

Mintzberg, H. (1994), *The Rise and Fall of Strategic Planning*, Prentice Hall, Englewood Cliffs, NJ.

Mintzberg, H. and Waters, J.A. (1982), 'Tracking study in an entrepreneurial firm', *Academy of Management Journal*, Vol. XXV, No. 3, pp. 465–99.

Porter, M.E. (1980), *Competitive Strategy: Techniques for Analyzing Industries and Competition*, The Free Press, New York.

Rich, S.R. and Gumpert, D.E. (1985), 'How to write a winning business plan', *Harvard Business Review*, May–June, pp. 156–66.

Tradenz (1997), *Competing in the New Millennium*, Tradenz, New Zealand.

Wildavsky, A. (1973), 'If planning is everything maybe its nothing', *Policy Science*, Vol. 4, pp. 127–53.

Woodward, J. (1965), *Industrial Organisation: Theory and Practice*, Oxford University Press, Oxford.

Zuckerman, L. (1997), 'IBM seeks new image in quest to unseat Microsoft', *New York Times*, 1 September.

4 ENTREPRENEURIAL PROMOTION

An important area of expertise required of the marketer is an understanding of all the activities associated with the customer reaching a purchase decision. Such knowledge is acquired through both trading experience and market research, leading to the development of a buyer behaviour model of the type shown in Figure 4.1.

Models of this type are typically based on the behaviour over time of the majority of customers. By building this type of model for a specific product or service purchase scenario, the marketer is provided with a map of the prevailing buyer behaviour conventions which can be used to plan promotional campaigns. Conversely, the entrepreneur can use this same knowledge to develop promotions which are effective because they breach existing conventions.

The entry point into the model shown in Figure 4.1 is the customer first recognising a need to purchase the product or service. The next stage is the customer beginning to acquire information about potential products or services which might fulfil his or her specific needs. After acquired information has been processed by the customer, a purchase decision is reached.

As the customer moves through the early phases of the purchase process, information which has been acquired will create expectations about actual product performance. These expectations are tested in the post-purchase evaluation phase. If the product lives up to or exceeds expectation, positive feedback ensues; thereby raising the probability that the customer will purchase the same product in the future. Conversely, if the product fails to meet expectations, negative feedback occurs which reduces the probability that the customer will consider purchasing the same product in the future.

In Figure 4.1, the sources of external information are those data supplied through the promotional activities of the supplier and/or any intermediaries who might be involved in the product distribution process. Internal information comes from those sources which are beyond the direct control of

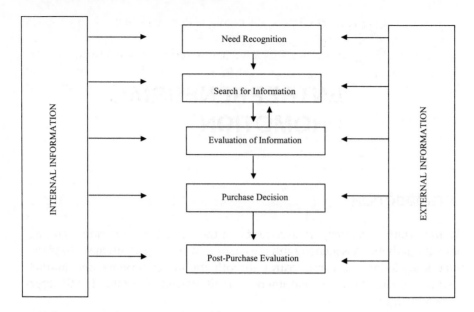

Figure 4.1 Five-phase purchase process model

supply chain members (for example, product experiences communicated by friends or relatives; recommendations made by colleagues at work; consumer programmes on television).

THE ROLE OF INFORMATION

The traditional view of promotion is that it comprises all of the activities associated with communicating information about a product or service. The aim of these activities is to achieve the outcome that the information provided causes the customer to purchase the organisation's output. Marketers have a variety of alternative information delivery systems available to them which can be used to construct an appropriate 'promotional mix strategy'. These include:

- *Advertising*, which permits the delivery of a non-personal message through the action of renting time and / or space within an advertising channel (for example, radio, television, cinema, newspapers, magazines and billboards).
- *Collateral promotion*, which covers a variety of message delivery approaches including brochures, packaging, merchandising materials, logos / company information on delivery vehicles, layout of office areas where service

providers have contact with the customer, and the corporate clothing worn by company personnel.

- *Direct marketing*, which exploits advances in technology to create an ever-increasing portfolio of techniques to interact with the customer (for example, mailshots, telemarketing, e-mail, fax, voice mail and Internet home pages).
- *Personal selling*, which involves one-to-one interaction between the customer and the producer's sales force (and/or the sales staff of intermediaries) within the marketing channel.
- *Public relations and publicity*, which constitutes a broad range of activities designed to promote the organisation and/or the organisation's products (for example, an article about the organisation in a trade magazine; sponsorship of a popular sporting event such as a round-the-world yacht race).
- *Sales promotions*, which involve activities that offer the customer some form of temporary, increased value (for example, a coupon good on next purchase; participation in a competition offering the chance to win an overseas holiday) (Kotler 1997).

Given the critical role that information plays in the effective execution of a promotional campaign, extensive research has been undertaken by academics seeking to determine exactly how delivered information can influence customer attitudes and/or values. A large proportion of these studies have focused upon the effectiveness of advertising, but many of the conclusions that have been reached are equally applicable to other activities, such as personal selling and public relations.

One of the issues which has concerned researchers is the degree to which involvement in the product influences customer response to promotional information. Houston et al. (1987) have suggested there are three types of involvement:

1. product involvement – the influence of the customer's prior purchase and consumption experience on his or her individual needs and values
2. situational involvement – the individual's concern for his or her behaviour at each stage in the buying process
3. response involvement – the persuasiveness of the information provided to the customer.

Munch and Hunt (1984) feel that response involvement is a critical variable in terms of determining the effectiveness of a promotional message. They propose that 'involvement is the level of perceived personal importance and/or interest evoked by a stimulus (or stimuli) within a specific situation'. From this definition it can be concluded that in cases of low involvement goods (for example, the decision to purchase a commodity good such as potatoes), the customer will progress rapidly through the problem solving model of the type shown in Figure 4.1. Over time, however, the repeated consumption of that good will evoke memory patterns that create feelings which may ultimately influence future purchase patterns.

Many manufacturers of long-established brands – for example, Maxwell House coffee and Kellogg's Cornflakes – recognise the importance of using promotion to reinforce the memory patterns evoked by regular product usage. They have remained successful over the years by using an unchanging promotional strategy based around a conventional execution delivered through a mass advertising channel such as television to sustain customer loyalty.

Other researchers feel that it is also important to recognise that promotional information can generate both cognitive and emotional reactions. Thorson and Friestadt (1989), for example, maintain that emotions triggered by a promotional message will 'condition' customers' feelings and thereby influence subsequent purchase decisions. By the 1980s, the issue of emotional content had resulted in the emergence of a school of thought which believes that the customer's attitudes towards the level of effective persuasion which is achieved by a promotional campaign will be influenced by whether he or she finds the promotional message likeable or not. Brown and Stayman's (1992) research demonstrated that attitude towards an advertisement has a distinct effect on brand cognition and a positive impact on customer attitude towards a brand.

It is also felt by some academics that in assessing potential response to promotional messages, it is also necessary to recognise the influence of customer personality. Wilson (1973) defines personality as a 'general disposition to behave', and contrasts this with attitude, which he describes as 'opinions on something in the world outside'. He further posits that personality is a continuum: at one extreme, there are the customers who seek consistency in their lives through the purchase of items that are familiar, comforting and re-assuring; at the other extreme are the customers who continually seek exposure to new and different experiences. Foxall and Goldsmith (1994) have concluded that this latter group are more likely to respond to entrepreneurial (that is, unconventional) promotion because they are flexible thinkers, are able to tolerate a higher level of ambiguity, and have high self-esteem and a positive attitude towards seeking out new sources of sensation.

CHALLENGING CONVENTION

In planning a promotion, most organisations opt for following the current conventions which prevail in their industrial sector. There are, however, two potential problems with this philosophy. First, if one or more competitors decide to act aggressively and increase their level of promotional expenditure, then the conventional firm is typically also forced into upweighting its own promotional activity in order to avoid losing market share. Second, smaller brands rarely have the scale of financial resources required to support the same level of promotional expenditure as the larger brands, and hence find it extremely difficult to increase their market share.

Given the potential drawbacks of following prevailing conventions, a feasible alternative is for a firm to adopt a more entrepreneurial attitude towards its promotional activities. As summarised in Figure 4.2, the four available options are:

1. target a different customer group
2. find an alternative approach to the delivery of promotional information
3. identify a new way of managing the purchase process
4. find an unconventional way of managing the flow of promotional information within the market system.

ENTREPRENEURIAL CUSTOMER TARGETING

The TSB

Similar to branded, tangible consumer goods, the financial services market tends to be dominated by a small number of large companies who have

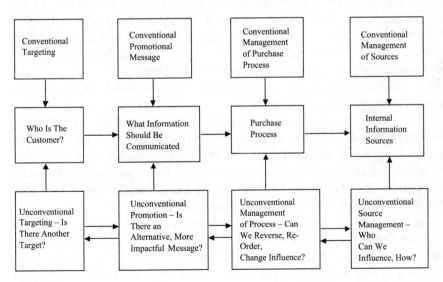

Figure 4.2 A process model for analysing opportunities for entrepreneurial promotion

established conventions for the promotion of banking and insurance services. In the UK consumer banking sector, the four largest high street banks – Barclays, Lloyds, HSBC (formerly Midland Bank) and NatWest – all tend to communicate very similar benefit claims, and their combined spending contributes well over 80 per cent of the sector's total promotional expenditure in the UK consumer banking sector (Channon 1985).

All the high street banks compete intensely for a share of new accounts opened. Since the main opportunity to recruit new customers is to attract them when they open their first ever account, the primary battleground is the youth market. In the early 1980s, the conventional promotional strategy was to seek to attract new accounts from among young people entering higher education. The TSB was a very small bank and it recognised that it lacked the resources to compete effectively in the student market. What it realised, however, was that its competitors were ignoring young people who, at the age of 16, had decided against further education and were leaving school to start work.

Research on school leavers revealed that these individuals are tugged in two different directions. On the one hand, they need to demonstrate their new independence by publicly rejecting the rules established by their parents' generation. This is clearly apparent in their mode of dress, their popular music preferences and their use of language. On the other hand, earning money and being able to be seen as moving towards adulthood pulls them in the direction of wishing to be perceived as responsible. It was apparent, however, that because most parents bank with the major high street institutions, school leavers are somewhat suspicious about using these same institutions. In the past, these larger banks were perceived by school leavers as not being interested in them because the new account promotional message centred on communicating services such as the availability of free student railcards and overdrafts at a special low rate of interest for students.

The TSB's solution, based on the theme 'the bank that likes to say Yes', featured trendy teenagers and used the latest popular music as the soundtracks of its commercials. Furthermore, these commercials also communicated that at the TSB, by opening a new account, teenagers would receive free banking, a discount card for use in Virgin record stores and a mail order programme offering savings on records, cassettes, hi-fi equipment and musical instruments. The bank also launched a free magazine, *TS Beat*, which was distributed through schools, clubs and rock concerts.

The impact of this entrepreneurial campaign exceeded all expectations. In 1984, the first year of the new promotional approach, the number of new youth accounts opened was 66,000 – twice the level achieved in the previous year. The bank's share of the youth market rose from 7 per cent to 22 per cent, and in 1985 the number of new accounts being opened reached 126,000. Research showed that unlike other banks, where recommendations by parents was still the dominant factor influencing bank choice, this factor was relatively unimportant to the new TSB customers. They decided on the bank for themselves and their primary reason was that they felt the TSB to be more approachable and helpful than other banks in relation to being genuinely interested in meeting the needs of teenage customers.

The Co-operative Bank

The Co-operative Bank has always been a somewhat unconventional member of the UK banking scene (Baker 1994). It is owned by the Co-operative Wholesale Society and is therefore not controlled by the same London stock exchange interests that have a major influence over the lending and borrowing strategies of other UK banks. The Co-operative Bank has retained strong ties with the UK co-operative movement, thereby acquiring specific lending expertise in areas such as labour unions and community action groups. This heritage has created a lending policy which has always been governed by an unwritten ethical code that money will never be lent to environmentally or politically unsound organisations.

Following deregulation of the UK banking industry in the 1980s, the intensity of competition between financial institutions increased dramatically. A major component of this competition was that the major banks significantly increased their promotional spending. The convention sustained by this activity was to continue to communicate the features of the wide range of financial services available to customers. The Co-operative Bank also utilised this type of promotional strategy. However, because it is an extremely small bank, its annual share of voice was less than 1 per cent and, by 1988, spontaneous awareness recall of advertising was only 7 per cent among UK consumers.

By 1991, the Co-operative Bank's share of the consumer banking market had fallen to 2.1 per cent. Research revealed that among the general public, the bank was seen as old-fashioned and working class, with left-wing tendencies and 'not really a proper bank'. However, research on customers revealed a very different picture. They valued the bank's heritage and a significant proportion had opened an account because they saw the organisation as being much more ethical than its competitors.

At the time of this research, the UK had just experienced a decade that in hindsight was perceived by many as the decade of uncaring, selfish materialism, promoted in part by the policies of Margaret Thatcher's Conservative government. There was now increasing public awareness of the wider social and environmental implications arising from large firms acting unethically. As evidenced by the success of Anita Roddick's Body Shop operation, this change in consumer attitudes was reflected by a swing in consumer buying behaviour towards purchasing environmentally friendly products that were not tested on animals.

The decision was made to break with the convention of advertising the range of financial products which the bank could supply, and instead to articulate overtly the institution's position as a highly ethical organisation. The promotional platform was founded on the proposition that 'the Co-operative Bank is committed to the responsible sourcing and distribution of funds'. Research revealed that this was perceived as a highly appealing claim. These studies also assisted in clarifying the type of organisations with whom the bank should not do business; namely, firms that use animals to test their products, firms that pollute the environment, and firms that are involved in the arms trade and/or trade with oppressive political regimes.

The bank used this consumer feedback to construct a written ethical policy that stated with whom it would do business, and undertook a detailed audit of corporate customers to ensure that they lived up to the bank's stated ethics. This resulted in the bank refusing to have any further dealings with some of its existing corporate customers.

The implemented promotional strategy was built around different ethical issues and each execution told the story of a normal family undertaking an everyday purchase activity that required borrowing money from the family's current bank. In every case, there was the ironic twist that the family's bank had loaned money to a company that was detrimentally linked in some way to what the family was purchasing.

Although the campaign had no significant impact on market share, the bank found that a greater proportion of new accounts were being attracted from the ABC1 customer group. These individuals had a high level of personal wealth which resulted in the bank's personal current account deposits increasing by 9 per cent in the first year of the campaign. In addition, this type of customer greatly increased the opportunity for cross-selling and, consequently, the bank's personal savings deposits rose by 49 per cent. Furthermore, although the campaign was directed at UK consumers, the bank also experienced a significant increase in its corporate account business. Corporate current account balances rose by 116 per cent and deposits by 161 per cent. Most of the new business came from sectors that had an affinity with the promotional campaign's ethical message (that is, education, health care and charities).

ENTREPRENEURIAL MESSAGE CONTENT

Nestlé Gold Blend

In a well established, mature market, the brand leader's promotional message usually defines the conventions for how benefit statements are communicated.

The standard approach to attempting to steal brand share from a leader is to communicate a similar message, but to spend even more money on promotion (for example, the advertising wars between Pepsi and Coca-Cola, and between Burger King and McDonald's). An alternative proposition, appealing especially to a firm with limited promotional resources, is to act entrepreneurially by communicating a very different message that breaches market sector conventions. Of course, if this entrepreneurial challenge is highly successful and the nature of the firm's promotional message is seen to be more effective, then other firms will adopt the same philosophy. Thus the entrepreneurial firm may eventually become the source of the new market convention.

One example of the successful challenging of convention is provided by the promotion of Nestlé's Gold Blend coffee in the UK. Launched in the mid-1960s, the firm used freeze-dried technology to provide a smoother, richer taste and Gold Blend was sold at a 25 per cent price premium over Nestlé's mass market brand, Nescafé (Baker 1992). Until 1987, Gold Blend's advertising, similar to other coffee brands, focused on communicating a rational, logical product-based performance claim. The apparently insurmountable task facing the advertising agency McCann-Erikson was, despite an available promotional budget somewhat smaller than the mass market brand leaders, to increase the sales of a brand perceived as a niche product by consumers.

At that time in the UK, the most popular television programmes were the soap operas such as *Dallas* and *Dynasty* which focused on the lives of extremely rich people in the American oil industry. The entrepreneurial decision was made to exploit this prevailing viewer interest by producing a coffee commercial based around the story of two single, personally successful but highly combative protagonists who clearly were romantically meant for each other. The various commercials in the campaign progressed the romantic relationship, but each was structured as a soap-type 'cliffhanger', leaving the viewer wondering what would happen next in the lives of these two individuals.

The campaign was launched in 1987 and, after 11 different episodes, climaxed with the 'happy couple' disappearing into the sunset in 1993. The unusually effective nature of the campaign in terms of capturing the interest of the general public was so powerful that it spawned compact discs (one of which entered the Top 10 on the album chart), a book and a video. The impact of Nestlé's move to break with the convention in coffee advertising of merely communicating a product performance benefit claim and instead featuring a love story, is reflected by the fact that over the period 1987–93, Gold Blend sales rose by over 60 per cent in a market where total category sales remained unchanged. More importantly, the brand's gain was incremental to the company, because growth was achieved without cannibalising the sales of other brands in the Nestlé portfolio.

Felix cat food

Another consumer goods category in which the promotional convention is to focus on the product benefit is cat food (Baker 1994). Typically, the convention is sustained by television advertising which reassures owners that their cats are eager to eat the brand. This message is communicated using the rational manner of owner endorsement with lingering shots of the cat food being forked from tin to bowl, accompanied by voice-over information about vitamins and minerals. By 1989, the UK wet cat-food market was worth £400 million, had achieved almost 100 per cent penetration among cat owners, sales had plateaued, and Whiskas Supermeat was the market leader with a share of nearly 50 per cent.

Felix, positioned in the sub-premium sector of the cat-food market, had a share of 6.5 per cent in the late 1980s. This poor performance, linked to the fact that it never received any advertising support, meant that the brand was under threat of being delisted by the major supermarket chains. The advertising agency BMP undertook a series of focus groups to determine consumer perceptions about conventional advertising which portrays idealised images of immaculately groomed cats and owners. These groups soon revealed that owners had a very different perception of their own cats. The immaculate pedigree bundles of fluffy affection represented in main brand advertising bore little resemblance to the cats owned by the research group's consumers. Instead, they reported that their cats were extremely lovable but mischievous characters who frequently exhibited exasperating habits such as clawing the furniture or bringing home dead animals which were proudly presented to the cats' owners.

The agency also discovered that consumers liked the black and white cat on the brand's new packaging. The creative team christened him 'Felix' and brought him to life by featuring him engaged in, or coming home from, various roguish activities and wanting to be fed. The end-line for all of these stories was 'Cats like Felix like Felix'. Initially, in 1989, Felix was featured in a black and white press campaign, but as sales began to increase, it was possible to afford a move into television advertising in 1991.

The impact of this highly entrepreneurial promotional approach is demonstrated by the fact that, by 1994, the Felix brand had risen to market leader. Achieved growth rates were not just impressive in terms of the cat food market. In 1991, Felix was the fourth fastest growing brand in any grocery category and, in 1992, was the second fastest growing grocery category brand in the UK.

Gateway 2000

Gateway 2000 is a mail-order computer manufacturer founded by Ted Waitt, who began by operating out of empty office space in a farmhouse. An important cornerstone of his operating ethos is the minimising of overheads, which perhaps explains why he manages the company's promotional campaigns without seeking input from an advertising agency. One of his earliest campaigns feautured a picture of his father's cattle herd. The logic behind this idea was that many PC clone producers often suddenly disappear from the market, leaving their customers without any technical post-purchase service support. The cow advertisement, linked to some 'down home' style copy was extremely effective in persuading potential customers that Gateway was a solid company based in the heartland of the US (Hyatt 1991).

Subsequent advertising campaigns have sustained this somewhat unconventional approach: one featured Waitt in an 1890s double-door saloon, playing poker and holding a royal flush; another featured a buffalo – which fortuitously coincided with the release of the blockbuster movie, *Dances With Wolves*. Having found that the star of the film, Kevin Costner, was to play Robin Hood in his next movie, Gateway exploited this theme in a campaign which featured Waitt as the champion of the poor.

ENTREPRENEURIAL APPROACHES TO PROCESS

Media Images

Media Images was a small design studio, operating regionally and founded by an individual with expertise in the development of educational products and activity packs for the UK road safety market. In seeking to diversity the firm's activities, he recognised that a significant revenue source for tourist attractions such as zoos and castles outside the holiday season is visits from local schools.

The firm assumed that its activity packs could easily be modified to meet the needs of schools using their visit to a tourist attraction as a component within the learning process (for example, studying history at a transport museum, or conservation at a bird sanctuary). The usual way in which suppliers market goods and services to tourist attractions in the UK is to adopt the conventional promotional process of mailshots followed by a visit from a salesperson. Media Images adopted this approach, but soon found that (a) it was extremely expensive relative to the company's limited financial resources and (b) the number of successful sales versus total number of calls was extremely low.

In reviewing this experience, the firm decided that one of the problems was that the potential client was not prepared to spend a sufficient amount of time listening to the sales presentation. The firm decided to re-visit the purchase process model and wondered whether entering the model prior to the customer collection of information might enhance the effectiveness of its promotional message.

It was decided that what was needed was a means of influencing the customer at the need recognition process phase. The firm achieved this through the entrepreneurial idea of (a) linking up with regional Tourist Boards in the UK and (b) mounting seminars on the effective exploitation of the school visits market. During the event, Media Images staff would cover issues such as how to promote the attraction to schools, assessing appropriate facilities, managing the booking process, pricing, and ensuring that teachers could be confident that their pupils would be provided with a genuinely educational experience. By forming a partnership with the Tourist Boards, Media Images gained the additional advantage of enhanced credibility with the tourist industry. The Tourist Boards were more than happy to use their own database and industry knowledge to ensure a high level of attendance at the events.

The seminars were extremely successful because this entrepreneurial 'customer education approach' to promotion assisted the audience in understanding the real complexities associated with succeeding in the school visits market. Furthermore, because they recognised that their organisations lacked many of the skills being exhibited by the Media Images team, it virtually guaranteed that by the end of the event many in the audience would seek a contract with the firm to assist them in managing the educational market. In only a few months, Media Images was able to rely on seminars and word-of-mouth recommendations from satisfied clients as the only promotional activities necessary to build a highly successful national business.

The book industry

One of the most radical changes in the opportunities available to firms for delivering promotional information to potential customers is the advent of the World Wide Web. Via this new medium, organisations can provide information, respond to enquiries and permit customers to execute their purchase decisions from the comfort of their own homes. In fact, it has become so popular that in many markets it is now a convention that firms must either have, or be considering the creation of, a website to service customer needs.

Even though the Internet is rapidly becoming a conventional promotional channel, one can find examples of firms who have moved first and can therefore be considered entrepreneurial in their exploitation of this new technology. In the book industry, one of the early entrepreneurs was the Amazon corporation in California. This firm is essentially a book store which realised that by moving its shop window on to the Web, it would be able to promote its range of products to the whole world, rather than just to people in the immediate vicinity of the store. Although Amazon has rapidly been followed by other players in the book industry, it was one of the first to use the Web to create a new global trading operation.

Another example is provided by the academic books division of Macmillan. The conventional way of marketing academic texts is to mailshot college lecturers and offer them the opportunity of being sent an inspection copy. This is a promotional device that permits the reader, without making a purchase, to reassure him- or herself that the new text is appropriate for the use of his or her students. If the lecturer decides to adopt the text, then he or she is permitted to keep the inspection copy.

The huge number of lecturers in the world means that publishers face a major logistics problem when seeking to ensure that where the lecturer does not adopt the text, the book is either returned or the lecturer is sent an invoice. Given the expensive nature of this conventional promotional process, Macmillan have come up with an extremely entrepreneurial solution. They now feature new texts in their entirety on their website. Interested lecturers no longer have to request an inspection copy because they can gain immediate access to new publications at the touch of a button.

ENTREPRENEURIAL APPROACHES TO INFORMATION SOURCES

Nestlé baby food

In the 1980s, Nestlé's baby food division in France was running an extremely poor second to Bledina, a brand owned by BSN, an $18 billion European branded goods company. Bledina had achieved its leadership position through aggressive promotional spending based around the conventional approach of spending heavily on television advertising (Rapp and Collins 1994).

Nestlé France was not prepared to enter into the expensive, and probably extremely risky, process of a head-to-head promotional spending battle with Bledina. Instead, it re-examined the conventions of how the customer acquires promotional information in the baby food market and the nature of the information contained within conventional promotional messages. Its unconventional solution was to identify another way of delivering the information that Nestlé cares about its customers' babies: the company opened rest-stops alongside the main autoroutes in France during the summer holiday season, where parents – at no charge – could stop, feed and change their babies. At each location the parents could visit the Relais Bebe Nestlé (the Nestlé 'Baby

Café') to be greeted by different baby food selections specially recommended by Nestlé dietitians to suit both different age groups and the time of day.

The next step in the alternative delivery of information was achieved by Nestlé building a database of new mothers to whom it mails a gift pack on a regular basis. Concurrently, the firm established a toll-free number via which parents could obtain free information and advice, and reassurance from a Nestlé licensed dietitian. The impact of this entrepreneurial approach to promotion is demonstrated by the fact that in only a few years, Nestle's market share in France went from 20 per cent to over 43 per cent.

Harley-Davidson

Although all organisations are aware of the existence of post-purchase evaluation, the conventional majority tend to create only minimal marketing structures to accommodate the promotional needs of the customer following purchase. For consumer goods, this is frequently achieved by having a department for handling complaints and/or offering a contact point where the customer can be provided with answers concerning any problems encountered during product usage. In those cases where the goods will require repairs and/or regular servicing over the life of the product, the supplier will create a system through which such services can be provided directly by its own technical specialists (for example, the teams at Boeing who work in close partnership with their customers in the airline industry) or contracted out to other specialist members of the supply chain (for example, the service departments operated by the car dealerships appointed by the major automotive manufacturers).

However, an effective example of how one can break with convention and really exploit the opportunities offered by the post-purchase evaluation phase is provided by the American motorcycle manufacturer, Harley-Davidson (Rapp and Collins 1994). In the early 1980s, this firm – whose name has for many years been synonymous with large powerful motorbikes – was faced with intense competition from Japanese firms such as Honda and Kawasaki that had invaded the American market, offering lower-priced, well made, heavyweight machines.

Having recognised the need to greatly improve build quality and thereby reduce defect rates, the next problem confronting the firm was how to rebuild customer loyalty. The solution was to recognise that in the minds of its customers, along with apple pie, John Wayne and the *Stars and Stripes*, the name Harley-Davidson is synonymous with the American dream of a free, democratic, wide-open-spaces lifestyle.

Instead of attempting to promote this concept through the traditional approach of large-scale pre-purchase promotions, what the firm decided to do was to adopt the entrepreneurial approach of exploiting the post-purchase evaluation phase. This it planned to achieve by communicating the promotional message that it was supplying a dream in which its machines were part of both a special relationship between owner and motorcycle and a special social relationship which can only come from being a Harley-Davidson rider.

In 1983, they formed the Harley Owners Group which rapidly became more commonly known as the HOG Club. Members were charged an annual fee of $35, for which they received an amazing range of benefits and the opportunity to participate in numerous social activities. Benefits included items such as an emergency pick-up service, a fly-and-ride rental programme, low-cost insurance, a touring handbook and the *Enthusiast* magazine.

In 1985, the formation of the club was followed by the firm promoting the creation of local HOG chapters aimed at encouraging owners living in the same area to get together to share their enjoyment of motorcycle riding. The firm also realised that its network of motorcycle dealerships had a critical role both in generating sales and, just as importantly, in assisting to sustain a positive post-purchase evaluation experience. The company formalised its aim of establishing an apparently seamless customer care web through the articulation of a vision statement of 'a commitment to continuously improve the quality of its profitable relationship with stakeholders (customers, employees, suppliers, shareholders, government and society)'. The dealers elect their own members to the Dealer Advisory Council and meet at least three times a year to provide feedback to the firm, which perceives its dealers not as links in the supply chain but as genuine friends of the organisation.

THE ENTREPRENEUR'S DREAM – THE INTERNET

If one were to ask entrepreneurs to describe the features they desire in a perfect promotional platform, their wish list would probably include the following attributes:

- the ability to communicate with customers anywhere in the world
- the ability to be available to customers 24 hours a day, 365 days a year
- the ability to design and produce advertisements without any expenditure on outside experts
- the ability to revise and change copy almost on a daily basis
- the ability to instantly communicate product line and/or price changes which have been revised in response to market trends

- the ability to process customer orders automatically at the 'touch of a button'.

The arrival of the Internet has of course permitted all of these entrepreneurial dreams to be fulfilled; so much so that this new medium is rapidly moving from an unconventional to a conventional medium through which firms can communicate with customers more effectively in virtually every industrial sector.

The entrepreneurs that have embraced the new medium with possibly the greatest enthusiasm are the owner/managers of small businesses. The reason for this is that, even with minimal technical skills and/or financial resources, they can now consider entering new markets anywhere in the world. If the reader wants examples of small business Internet success stories, then they should visit the Microsoft home page (www.microsoft.com/smallbiz/success). One recently published story on this site describes the trading experiences of a company called Dogtoys. As the name suggests, the company specialises is supplying a range of dog toys selected on the basis of both known favourites of their customers and meeting the requirements of different breeds of dog. The company perceives the Internet as a means of building a global customer base without the need to open any outlets in any country. Essentially, the business consists of a website and a warehouse. Not surprisingly, given that the company is featured by Microsoft, Dogtoys operates its entire Internet and direct marketing operation via a suite of Microsoft software products.

For those firms that as yet have not decided to enter the world of cyberspace, Hamel and Sampler (1998) have proposed that the Internet represents a new age in which many of the traditional marketing conventions will be broken. They point out that for the customer, traditional advertising tends to be a passive medium which has only a few seconds of airtime or limited print space during which to communicate the product story. Customers who enter cyberspace have much more control over reacting to the promotional messages provided. They can either seek more information or, if unstimulated by a supplier's website, can click a button to locate a more satisfactory source of knowledge. Given that freedom and control now rest in 'the hand controlling the mouse', effective Internet promotions must involve education, entertainment and enticement.

Another critical aspect is that the Internet provides access to truth. In a normal retail environment, the customer will visit only one or two outlets seeking information. On the Internet, the customer has access to sites run by 'neutral brokers' who are willing to provide detailed information on the relative merits of all products within an industrial sector. These sites also permit the user rapidly to acquire information on prices. In some cases, the user can state his or her product interest and sit back to await bids from potential suppliers. Furthermore because these potential suppliers are located around the globe, any Internet shopper can now purchase from whichever country offers the best deal.

In the past, many manufacturers only had contact with customers via an intermediary such as a retailer or an industrial distributor. The Internet now permits direct contact between supplier and final customer. This means that the two parties can communicate directly about product needs, thereby providing the highly flexible manufacturer the opportunity to customise its products to suit the specific needs of each individual customer. Some firms have already recognised the immense power that this type of relationship offers in terms of delivering total customer satisfaction. For example, a visitor to the Dell Computers website can not only request a customised specification for his or her PC, they can also automatically be advised on whether requesting a specific component will delay product shipment or whether it would create incompability problems for other aspects of his or her computer system. Nevertheless, it is important to recognise that even the most avid cybershoppers have a limited attention span and will tire of searching after a while. For this reason it is increasingly important that a supplier's website contains a very broad range of items if it wishes to build a long-term relationship with its customers.

For the entrepreneur who is considering building a major national or international business based solely upon marketing through the Internet, it is also important to understand that the promotional costs of establishing the business will be very high. This fact is demonstrated by the recent creation of the first online mass market toy store, eToys (Sellers 1999). The entrepreneurial founder of the business, Toby Lenk, originally hoped to establish a small business selling upmarket toys to the young, upwardly mobile market. The response of the venture capitalist approached by Lenk was that the idea was too small and that Lenk should consider starting a mass market Internet operation, competing with traditional warehouse retailers such as Toys 'Я' Us.

In the US, toys are a $22 billion industry and competition between retailers is therefore extremely intense. The eToys concept was targeted at those customers who do not enjoy spending hours searching through shopping malls for their children's toys. To attract these individuals, eToys positioned themselves as the place where shoppers can 'save time versus regular retail shopping'. The critical element affecting the success of any national/international Internet retailer, however, is the organisation's ability to rapidly attract customers to its website. It is estimated that, on average, the cyberspace retailer will need to spend at least 65 per cent of revenue on promoting its brand. This contrasts with the 5 per cent of revenue that the traditional retail outlet spends on supporting its customer base.

ENTREPRENEURIAL MARKETING

To launch eToys, Toby Lenk spent $3 million for a feature by America Online. In addition, he offers a 25 per cent sales commission to other net members who direct customers to the eToys website. Other promotional expenses include running advertising in the traditional media, such as televisions and magazines, as well as operating an online sweepstake. During the 1998 Christmas season, the sweepstake offered potential customers the opportunity to win the toy most in demand, the Furby robotic animal. The reason for operating the sweepstake is that the entrants provide eToys with new e-mail addresses to which the company can subsequently direct promotional messages.

The other critical aspect of Internet retailing is to ensure that customers remain satisfied with the speed of product delivery. To fulfil this requirement, eToys is required to make a massive investment in an extensive range of stock. Managing this aspect of the operation is not made any easier by the fact that the toy industry is characterised by having over 500 major suppliers. Additionally, during the Christmas selling season, eToys expends significant funds on actions such as offering free upgrades from regular to express shipping and automatically issuing a $5 coupon on any order for an out-of-stock item.

TOE IN THE WATER TO TOTAL IMMERSION

Even before the advent of the numerous new promotional pathways offered by the Internet, promotion was the element of the marketing mix offering the broadest range of opportunities for organisations to implement entrepreneurial actions. The following are some of the reasons why promotion is such an attractive entrepreneurial vehicle.

1. *Scale of activity* The marketer has the option of launching a single, minor event (for example, a sales promotion) through to a complete revision to the mainstream promotional message used to communicate the product benefit claim.
2. *Range of choice* The marker has access to a whole range of activities within the promotional portfolio, such as advertising, personal selling, public relations and sales promotion, any of which can provide the platform through which to deliver an entrepreneurial message to the customer.
3. *Variety of communication media* The marketer, when considering either advertising or public relations, can choose from a wide range of media channels such as television, radio, cinema, newspapers, magazines and posters.

For an organisation that wishes to test the appeal of a new, entrepreneurial approach to promotion, possibly the simplest and lowest-risk proposition is to use sales promotion. Within the promotional mix, sales promotions are typically short-term events which involve a variety of activities such as price pack, coupons, money-back offers, premiums and competitions that offer the customer some form of a temporary added value. The commonest forms of sales promotion are price packs and coupons, and these can therefore be considered as conventional activities in widespread use across virtually every market sector. Opportunities for more entrepreneurial actions are somewhat limited unless the marketer can identify a new, unusual way of delivering temporary added value. One of the easiest ways of achieving this objective is through premiums that offer the customer a very different, and therefore rapidly noticed, proposition.

Within the world of consumer goods marketing, one of the classic entre-preneurial premiums was that offered by Kool, the leading menthol cigarette brand in the US. In the 1970s, this company offered a sailboat as a premium. The unusual features of this premium were (a) although the boat was available at below cost, consumers still had to find well over $1,000 to redeem the premium, and (b) there was no perceived relationship between product usage and the premium. To the surprise of the industry (and, one suspects, also to the Kool brand manager), the premium captured the appeal of the market and thousands of sail boats were redeemed. An interesting side effect of this situation was that because the sails on the boat featured the Kool brand logo, when boat owners took to the water the company was provided with additional, free, floating promotional billboards on reservoirs and beaches across the US.

Another more recent and very different sales promotion has been used by Tiny, a company that manufactures and retails PCs in the UK consumer computer market. As part of its diversification, it created a telephone company as a platform for generating revenue from people using the Internet. Instead of the conventional approach of offering a PC package with discounted access to an Internet service provider, in July 1999 Tiny announced that if consumers were willing to subscribe to its service then they would receive a totally free computer.

Public relations is that aspect of the promotional mix whereby a firm has an announcement which contains sufficient news value that the media will run the story. Hence the firm receives what is essentially 'free advertising'. Public relations clearly offers an extremely powerful vehicle through which to gain additional market exposure for a firm. As a result, a massive global industry has been created which is willing, for a fee, to assist firms in managing their public relations budgets. In the main, most of the messages contained within public relations press releases are extremely conventional, communicating stories about new products, plant expansions and changes in company personnel. In addition, where a company encounters some bad publicity (for example, Perrier's problems some years ago with contaminated product), the corporate public relations machine is often a critical element in seeking to rebuild customer confidence.

Occasionally, however, the publicity message is based around a more entrepreneurial idea. One example of this approach was provided by a medium-size UK robotics company. As a leading-edge firm, its local Chamber of Commerce liked to feature it in industrial plant visits offered to overseas visitors to the area. Due to workloads, the Managing Director had to decline participating in a forthcoming tour by some Japanese industrialists. When made aware of this situation, its public relations agency wrote a short article around the headline 'UK firm bans Japanese from their factory' which inferred that the ban was because of concerns about industrial espionage. The UK national papers ran with the story and the result was that the firm was contacted by a number of major UK firms interested in installing robotic manufacturing systems.

The other route to highly effective public relations campaigns is where the owner or managing director of a business is a highly personable individual whose activities provide the basis of entrepreneurial media events. Two examples of this opportunity are provided by Richard Branson of Virgin and Anita Roddick of the Body Shop. In the former case, the media is provided with newsworthy stories of Richard Branson's adventures, such as attempting to fly a hot air balloon around the world. This contrasts with Anita Roddick, whose 'green principles' of business are always a source of opinion when yet another example is found of humankind's unwillingness to treat Planet Earth with sufficient care.

In industrial markets, the primary promotional vehicle is the company sales force. The majority of firms use conventional approaches for defining the role and task of their sales personnel. Here again, however, opportunities will arise to enhance sales force effectiveness by acting entrepreneurially. The usual outcome is that the success of the idea is then recognised by competitors and eventually becomes a new conventional management approach within an industrial sector.

Ultimately, the effectiveness of a salesperson is dependent upon the degree to which he or she is perceived by the customer as being able to offer guidance which can resolve problems that may be confronting the customer. In the case of entrepreneurial actions to add capability in the area of assisting the customer, most of these are typically based around exploiting new technology. One example is provided by the American food brokerage firm, Francoise Schwarz.

In the American military, service personnel and their families are provided with access to on-base supermarkets (or 'commissaries') which are operated by the armed services. These commissaries are located around the world wherever the American military has a base. Francoise Schwarz is a brokerage company which specialises in acting as an agent for major American branded consumer goods, having brokers who call on commissaries both inside the US and elsewhere in the world. One of the major problems the company perceived was that some commissary managers lacked skills in the area of ensuring that their stores carried a balanced, adequate range of stock, especially of leading branded consumer goods. The Francoise Schwarz solution was, in the early 1980s, to equip each broker with a computer. The broker would analyse store movement and on-hand warehouse stocks during his or her store visit. These data would then be transferred via a telephone modem to the Francoise Schwarz Head Office where they were incorporated in a store modelling software package which had the capability of generating a detailed item-by-item purchasing recommendation. The results of the analysis were transferred back to the broker who could then make a detailed presentation to the commissary manager advising upon possible changes in future ordering and item stocking patterns.

Last but not least are the entrepreneurial opportunities offered through advertising. However, it is necessary to recognise that most leading brands tend to be extremely conventional, using the same mainstream message that remains virtually unchanged over many years. Examples of such conventional practice include Procter & Gamble, Unilever, Maxwell House, Kellogg's, Heinz, Coca-Cola and McDonald's. Clearly, the approach must work, or these brands would have lost market share and would have been forced to introduce radically different campaigns.

The net outcome of this situation is, therefore, that it is either existing smaller brands or new market entrants who adopt a more entrepreneurial approach in an attempt to gain high market awareness. A UK example is provided by the late 1980s 'Nicole' campaign, which featured vignettes of the life of a young lady in France as a platform for marketing the Renault Clio car in the UK. A more global example is the highly publicised campaign by the Benetton clothing company which featured visually dissonant materials – such as a nun and a priest kissing and a newly born baby still attached to a very bloody placenta – to communicate their 'total colours' campaign.

REFERENCES

Baker, C. (ed.) (1992), *Advertising Works 7, IPA Advertising Effectiveness*, NTC Publications, London.

Baker, C. (ed.) (1994), *Advertising Works 8, IPA Advertising Effectiveness*, NTC Publications, London.

Brown, S.P. and Stayman, D.M. (1992), 'Antecedents and consequences of attitude towards the Ad: a meta analysis', *Journal of Consumer Research*, Vol. 19, pp. 143–58.

Channon, C. (ed.) (1985), *Advertising Works 3, IPA Advertising Effectiveness*, Holt, Rinehart and Winston, London.

Foxall, G. and Goldsmith, R. (1994), *Consumer Psychology for Marketing*, Routledge, London.

Hamel, G. and Sampler, J. (1998), 'The e-corporation', *Fortune Magazine*, 7 December, pp. 53–63.

Houston, M.J., Childers, T.L. and Hoeckler, S.E. (1987), 'Effects of brand awareness on choice for a common, repeat purchase product', *Journal of Marketing Research*, Vol. 14, pp. 404–20.

Hyatt, J. (1991), 'Betting the farm', *Inc Magazine*, Goldhirsh Group, Boston, MA, p. 36.

Kotler, P. (1997), *Marketing Management: Analysis, Planning, Implementation and Control*, ninth edition, Prentice Hall, Upper Saddle River, NJ.

Munch, A. and Hunt, S.D. (1984), 'Consumer involvement: definition issues and research directions', in Kinnear, T. (ed.), *Advances in Consumer Research*, Vol. 11, Association for Consumer Research, Provo, UH.

Rapp, S. and Collins, T.L. (1994), *Beyond Maxi-Marketing*, McGraw-Hill, New York.

Sellers, P. (1999), 'Inside the first e-Christmas', *Fortune Magazine*, 1 February, pp. 52–5.

Thorson, E. and Friestadt, M. (1989), 'The effectiveness of emotion on episodic memory for TV commercials', in Percy, L. and Woodside, A.G. (eds), *Advertising and Consumer Psychology*, Lexington Books, Lexington, MA.

Wilson, G. (1973), *The Psychology of Conservatism*, Academic Press, London.

5

ENTREPRENEURIAL PRICING AND DISTRIBUTION

Price is one of the simpler facets of the marketing process to comprehend because there are a number of clearly identifiable rules and conventions which control the use of this variable in seeking to improve organisational performance. One of the most fundamental rules is that, with the possible exception of monopoly goods scenarios, customers, not suppliers, determine at what price goods will be sold in a market sector.

This rule can be demonstrated by undertaking research asking customers their probability of purchase in relation to an example price range (Gabor 1977). What usually emerges from such research is the bell-shaped curve of the type shown in Figure 5.1. This suggests that there is an average price acceptable to

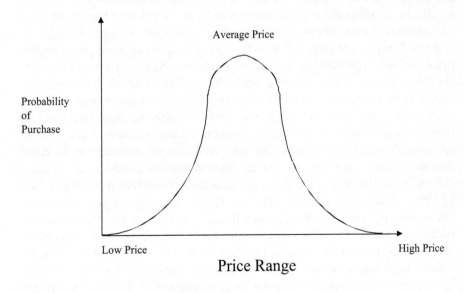

Figure 5.1 A price preference curve

the majority of customers. As the price changes on either side of the average, then the probability of purchase can be expected to decline. Thus, if a company decides to ignore the price preference of the average customer and, on the basis of internal operating costs and / or profit margin aspirations, sets a significantly higher price or much lower, then the organisation should not be surprised to find that its decision may adversely impact overall sales volume.

Average price expectations within most markets arise through a convergence between what customers are willing pay and at what price suppliers are willing to offer goods. Thus, if one were to interview customers in a supermarket, they will usually be able to describe the prices they expect to encounter when choosing the vast array of goods which are displayed on the shelf. Furthermore, as most people are forced to budget their total weekly household expenditure carefully, they will usually immediately recognise when prices for any necessity goods have altered dramatically. The aim of the suppliers in this situation is to make goods available at this expected price while concurrently managing production costs such that an adequate profit margin can be achieved.

Another important convention which will influence purchase decisions is what economists refer to as 'demand curves'. These curves posit that for most goods and services, demand is 'elastic'. This means that as prices decline, customers can be expected to purchase more goods, and, conversely, as prices rise, customers can be expected to reduce purchase quantities. There also exists what is known as 'cross elasticity'; that is, if the price is increased for an item in a group of goods which are perceived as similar, customers will switch their loyalty to an alternative good (for example, if the price of beef rises, then customers will probably switch their purchase to either chicken or lamb).

A third important convention is that most people expect to pay a higher price for higher-quality goods. The implication of this convention is that, as shown in Figure 5.2, depending upon the quality of goods being offered, suppliers face a number of different price scenarios. Conventional organisations which are positioned on the basis of offering superior product performance have three alternative pricing strategies they might wish to consider. Premium pricing involves charging a high price to support the claim that the customer is being offered the highest possible product performance (for example, the cost of hand-crafted furniture). Penetration pricing is used by firms wishing to build market share rapidly through aggressive pricing. Successful application of this strategy usually involves being able to offer the customer a reason to explain why the price is below that normally offered for this level of product performance. This is typically achieved because, by gaining high market share over the longer term, the supplier can reduce costs by exploiting economies of scale (for example, the Boeing corporation launching a new generation of jet aircraft). Offering a low price on a superior product usually involves the risk that the customer, applying the adage 'you get what you pay for', is suspicious about the validity of the performance claim (for example, the probable adverse reaction a company constructing executive-style homes would encounter if, during a period of rapidly rising house prices, the firm offers to sell a house at 50 per cent below the advertised price).

A skimming strategy involves customers deciding that there is a benefit to paying a high price for what they clearly recognise as only average-quality goods (for example, a night club which is currently very popular as the place to 'be seen' and exploits what is probably a temporary phenomenon, by charging prices somewhat higher than equivalent venues elsewhere in the same area). Average pricing is used by firms who service the needs of the majority of customers who are seeking an average level performance from products purchased. Sale pricing to retain customer confidence over quality is usually a temporary phenomenon used by firms to stimulate a sales upswing (for example, the January sales activities of high street retailers). This pricing strategy is aimed at serving the needs of the more price-sensitive customer seeking to purchase average performance goods.

PRICE

		High	Average	Low
	Level			
QUALITY PERCENTAGE	High	**PREMIUM PRICE** Quality is overt influence in buying decision	**PENETRATION PRICE** Opportunity to lower costs over longer term through economy of scale of new technology	**EXTREME VALUE PRICE** Risk that acceptance of quality claim is undermined by price
	Average	**SKIMMING PRICE** For either status reason or desire to immediately acquire product, customer willing to pay higher than necessary price	**AVERAGE PRICE** Product quality adequate for majority of customer needs in market	**SALE PRICE** Usually a temporary action by 'average pricers'
	Low	**SINGLE SALE PRICE** Single purchase of very short duration Product Life Cycle	**LIMITED REPEAT PRICE** Customer in market for limited period	**ECONOMY PRICE** Customer's personal circumstances cause price to be dominant purchase factor

Figure 5.2 A Price/Quality Matrix

Source: adapted from Chaston (1990).

ENTREPRENEURIAL MARKETING

A policy of low quality and high price is rarely able to sustain any degree of long-term customer loyalty. Those organisations who use this strategy usually survive only if customers who are lost after a single purchase are easily replaced by new buyers entering the market segment. Similarly, organisations using a low performance/average price strategy can only survive in those markets where customers who change their loyalty after two or three purchases are regularly replaced by an influx of new, less informed customers. Economy pricing involves offering low but acceptable quality goods at highly competitive prices to customers whose price sensitivity is usually a reflection of limited financial means. It can be an extremely successful market position, but the low margin per unit of sale does mean that the supplier has to sustain a very high level of customer transactions in order to achieve an adequate level of overall profit.

EXPLOITING ILLOGICAL BEHAVIOUR

If a supplier researches customer behaviour carefully, it is sometimes possible to identify apparently illogical behaviour patterns that can offer an opportunity to adopt an entrepreneurial pricing policy. This scenario is most likely to occur in relation to breaking the convention that demand should decrease as prices rise, by exploiting the convention that customers expect to pay higher prices for what they perceive to be premium quality goods. When the German car manufacturer BMW first entered the UK market, similar to their strategy in Germany, the company priced its cars somewhat lower than its competitor, Mercedes-Benz. Sales in the UK were lower than expected. Research revealed that potential UK customers perceived the BMW to be a 'racier version' of a Mercedes-Benz, but were apparently somewhat surprised by the price differential. In response to this situation, for some years BMW UK raised prices at a rate higher than the annual rate of inflation and, as the price spread between themselves and Mercedes-Benz narrowed, it sold more and more cars.

A similar small business example is provided by a UK firm in Devon which invented a highly entrepreneurial product designed to reduce the risk of infants dying from the illness known as 'cot death' syndrome. The product operates by monitoring certain physiological characteristics of babies when asleep and sets off an alarm if it appears that the child is at risk. The firm did not research customer price expectations but instead launched the product at what it considered to be a reasonable price that was capable of fulfilling its aspirations to achieve a reasonable profit margin per unit sold. Sales following product launch were disappointingly much lower than expected. The company subsequently discovered that although the medical profession were impressed with the product claims, these individuals were surprised that the technology could be delivered at the quoted price. The firm therefore moved to increase the list price significantly and enjoyed a massive upswing in sales.

SPOTTING CONVENTION SHIFTS

Most of us at some time in our lives have observed a very successful business idea and have asked ourselves, 'Why didn't I think of that?' It is often the case when one analyses such scenarios that an entrepreneur has observed the early signs of a shift in customer convention and has moved rapidly to exploit the identified opportunity ahead of competition. Such is the case of the recent threat that emerged in the branded soft drinks market in both the US and Europe.

In the decades following World War II, major brands in consumer goods markets were able to sustain a high price because apparently many customers perceived greater added value from purchasing branded goods than the equivalent own label brands offered by the major supermarkets. In the late 1980s/early 1990s, however, there was a major shift in Western consumers' attitudes regarding their willingness to purchase branded goods. An entrepreneurial thinker who recognised ahead of the competition that consumers were questioning the conventional view that branded goods deliver higher value was Dave Nichols, the President of the Canadian supermarket chain Loblaw's. Having validated the benefits of offering excellent value through his President's Choice/Master Choice ranges of own label brands in Canada, he then licensed the concept to a number of American supermarket chains. The earliest casualties in this move were Coca-Cola and Pepsi, who found that their in-store sales were impacted by the arrival of Master Choice Cola (Rapp and Collins 1994). Similar success has subsequently been achieved by the British entrepreneur Richard Branson who adopted the same philosophy in his very successful introduction of Virgin Cola into the UK market.

EXPLOITING DISTRUST

In the years following the 1970s OPEC oil crisis, the conventional strategy of most Western firms facing high inflation and flat demand was that, in order to avoid a decline in share prices, they sought ways to reduce operating costs while sustaining their quoted share price. Fish finger producers switched from cod to Alaskan pollock and car manufacturers produced cars with such thin metal bodies that vehicles sometimes rusted away to nothing in less than five years. Quite understandably, their long-suffering customers began to adopt a philosophy of 'if you want good quality, then be prepared to pay a higher than average price'. Furthermore, they became highly suspicious of any firm which claimed that its goods were of adequate or high quality, but offered them at a lower than usual price.

The other convention which existed at that time was that when a firm wished to enter a new overseas market, a very successful strategy to adopt was to charge a lower price and thereby achieve rapid market penetration. After a series of mistakes in the American market caused by offering poor-quality goods, the Japanese car manufacturers in the 1980s were eventually able to acquire the skills required to produce above-average-quality mass market cars at a much lower price than the equivalent vehicles offered by American producers. They recognised, however, that if they reflected these savings in the list price, the American consumer would probably be deeply suspicious of any quality claims which were made for the products.

At that time the conventional way of marketing cars in the US was that the dealer would quote a price for the basic vehicle specification and if the customer wanted to include 'options' such as air conditioning, electric windows, and so on, these were then added to the 'sticker price'. In many cases, the addition of these options virtually doubled the list price for the car. The entrepreneurial solution adopted by the Japanese car manufacturers in this situation was to equip their vehicles with all these additional options and still quote a single basic price for their vehicles. Their subsequent over-whelming success in the American market clearly demonstrated the wisdom in this unconventional approach to pricing. In fact, the impact of this break with convention was such that in recent years American producers have been forced to include many of the more popular options as standard items covered within the basic sticker price for their vehicles.

Over time, the Japanese reputation for build quality and reliability across a whole range of both consumer and industrial goods gave rise to the unexpected bonus that Western consumers now trust Pacific Rim suppliers, while still being distrustful of similar performance or quality claims being made for goods produced by Western firms. Having recognised this trend, the Toyota company decided to break another pricing convention. Traditionally, if one offers a premium-quality good, customers will expect to pay a premium price. In the late 1980s, Toyota took the lessons it had learned in the management of quality and 'lean manufacturing' during the production of mass market cars and applied these in the development of a luxury limousine capable of competing with the leading player in this market, Mercedes-Benz. The car Toyota developed was the Lexus. If the company had been a conventional thinker, it would have launched the new product at a price very similar to its German counterpart. Instead, the Lexus was introduced at a price some 25 per cent lower. Industry experts immediately claimed that the car would never appeal to the luxury market segment at that price. Of course, they were seeing the product as occupying the top-right cell in the Price/Quality Matrix shown in Figure 5.2. Within months, however, these predictions were proved completely invalid. Initial sales were extremely high and, within 18 months, Lexus moved to a leadership position in the American luxury car segment. The explanation was, of course, that Toyota had realised that once you have gained the trust of the customer, then you can act as an entrepreneurial pricer because potential customers will have no qualms about accepting both your premium quality claim and your highly competitive price.

PLANNING ENTREPRENEURIAL PRICING STRATEGIES

For both conventional and entrepreneurial organisations, as illustrated in Figure 5.3, there are two dimensions offering the opportunity to use price-based competition to establish a new market positioning. One dimension is

	Conventional Production Process	New
New	Existing low cost process to support price competitive entry into new market	New process to support price competitive entry into new market
Market Positioning		
Now	Current strategy	New prices to support price competitive position in an existing market

Figure 5.3   Price/Process Position Matrix

that of moving into a new market sector; the other is to find a way of reducing current operating costs through introducing revisions into the existing process technology and to pass on these savings to the customer through the medium of a price reduction. By combining the two dimensions, the organisation can simultaneously enter a new segment and use process revisions to support a price-based competitive positioning. The only real difference between entrepreneurial and a conventional firms is that the former are those organisations that are the first to recognise the new opportunity and move to exploit the situation ahead of the majority of firms that will tend to continue basing their operations around existing industry standards.

Direct Line insurance

An example of an organisation which used existing processes to instigate an entrepreneurial move into a new market sector is the UK insurance firm Direct Line. In the 1980s, this organisation was one of the first to move to the marketing of low-cost car insurance by exploiting the savings offered by the establishment of a centralised and highly computerised telemarketing operation. Direct Line's subsequent investigation of another insurance market, that of domestic property insurance, revealed that the existing convention in this sector is that the lending institution that supplies the mortgage also expects the borrower to allow the lender to arrange insurance cover on the borrower's behalf with a leading insurance company. These lenders' virtual monopoly is ensured because the high operating costs facing the smaller insurance firms seeking to market alternative cover through the conventional approach of using a direct sales force and/or a commission agent means that these latter organisations do not represent any real threat to the lending institutions.

Direct Line adopted the entrepreneurial view that, because it had already recovered the original investment in its direct marketing operation from its car insurance business and owned a massive existing data base of clients purchasing insurance, it would be a relatively simple, low-cost task to enter the domestic property insurance business on a platform of offering significantly lower premiums to potential customers. The firm realised that the lending institutions would probably attempt to put administrative obstacles in the way of clients seeking to switch their cover to Direct Line and/or charge clients an administrative fee to cover the paperwork associated with moving the cover to another insurer. Direct Line's entrepreneurial solution was that (a) it would, at no charge, handle the necessary administrative liaison with the lending institution, and (b) should the lending institution charge the customer a fee to move his or her insurance cover, Direct Line would reimburse the consumer for any reasonable costs incurred.

The Nucor corporation

The entrepreneurial strategy of fundamentally revising an organisation's production process to support the implementation of a price competitive position in an existing market is very effectively illustrated by the activities of the Nucor corporation in the American steel-making industry (Slywotzky 1996). The sectoral convention which drove the American steel industry in the 1950s and 1960s was that of producing a broad line of products delivered at a competitive price through investment in high fixed cost, high-productivity steel plants. By the mid-1960s, these massive, highly integrated plants were generating huge revenue flows, and nobody in the American steel towns such as Pittsburgh was too concerned about the fact that the Japanese were gearing up to challenge the Americans through the simple process of following the same conventions but building even more efficient steel plants.

By 1971, Japanese and American output was almost equal. Then, to add to the industry's problems, some major customers such as the soft drinks industry switched from steel to aluminium as the raw material for drinks cans. One individual, Kenneth Iverson of the Nucor corporation, then developed a new vision. Why not use scrap steel as a raw material instead of iron ore; build small, low-cost, highly flexible factories located close to customers, and offer low-cost steel using a JIT philosophy? From this vision emerged a whole new industry know as the 'mini-mills'. By the 1980s, the £1 billion shareholder value of Nucor was almost equal to one of the largest and oldest steel-makers in the world, Bethlehem Steel.

Nirma detergent

A nice small business example of changing process to mount a price-based attack on a much larger firm is provided by Nirma detergent in India (Rogers 1990). In the 1970s, the Unilever brand, Surf, dominated this market, using the latest technology to produce a high-quality product and adopting the conventional philosophy of supporting the brand through a high level of promotional spending. An Indian entrepreneur, Katsanbhai Patel, decided that Unilever might be vulnerable to attack through price competition.

He adopted the classic Schumpeterian principles of simplifying manufacturing processes to minimise costs. Instead of utilising modern manufacturing techniques, he started a chain of workshops in which people mixed the ingredients by hand – thereby using no electrical power. His labour costs are estimated to be about one-fifth of Unilever's costs and his workforce is non-unionised. His overheads are further reduced by having a workforce of some 10,000 persons supervised by only 200 or so supervisors. By 1987,

Nirma was outselling Surf by a ratio of three to one and turnover had reached £150 million.

THE SAVIN CORPORATION

After Xerox launched its first photocopier in 1958, the company then enjoyed a 20-year virtual monopoly position. The company's strategy over this period was, having persuaded industry to accept photocopying as the standard approach for information handling and storage, to invest in making available ever more complex, technically sophisticated machines (for example, capable of collating and binding lengthy documents, and able to perform high-speed, two-sided copying) which it sold or leased at a premium price.

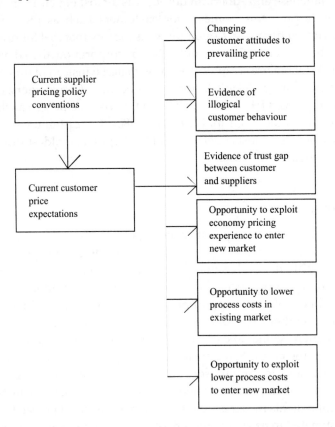

Figure 5.4 Alternative pathways for implementing entrepreneurial pricing policies

In the late 1970s, the Savin corporation in the US recognised that Xerox's strategy was orientated towards serving large organisations, and ignored smaller businesses that merely wanted access to a low-cost, low-speed way of copying merely A4-sized paper (Grant 1997). Having identified an entirely new market sector for photocopying, Savin developed and patented a machine based around new technology. Furthermore, by adopting a product design which used standardised parts, Savin was able to outsource the entire manufacturing operation to Ricoh in Japan. As a result, Savin was able to offer extremely competitively priced photocopiers in the American market, and for some years, until competitors such as Canon entered the market, the firm enjoyed a virtual monopoly in both the small business and in-home market sectors.

In summary, it is apparent that there exists a diversity of alternative actions open to the firm seeking to identify ways of using price to break conventions and establish new, more appealing market conventions and/or to open up completely new market sectors. A number of these alternative pathways are summarised in Figure 5.4.

THINKING THE UNTHINKABLE

The conventional marketer would never think of starting a new business based on a strategy of using low price to compete with a blue chip fast-moving consumer goods company, because the latter can be expected to utilise its much greater 'marketing muscle' to demolish the threat of the new firm driving down sector prices. Entrepreneurs, of course, tend not to be logical because they are prepared to think the unthinkable. One such individual is David Pitassi, who has successfully implemented a price-based competitive strategy in the American disposable nappies market to steal share from Proctor & Gamble's top-of-the-line brand, Pampers (Posner 1993).

Pitassi first entered the nappy market in Vancouver, Washington, by using local materials to produce a low-cost product. Launching the business required a $1 million investment. The funds were raised through the unusual approach of forming a limited partnership with investors who would own the production equipment. By June 1985, only a few months after start-up, the company was hitting its Year 5 projected sales volume and needed to invest another $2 million in new production equipment. Unfortunately the investors were not interested in injecting new capital, and in November 1985 they voted to eject Pitassi from the company. Having proved that consumers were attracted to a quality product priced $1 lower than national brands, and that retailers appreciated stocking regional brands that made money in a category which traditionally generates a very low profit per square foot of retail space,

Pitassi and his business partner Wally Klemp decided to start all over again. They moved to Houston because it offered low-cost raw materials and low distribution costs.

It took more than a year to find new investors but, by August 1987, the new company had raised $2.4 million from about 60 investors. The strategy remained unchanged: to sell a nappy offering the same features as Procter & Gamble's Pampers and Kimberly Clark's Huggies which would retail at $1 lower than the national brands and offer retailers higher in-store profitability. During the 1980s, many supermarkets had seen their margins on disposable nappies eroded as mass merchandisers such as Wal-Mart and K-Mart promoted the national brands as 'loss leaders'. Thus the launch of Pitassi's new brand, Drypers (a play on the American name for nappies, 'diapers' and the word 'dry' which suggests a quality of the nappy), was assisted by the fact that the product offered supermarket chains the opportunity to return to making a reasonable profit from nappies.

The company could not afford to pay store slotting allowances to buy on-shelf space and therefore offered to compensate for this inability by running television and newspaper advertising along with heavy consumer coupon drops. Within months, Procter & Gamble responded with a coupon blitz. Pitassi's response was to take out newspaper advertisements which invited consumers to 'Pamper, Hug and Luv Us' and invited them to redeem coupons from any brand to purchase their next box of Drypers. This then ensured that even in the face of Proctor & Gamble's attack, Drypers could sustain its $1 price differential. Within weeks production was running at three shifts per day, seven days a week, and in Houston the brand achieved a 15 per cent market share.

Pitassi realised that to survive in the market, he needed to keep careful control over costs. His solution has been to keep the organisation as flat as possible and to stress the importance of multi-skilling so that employees can switch between job roles as needed. The company also recognises that to survive it should not aspire to achieve brand leadership, but is better off remaining a very successful number three in the market. By letting the bigger brands expend funds on educating consumers about why different products are effective, the company can piggyback these promotional activities by spending funds on local and in-store advertising campaigns which stress Drypers' greater value proposition. By 1991, sales across the Southern USA had reached $35 million. At this stage, instead of following the conventional marketers' approach of seeking to take the brand national, Pitassi opted to purchase two other regional brands. His first purchase was the company in Washington from which, five years earlier, he had been ejected by the investors. Then, in 1992, he purchased a second company based in Marion, Ohio. Together these acquisitions have moved the company to a 6 per cent share of the total American nappy market.

DISTRIBUTION CONVENTIONS

Distribution systems are presented as vertical systems where responsibility for goods is transferred from one level to the next (Figure 5.5). Until very recently, both academics and practitioners have tended to consider distribution to be one of the most unexciting areas of marketing. This is because the

	Current	New		Current	New
New	Entry into new sector drawing upon existing channel expertise	Entry into new sector drawing upon new channel opportunity	**New**	Entry into new sector drawing upon existing technology expertise	Entry into new sector drawing upon new technology opportunity
Current	Conventional practice	Improved operation through change of channel	**Current**	Conventional practice	Improved operation through new technology
	Current	New		Current	New
	Distribution Channel			Distribution Technology	

Figure 5.5   An Alternative Distribution Opportunity Matrix

activity has been perceived as being concerned with minimising the cost of moving goods from the producer to the point of final consumption within a market system utilising a number of trading conventions that have remained virtually unchanged for many years.

One important decision issue is the choice facing a supplier of whether to work directly with customers or to involve one or more distributors. Direct supplier–customer distribution tends to occur in those market systems where conventions prevail – for example, where each end user purchases a large proportion of total output, where goods are highly perishable and/or where the complex nature of the goods requires a close working relationship between supplier and final customer. This scenario will be encountered, for example, in many large capital goods markets, such as the office block and petrochemical plant construction industries.

In those markets where an indirect distribution system is perceived as being more cost effective, the usual convention is that one or more distributors will become involved in the distribution process. These distributors will typically receive a truckload-size shipment which they break down into smaller lot sizes. These are sold to an end user outlet that will be responsible for managing both the final customer purchase transaction and any post-purchase service needs (for example, cash and carry warehouses supplying branded food products to small local grocery stores).

Multi-layered distribution systems were a feature of Western consumer good markets in the nineteenth century. They remain the predominant system in most developing nations and also in many of the Pacific Rim Tiger economies. Japan, for example, is often characterised as having long, complicated, multi-level networks serving a multitude of numerous retail outlets. The existence of these systems are, in fact, often seen as a major obstacle to Western firms seeking to enter this market (Min 1996).

A common convention in Western economies during the twentieth century has been that of retailers perceiving scale benefits in purchasing directly from suppliers. In these cases, the outcome is usually that of 'cutting out the middleman', with the retailers establishing vertically integrated procurement, warehousing, distribution and retailing operations. Early entrepreneurial exploitation of this opportunity ahead of competition provided the basis for the establishment of what are now considered highly conventional trading dynasties such as Sears Roebuck in the US and Marks and Spencer in the UK.

An orientation towards distribution systems being selected on the basis of cost minimisation is reflected in many of the earlier writings on the marketing management process. Authors presented models describing how entrepreneurial intermediaries, by moving ahead of competition and consolidating purchases from a number of sources, could concurrently reduce the number of transactions and increase the variety of choice offered to customers within a market system. In the US, for example, one of these entrepreneurs was the Atlantic and Pacific (A&P) company which, at the beginning of the twentieth century, began to construct a trading model which has subsequently evolved into the conventional paradigm for successfully creating and operating national supermarket chains.

In many of these earlier writings on distribution, the reader was also advised to be concerned about the possibility that, when a convention becomes an industry standard, power imbalances can emerge which will be to somebody's disadvantage during pricing negotiations. For example, in the UK, the top four supermarket chains control almost 80 per cent of all food sales, which places manufacturers at a significant disadvantage when seeking to sustain an adequate profit margin on their output. Another commonly described scenario requiring managerial caution is the emergence of a new entrepreneurial force within a distribution channel. The risk in this situation is that the supplier may lose sales because it does not move rapidly to develop a relationship with this new entrepreneur within a distribution channel (an example being the UK out-of-town warehouse operations which, in the 1970s, replaced department stores as the primary outlet for soft furnishings such as carpets, and sourced their products not from UK suppliers, but mainly from large carpet mills based in the Southern USA).

DISTRIBUTION: THE NEGLECTED BATTLEFIELD

After decades of virtually being ignored as an important aspect of the marketing management process, the more entrepreneurial organisations began to realise in the mid-1980s that effective management of distribution channels can actually provide additional opportunities to gain advantage over competition. A number of factors have contributed to this situation. Possibly two of the more important have been:

1. the impact of new or improved technology in the reduction of transportation costs and/or delivery times (for example, the construction of motorway networks in Europe which has made it feasible for a manufacturer based in one country to service effectively, from one single plant, the needs of customers in all other Eastern and Western European countries)
2. exponentially declining prices for IT systems across all facets of the distribution process (for example, linking supermarket computers with the production scheduling systems of key suppliers to manage more effectively the process of matching supplier production schedules with sudden changes in consumer demand).

Similar to entrepreneurial pricing, there are a number of pathways through which to exploit changes in distribution to service the needs of existing customers and/or enter new market segments more adequately. The only real difference, as shown in Figure 5.5, is that the range of options is possibly greater because a firm can consider both changing channels and exploiting new technologies as routes by which to break with existing conventions. By adopting a more entrepreneurial attitude towards distribution, an organisation may thus be able to fulfil one or more of the following aims:

- increasing sales
- improving customer service
- reducing distribution costs
- speeding up deliveries
- entering new market sectors.

ENTREPRENEURIAL MARKETING

Habitat

An example of success in an existing channel offering an opportunity to attract new customers is provided by the activities of the UK entrepreneur Joseph Conran who, in the 1960s, founded the highly successful furniture chain, Habitat. Until the advent of Habitat, the long-standing convention of furniture stores was to supply a range of products aimed at appealing to the entire customer age profile. Conran broke this convention by focusing on selling very modern furniture, fabrics and houseware targeted at the market sector of young people and couples setting up their first home. The firm soon realised, however, that its unusual product range was attracting the attention of firms seeking small quantities of competitively priced modern furniture and fittings for offices, hotels and restaurants. Having perceived the existence of this unexpected new customer opportunity, Habitat rapidly moved to add specialist staff in its stores to handle this new source of business.

Tupperware

In relation to a move towards changing channels to increase sales to current customers, an excellent but now somewhat dated example of entrepreneurial thinking is provided by the Tupperware corporation. Having developed a range of plastic containers with seals that kept food fresher for longer, the firm soon discovered that selling these products through the traditional channel of major retail stores was not very successful. The solution was to recruit housewives as sales agents and to market the product direct to consumers through the creative idea of holding 'Tupperware parties' hosted by commission-only sales staff in the customers' own homes. In recent years Tupperware found that many of its traditional customers, American housewives, are now not staying at home but going out to work. Tupperware's entrepreneurial response to this scenario has been to open its own shops located in the works canteens of major corporations.

Ginsters

An example of a new channel giving access to a new group of customers is provided by Ginsters, the bakery products manufacturing division of the privately owned UK food conglomerate, Samworth Brothers. Ginsters started life producing branded goods sold via a van sales operation to small independent catering and retail outlets. The company's quality story soon attracted the attention of the large UK supermarket chains who wanted it to produce large quantities of own label goods. As the own label business fuelled rapid growth, the company started to think about establishing its own brand on a national basis. However, it soon found that the power of the national supermarket chains was such that an impossible scale of investment would be needed to break into this distribution channel. The solution was to examine the alternative food distribution channel offered by forecourt garage shops and shopping malls in motorway service areas. In seeking to build a national branded goods operation, the new customer target that Ginsters selected was not the conventional food buyer, the UK housewife, but people who, as part of their working lives, spend extensive periods of time travelling up and down the country by road. The success of this entrepreneurial strategy is evidenced by the fact that for one of their products, sausage rolls, Ginsters is now the UK brand leader even though the company's inability to gain distribution in national supermarket chains has meant that the small independent grocery store remains the only conventional retail food outlet where you will encounter the Ginsters brand.

Torr Systems

In relation to exploiting existing technology as a mechanism for attracting new customers, one example is provided by a small, entrepreneurial UK manufacturing firm, Torr Systems Ltd. This company manufacturers uPVC replacement windows which they supply to window installers and builders. Because Torr is too small to capture the economies of scale available to its larger national competitors, upon establishment of the business the owners determined that they would be unable to compete on the basis of lower prices. They consequently selected the positioning of offering (a) high-quality products, (b) exceptional customer service, and (c) a free technical advisory service for customers confronted with a difficult or unusual window replacement contract.

Over the years, the company has invested in new technologies to sustain quality and to further enhance its speed of response in order fulfilment. It was one of the first replacement window firms in the UK to invest in a computer aided design/computer aided manufacturing system (CAD/CAM). Although the intended use for this system was to optimise the organisation's manufacturing productivity, it soon found that the system was useful when negotiating an order with customers needing one-off designs to overcome complex installation problems.

Within a very short time, Torr Systems' problem-solving reputation resulted in the company being approached by a completely new customer group: architects and larger building firms involved in complex renovation contracts, such as the refurbishment of older hotels and office buildings. Torr Systems had for some years been producing a range of conservatories for domestic homes. When one of its new architect customers, who was working on the renovation of a 150-year-old hotel, became aware of Torr's involvement in the conservatories area, he asked if it would be possible for the company to develop a massive, customised conservatory reminiscent of the orangeries popular during the Victorian era. By using its CAD/CAM system, Torr Systems was able to develop, manufacture and deliver the components for the conservatory in eight weeks. Press coverage of the conservatory immediately brought new enquiries, thereby creating an opportunity for the firm to exploit its investment in technology to service a completely new customer group.

American Hospital Supply

A classic example of a firm seeking to use new technology to improve its services to existing customers is provided by the company American Hospital Supply, which distributes medical products. The company had traditionally used a sales force, complemented by a telesales operation, to generate customer orders. As its product range was not unique, in seeking ways to create competitive advantage it hit upon the idea of supplying its major customers, such as hospitals, with a computer system linked directly to its own in-house order-entry system. Thus, a hospital administrator could, at a time most convenient to him- or herself, turn on the computer in his or her own office, link up to a system providing detailed information on the pricing and availability of medical products he or she wishes to purchase, and immediately place an order. Within only a few years this entrepreneurial use of technology moved American Hospital Supply to a leadership position in the American medical supplies market.

West Coast Salmon

An example of exploiting technology to enter a new market is provided by a group of West Coast fresh salmon producers in the US (Chaston 1985). Keeping salmon fresh is difficult and this has traditionally meant that the geographic market boundary for a producer is defined by how far a delivery truck from the plant can travel in 24 hours – the maximum delivery time if the salmon is to be kept fresh. The problem facing this small group of producers was that, to sustain sales, they were forced to compete on the basis of price when attempting to steal business from the much larger producers also based around the Seattle area.

One of the members of the group had the idea that a much higher price could be achieved by shipping West Coast fresh salmon to the restaurant market in New York. The problem was how to manage the logistics of ensuring that the delivery could be made to a specific customer within 24 hours after the processing of the fish. He was aware that the advent of the Jumbo jet in the air freight industry had significantly reduced transportation costs, and so he approached one of the major airlines to gain its perspective on the viability of shipping salmon by air. The airline recognised that salmon could not be shipped using its existing freight containers, but was willing to develop a new container designed specifically to handle fresh seafood. Furthermore, it was also able to suggest a container tagging system which would ensure that the containers received priority during shipment, and also that if a flight was delayed, the New York distributor could rapidly find out when and where any delayed shipment would arrive on the East Coast. Within months this new concept in seafood distribution was established and was so successful that virtually the entire output from this small group of producers is now sold at a premium price on the Eastern Seaboard of the US.

ENTREPRENEURIAL DISTRIBUTION PLANNING

Rangan et al. (1992, 1993), in reviewing the future strategic implications of new approaches to channel management, have suggested that managers must now view the flow of goods and services in relation to the question of whether the exploitation of alternative channels can serve to create competitive entry barriers, enhance product differentiation and enable greater customer intimacy. These authors' proposal is that it is now necessary to 'unbundle' the channel functions of information provision, order generation, physical distribution and after-sales service. The next step is to then determine how customer needs can best be met by channel members working together as a team of channel partners, each performing those tasks at which they excel. The concepts underlying their ideas can be summarised in a distribution planning process of the type shown in Figure 5:6.

Moriaty and Moran (1990) have referred to these new, more customer orientated, entrepreneurial approaches to channel management as 'hybrid marketing systems'. They present the example of IBM which, over the years, has been surprisingly entrepreneurial, having moved from a single channel based around its own sales force to expanding into a hybrid operation involving dealers, value added resellers (VARs), a catalogue selling operation, direct mail and telemarketing. In the last ten years, this has been reflected in a doubling of the size of its own sales force and the opening of 18 new channels to serve the highly diverse nature of its customers' needs.

Moriaty and Moran's view is that the two forces driving this type of change were the need to expand market coverage and the concurrent requirement to contain costs by improving the efficiency of channel members. Another way of viewing these hybrid systems is to perceive them as providing the opportunity to create a spider's web structure of distribution with the firm at hub identifying and managing numerous different strands through which to link themselves more closely to the customer.

An excellent example of this approach is provided by a group of ex-IBM employees who founded the German software firm which developed systems application programming (SAP). This software offers a totally integrated system for managing all aspects of a firm's operations. The Germans realised, however, that, as a small player in the world computer market, merely relying upon one channel of distribution would never ensure achievement of their

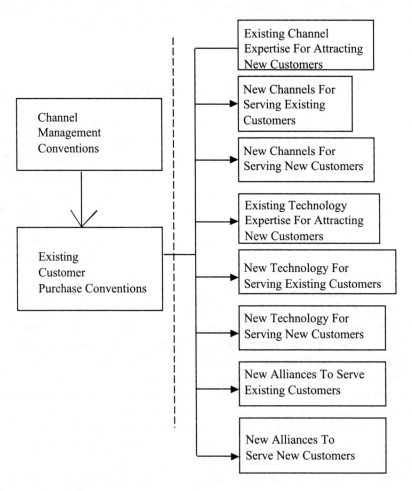

Figure 5.6 Alternative opportunities to exploit changes in channel management to optimise customer satisfaction

aspirations to become a global player. Their solution was to link up, mainly through the medium of user accreditation and licensing, with other organisations in the IT industry ranging from hardware producers (IBM, for example), major IT-based consulting firms (such as Arthur Anderson & Co.) and smaller systems developers that specialise in creating customised solutions for clients in specific market sectors. The success of this entrepreneurial example of a spider's web approach to distribution is evidence by the fact that, in 1998, the company became the fastest-growing integrated systems software firm in the world.

REFERENCES

Chaston, I. (1985), *Strategic Business Management in Fisheries and Aquaculture*, Blackwell Scientific, Oxford.

Chaston, I. (1990), *Managing for Marketing Excellence*, McGraw-Hill, Maidenhead.

Gabor, A. (1977), *Pricing: Principles and Practice*, Heinemann, London.

Grant, R.M. (1997), *Contemporary Strategy Analysis: Concepts, Techniques, Applications*, Blackwell Business, Malden, MA.

Min, H. (1996), 'Distribution channels in Japan: challenge and opportunities for the Japanese market entry', *International Journal of Physical Distribution and Logistics Management*, Vol. 26, No. 10, pp. 13–24.

Moriaty, R.W. and Moran, U. (1990), 'Managing hybrid marketing systems', *Harvard Business Review*, November–December, pp. 146–55.

Posner, B.G. (1993), 'Targeting the giant', *Inc. Magazine*, Goldhirsh Group, Boston, MA, p. 92.

Rangan, V.K., Moriaty, R.T. and Swartz, G. (1992), 'Segmenting customers in mature industrial markets', *Journal of Marketing*, Vol. 56, October, pp. 72–82.

Rangan, V.K., Moriaty, R.T. and Swartz, G. (1993), 'Transaction cost theory: inferences from field research on downstream vertical integration', *Organization Science*, Vol. 4, No. 3, pp. 454–77.

Rapp, S. and Collins, T.L. (1994), *Beyond Maxi-Marketing*, McGraw-Hill, New York.

Rogers, L. (1990), *Pricing for Profit*, Blackwell, Oxford.

Slywotzky, A.J. (1996), *Value Migration: How to Think Several Moves Ahead of the Competition*, Harvard Business School Press, Boston, MA.

6

ENTREPRENEURIAL NEW PRODUCT DEVELOPMENT

DETERMINING PRIORITIES

New product development, whether undertaken by a conventional or an entrepreneurial organisation, is a high-risk activity. The 'hall of famed failures' contains numerous exhibits ranging from major mistakes by individual entrepreneurs (for example, the American millionaire Howard Hughes's giant wooden seaplane – the 'Spruce Goose'; the UK entrepreneur Clive Sinclair's electric car – the C5) through to those made by major corporations (for example, Du Pont's artificial leather product – Corfam; Ford's launch of the Edsel car).

Failure can be expensive in terms of both unrecovered investment and the time that staff have been diverted away from mainstream activities which could have been financially more worth while. Before embarking upon a race to develop new products, organisations thus need to clearly assess the relative merits of medium-term alternatives to creating new products in order to generate the majority of any sales revenue growth or, for the time being, revenue growth being sought from exploiting existing products further.

The other issue which should be considered is whether the organisation wishes to behave in a conventional manner or opt for a more entrepreneurial approach. Reaching a decision over this latter issue requires recognition of an important aspect of new product development: that the adoption of an appropriate orientation to innovation should be perceived as a selection point somewhere along a continuum. At one extreme is the decision to progress development based purely upon conventional thinking (for example, a wine producer experimenting with different types of grape to improve the 'body and fragrance' of its most popular wine). At the other extreme on the continuum is the adoption by the organisation of a totally entrepreneurial approach to create a radically different, entirely unconventional product (for example, the inventive decision taken to combine a surf board and a sail to create the first ever wind surfer).

Combining the source of sales growth dimension and the organisational behaviour dimension generates the Alternative Medium-term Option Path Matrix of the type illustrated in Figure 6.1. Cell 1 is associated with concentrating on exploiting existing conventional products, and new product activity will therefore have minimal impact on the organisation's future performance. This path is probably the most frequently utilised of all the options proposed in Figure 6.1; it can be found both in many small firms (for example, an accountacy practice, offering basic tax and audit services to local firms, moving towards having some clients beginning to use self-diagnostic, computer-based audit tools) and in the majority of large corporations (for example, Cadbury's launching of a new, improved chocolate bar).

Cell 2 proposes the option of emphasising the importance of new products while retaining a conventional orientation to innovative activities. This scenario is often exemplified by large multinational firms recognising that their existing products are beginning to 'show their age' and needing to be replaced in the near future (for example, in the 1980s the Toshiba company in Europe was performing poorly in a highly price orientated market, and therefore decided to leapfrog competition by introducing a range of flat screen technology (FST) televisions that offer superior picture quality). It is usually the case that firms which adopt the Cell 2 position are assuming that, as their new products gain market share, they will be able to move back nearer to a

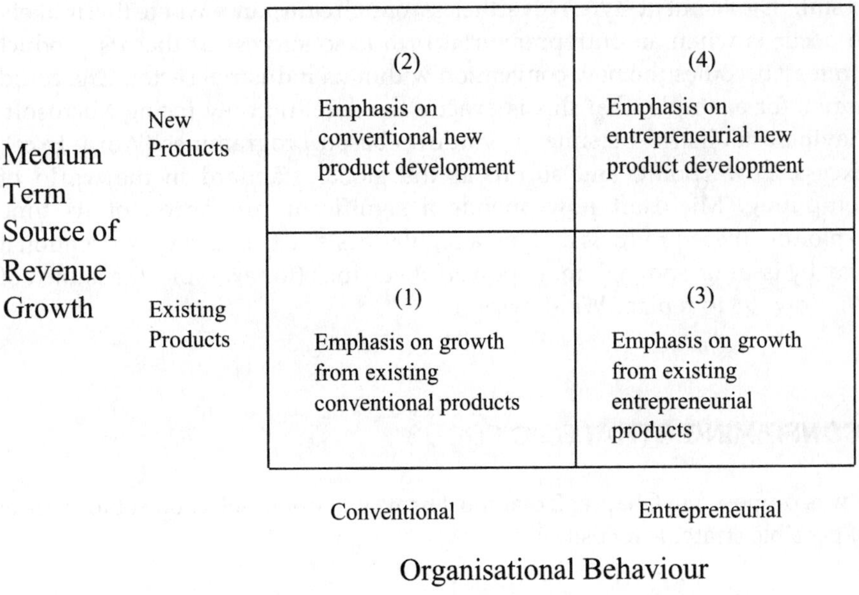

		(2)	(4)
Medium Term Source of Revenue Growth	New Products	Emphasis on conventional new product development	Emphasis on entrepreneurial new product development
	Existing Products	(1) Emphasis on growth from existing conventional products	(3) Emphasis on growth from existing entrepreneurial products
		Conventional	Entrepreneurial

Organisational Behaviour

Figure 6.1   A Medium-term New Product Option Path Matrix

Cell 1 situation where new products revert back to being a significantly less important source of revenue growth.

Cell 3 suggests that an entrepreneurial firm, having successfully developed a range of unconventional products, will, at least for the foreseeable future, concentrate on generating revenue growth without committing additional resources to the development of a completely new product concept (for example, the highly successful American theme restaurant chain, the Hard Rock Cafe, which is currently in a phase of generating incremental revenue from the opening of new outlets around the world).

Cell 4 positions the firm as concentrating the majority of its resources upon entrepreneurial new product development. It is possibly the riskiest of all of the options available within the matrix. Accordingly, most firms are likely to adopt this position only for a defined period of time, in the hope that once the new products are launched, they can gradually move towards a Cell 3 situation where this latest generation of products will come to represent a long-term source of revenue growth. A possible exception to this scenario, however, is the small firm run by an intuitive entrepreneur who achieves real personal satisfaction only from trading activities that involve developing and launching radically new products.

The proposed model in Figure 6.1 is posited as a dynamic process, changing over time depending upon the circumstances confronting the organisation. What is often a very rare direction within the dynamic model, probably because it requires a fundamental shift in organisational culture, is for a firm to shift management style. Nevertheless, one circumstance where this is likely to occur is when an entrepreneurial firm is so successful that its product strategy becomes the new convention within an industrial sector. One could argue, for example, that this is exactly the scenario now facing Microsoft. Having established its suite of windows-based programmes (Word, Excel, Excess, Powerpoint, and so on) as the global standard in the world of computing, Microsoft now spends a significant proportion of its time exploiting these products and, on a regular basis, acts in a very conventional way by issuing updated, more powerful versions (for example, the launch of Windows 98 to replace Windows 95).

CONFIRMING STRATEGIC FOCUS

It was proposed in Chapter 2 that most firms will opt to select one of four areas of possible strategic focus:

1. product performance excellence
2. price performance excellence

3. transactional excellence
4. relationship excellence.

Given the high risks associated with virtually any form of significant innovation, it is probably much safer for a firm to retain its existing strategic focus than to consider new product development as an opportunity concurrently to reposition the organisation totally. Clearly, however, prior to finalising the project specification for a very significant product innovation, the organisation should re-visit this issue of organisational positioning to ensure that an appropriate decision has been made concerning the strategic pathway along which the firm's innovators will travel in seeking to identify an idea capable of supporting the organisation's financial performance goals.

Figure 6.2 provides some examples of sustaining strategic focus during the development of new products by following either a conventional or an entrepreneurial pathway. In the case of conventional innovation (Figure 6.2a), the microchip producer Intel has followed the path of continually seeking to make a more powerful product (for example, the move from the Pentium to the Pentium II processor). The Boeing corporation, in moving from its 747 to the 757/767 series, has continued to focus on applying its superior design and manufacturing expertise to building a new generation, larger jet aircraft. In the desktop sector of the photocopier market, a price excellence position is exhibited by Canon which, by exploiting superior manufacturing expertise, has continued to develop cheaper products and/or new products with upgraded features offered at the same price as its previous generation model range. In the area of relationship excellence, British Airways has sought to sustain its market domination of international routes by focusing on new mechanisms with which to enhance customer service continually throughout all phases of the customer purchase and usage process.

In the case of entrepreneurial innovation (Figure 6.2b), a product performance excellence example is provided by the computer disk drive company, Quantum. Having become the dominant player during the 1980s in the market for 8-inch disk drives sold to the microcomputer industry, Quantum was forced to reconfigure its technologies totally in order to enter the 5.25-inch and subsequently the 3.5-inch disk drive markets (Christensen 1997).

An example of price excellence is provided by the consumer electronics company Amstrad. This organisation was founded by the entrepreneur Alan Sugar, who started his career by selling cut-price electrical goods, such as radios. When Amstrad decided to enter the bottom end of the UK PC market in the mid-1980s, it achieved market leadership in the home computer market through the unconventional approach of (a) transferring into the computer industry, the manufacture technologies previously associated with other consumer electrical products (that is, mass production based upon using off

105

the shelf, standard components), and (b) selling its products through a national chain of discount retail outlets.

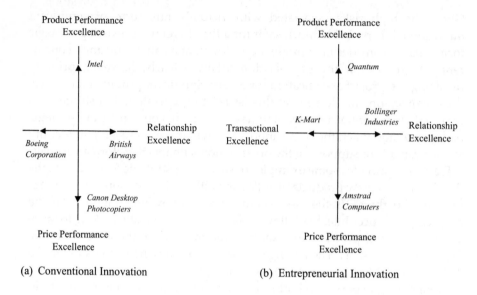

Figure 6.2   Examples of conventional and entrepreneurial focus during product innovation

Excellence in transaction management was exemplified in the late 1950s by the second largest variety chain store company in the world, S.S. Kresge. This organisation began to realise that a probable trend in the American retail environment was that customers would place increasing importance on price in reaching a purchase decision for domestic items such as clothing and small electrical appliances. The solution was to take all of the company's acquired retail operation expertise, to complement this by hiring certain new key staff, and to exploit the company's excellence in transaction management by creating an unconventional new discount retailing concept which was launched under the K-Mart brand name. A decade later, revenue from this new store chain approached $3.5 billion, while its nearest competitor, Woolworth's Woolco operation, languished at an unprofitable $0.9 billion (Christensen 1997).

Entrepreneurial relationship excellence is illustrated by Bollinger Industries, a leading American distributor of exercise accessories such as dumbbells and exercise mats. Bollinger recognised that American consumers entering stores to whom Bollinger distributed products (such as Wal-Mart and Sears Roebuck) were seeking not more equipment, but help with the injuries incurred while pursuing their drive to become fit and healthy. Bollinger's response to this situation was to develop a whole new range of sports medicine and health and safety products that its retail customers could stock in their stores – thereby dramatically increasing sales per square foot (Wiersema 1996).

DETERMINING PROJECT ORIENTATION

For the systematic entrepreneur, prior to initiating the idea generation phase of the new product development process, there is the task of deciding the degree to which conventions are to be challenged. In reviewing this issue, the entrepreneur has two product dimensions to consider: the functionality of the product (that is, the benefit offered to customers) and the form (that is, the physical nature) of the product. As shown in Figures 6.3 and 6.4, these two dimensions generate eight alternative options (and one option of no change), depending upon the degree to which the entrepreneur decides to challenge convention.

The lowest level of risk presented in Figure 6.3 is to change neither function nor form conventions. The example of this in Figure 6.4 is the recent move by

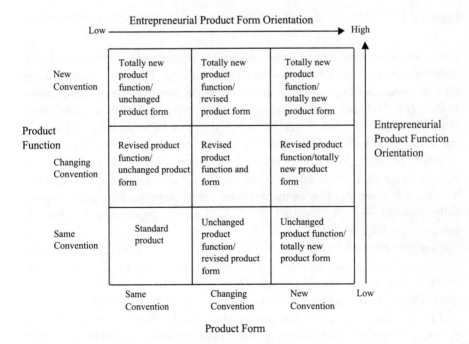

Figure 6.3 A Product Function/Form Planning Matrix

Product Function		Product Form		
New Convention		Armond Hammer baking soda as an odour absorber for refrigerators	Wind surfboards	The domestic video cassette recorder (VCR)
Changing Convention		McCain's oven-bake French fries	The Sony Walkman	Snowboards
Same Convention		Adding colouring agents to car wax	The introduction of 486 RAM PCs to replace 386 models	Roller blades to replace roller skates
		Same Convention	Changing Convention	New Convention

Product Form

Figure 6.4   Examples of product function and form convention challenging

producers of car wax to add colouring agents which improve their products' ability to revive a car's body colour during waxing. There is relatively little risk in repositioning product function while leaving the product form unchanged. In Figure 6.4, an example of changing convention is McCain's launch of French fries which can be prepared by baking in the oven rather than the traditional method of deep fat frying. An example of the creation of a new function convention without revising product form is provided by the Armond Hammer corporation. In the face of declining sales of baking soda following the introduction of instant cake mixes, Armond Hammer successfully repositioned its product as a food-smell deodoriser for use in refrigerators (Figure 6.4).

Changing product form involves a certain degree of risk because of the need to physically alter the product. In Figure 6.4, an example of form change without altering function is provided by the move in the 1980s to introduce 486 RAM PCs in the place of 386 machines. An example of changing both form and function is provided by the Sony Walkman. The Wind surfboard (Figure 6.4) represents a product change (adding a sail to a surfboard) that resulted in the creation of completely new watersport.

To develop a completely new product form is clearly very risky. Possibly the safest option in this situation is not to change product functionality because the new product can then be marketed simply as an unconventional product form replacement (for example, the roller blade, which uses the ice-skate technology of a single central blade but has a central line of wheels instead of a blade which permit skaters to move rapidly on roads and pavements). Changing product function while concurrently introducing a new product form is exemplified by the snowboard; snowboarding is now overtaking skiing as the most popular winter sport around the world.

Finally, the highest-risk proposition is both to introduce a new product form and to seek new users (that is, to develop a 'new to the world product'). An excellent example of this action is provided by the Japanese recognition of the wide commercial opportunities associated with the technology of storing visual images on to magnetic tape. While their American counterparts were experimenting with complex machines for possible application in the broadcast industry, the Japanese moved to create a product with a much greater appeal – the VCR. This offered a new form of in-home entertainment because, for the first time, consumers could record television programmes and watch films (without having to attend a cinema) by hiring or purchasing videos to play back at home.

IMPROVING FORM AND EXTENDING FUNCTIONALITY

In the US, Stan and David Gallery purchased two hot-dog carts at the beginning of the 1980s and were soon operating a fleet of 15. Following threats from the Denver Health Department over alleged failure to keep food hot or cold enough, they developed a new cart that incorporated new cooling units, high-capacity burners and running water (Richman 1989). These immediately attracted the attention of other business people who wanted to purchase the improved pushcarts. At this point in time, the two brothers realised that, with their new product, they had created a 'mobile merchandising system'.

The Gallery brothers began to seek non-traditional uses for their innovative pushcarts. They persuaded Pizza Hut to use them to sell products in corporate and school cafeterias. The food company Oscar Mayer has adopted the concept to stimulate paid sampling outside supermarkets which then stimulates higher in-store sales of its products. Multi-screen cinemas are rolling the carts down the aisles in their theatres to stimulate sales of popcorn and soft drinks to patrons who do not wish to queue for food in crowded lobbies. Having demonstrated the power of the concept, the two entrepreneurs have moved on to develop a 'smart cart' which uses microprocessors and telemetry to keep the Head Offices of cart operators appraised of hourly sales and inventory levels.

CHANGING FORM AND UPGRADING FUNCTIONALITY

David Giuliani was first stimulated to think about better ways of cleaning teeth during a conversation with David Engel and Roy Martin, professors at the University of Washington. These latter individuals were convinced that by using sound waves they could remove a much higher level of bacteria from teeth than was achievable with conventional electric toothbrushes (Freedman 1997). Guiliani founded the new firm, Optiva, but, after working on the prototype for six months, was unable to develop a viable product. He then decided that the approach could be improved if the sound waves were travelling through a fluid. Having convinced his academic partners of the need to try this alternative approach, Guiliani evolved a new design which was based around the concept of a tuning fork driven by an electromagnetic field. Together the researchers discovered that at 520 strokes per second, fluid in the mouth would erode plaque even when the vibrating brush head was not in contact with the teeth. This discovery meant that the product could actually remove bacteria from beneath the gum line, an area which remains untouched by conventional toothbrushes.

The company realised that the sophisticated claim that its new product, now branded as the Sonicare toothbrush, could remove bacteria from below the gum line could not be communicated effectively using conventional mass marketing techniques, so they decided to focus on gaining the support of the dental profession by advertising in dental journals and having their sales force call on dental practices. Research validated the effectiveness of this approach – 98 per cent of dentists who were shown the product were willing to recommend it to their patients. Having begun to make inroads into the market, an upmarket retailer, Sharper Image, that liked the high-tech nature of the product, offered to feature Sonicare in its catalogue. This move, coupled with talk show host Oprah Winfrey praising the product on her show, caused the product to gain widespread market acceptance.

Optiva re-invested 5 per cent of revenue back into in-house research and clinical studies by leading universities. The data generated by these studies were then used by the company's sales force to further expand awareness of the product's performance claims among the dental profession. At the same time, Optiva established a new sales force to work with mass merchandisers such as Wal-Mart and pharmacy chains such as Walgreens. By 1995, about a third of the nation's dentists were recommending Sonicare and over 250,000 retail stores were stocking the product. From launch, however, Optiva was concerned about competitors from the conventional electric toothbrush firms, such as Braun, entering the market with an equivalent product. Fortunately, it was successful in having patents approved for its technology and, in 1996, Teledyne – producer of the leading electric toothbrush brand, Water Pick – was forced to acknowledge the validity of the Optiva patents and had to pay the company an undisclosed sum plus royalties on future sales of their sonic toothbrush, the SenSonic. By the end of 1997, Optiva had captured 33 per cent of the $184 million American retail electric toothbrush retail market and over a 50 per cent share of the market for toothbrushes sold directly by dental practices.

ENTREPRENEURSHIP AND PRODUCT PORTFOLIO MANAGEMENT

Most organisations recognise that all products have a finite life. This concept provides the basis of a theoretical paradigm known as the product life cycle (PLC) curve which proposes that products and service pass through the four phases of introduction, growth, maturity and decline (Heldey 1977). In recognition of the risks associated with depending upon a single product which has a finite life, the majority of firms strive to have a number of products positioned at different stages on the life cycle curve with the objective that such a portfolio will ensure long-term revenue stability.

In the 1970s, the Boston Consulting Group evolved a decision matrix based on the two dimensions of market share and rate of market growth. The theories underlying the BCG Matrix are that (a) high market share products generate large profits and (b) the earlier a product achieves market domination, the more likely this share will be retained as the market moves into the maturity phase on the PLC. Although evolved by the Boston Group as a tool for assisting its essentially conventional clients to manage their portfolio of products more effectively, the concept has similar potential to assist the entrepreneurial firm.

Although the original model has proved extremely popular, it has faced a number of criticisms in relation to (a) market share possibly being a somewhat crude assessment of performance and (b) market growth rate being an inadequate description of overall industry attractiveness (Doyle 1998). One way of handling the criticism about using share of total market sales share is to accept the view recently expressed by Slywotzky (1996), that one should assess sales revenue of a product relative to proportionate share of total corporate value contained within a market sector. (For publicly quoted companies, corporate value can be calculated by summing the variables of quoted market value; that is, total shares issued × current market value/share and long-term debt).

The concerns over market growth rate being an inadequate description of overall industry attractiveness can possibly be overcome by concurrently replacing market growth on the BCG Matrix with the new dimension of product uncertainty (Chaston 1999). As suggested in Figure 6.5, it is then possible to determine appropriate marketing strategies for a product portfolio which is more reflective of the objectives of value maximisation and management of risk. During the introduction and growth phases of the PLC, uncertainty is high because suppliers need to convince customers that adopting their specific product is the correct decision. By the time a market moves into the maturity phase, most customers have become loyal to a specific product and their level of confidence is high.

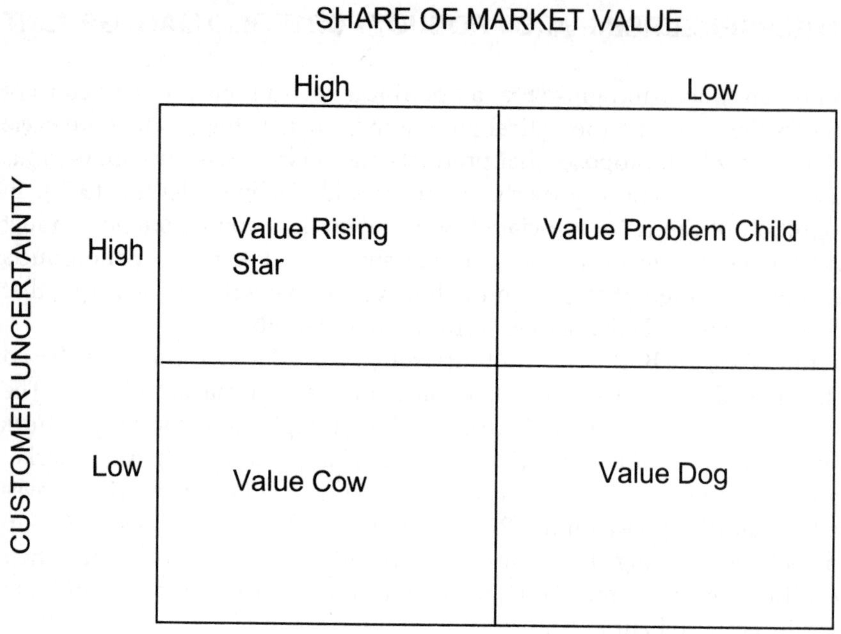

SHARE OF MARKET VALUE

	High	Low
High	Value Rising Star	Value Problem Child
Low	Value Cow	Value Dog

CUSTOMER UNCERTAINTY

Figure 6.5 Value-based BCG Matrix

Source: adapted from Chaston (1999).

If a supplier's product has achieved a dominant share of total corporate market value by the time the market has reached maturity then, because customers are extremely confident about their purchase choice, the supplier will have to expend only limited funds as a percentage of sales on promotional activity to sustain market position. Hence this product, the 'Value Cow', will contribute a significant proportion of the company's total corporate value, which in turn will be reflected by a high traded market price for the company's share.

In contrast, the 'Value Dog' product is in the unenviable position that (a) low value generation by the product will depress the company's share price and (b) the sales growth needed to increase the company's traded share price can come only from stealing sales from a market leader. Because this latter firm's customers are now highly certain about the correctness of their product choice, then the company with a Value Dog product will have to expend a massive level of funds and/or dramatically reduce price in order to stimulate switching by eroding customer loyalty. In most cases this strategy is not financially viable, which is why Value Dog products are rarely able to overthrow Value Cows in most markets.

An exception to this rule can occur where the leader company(s) has become complacent to the point of clearly not being interested in meeting the changing needs of the customer. Under these circumstances, disenchanted customers are only too willing to switch loyalty. This scenario has frequently been exploited by Pacific Rim firms acting to steal sales from their Western counterparts in mature markets by entrepreneurially challenging sector conventions (for example, the success of the Japanese camera companies in using new technology to challenge the German's use of high-quality optics and superior engineering of moving parts to dominate the world market for premium-priced cameras). Similarly, a service sector example of creating uncertainty in the minds of customers, causing them to reassess their previously strongly entrenched product usage habits and values, is provided by HSBC's decision to launch Direct Line, a 24-hour telephone banking which has successfully challenged the conventional habit of traditional banking based around the use of retail outlets in the UK.

If a firm has a low market value share product during high market uncertainty phase (that is, a 'Value Problem Child'), then the most appropriate time to act is when customers are still at the stage of finalising their decision about which supplier offers the best proposition. Consequently, firms with a low share of total market value, or who are entering an uncertain market sector for the first time, are well advised to assess whether, while customer uncertainty is still high, a more entrepreneurial approach to new product development might result in an unconventional proposition capable of effectively attacking the 'Rising Value Stars' (for example, the decision by ex-IBM employees to develop the Compaq PC, a product with a specification equivalent to IBM PCs but which could be offered at a much reduced price).

IDEA MAXIMISATION

Inventors and intuitive entrepreneurs will tend to embark on an idea search without worrying too much about any practical commercial considerations. This is because, in their own minds, they have already conceptualised the idea they wish to pursue (for example, UK engineer Frank Whittle's desire to increase the speed of flight by developing the world's first jet engine) or, alternatively, an idea has arisen as a side effect during their ongoing pursuit of new knowledge (for example, Alexander Fleming's observation of strange events in a petri dish in his laboratory which eventually led to the discovery of penicillin).

Rational entrepreneurs are usually not gifted with the capability of insight with which their intuitive counterparts are often blessed. Furthermore, the former tend to more concerned about the need to minimise risk effectively during their search for an unconventional new product opportunity. Prior to embarking on the idea generation process, they will thus tend to find some benefit in using tools such as those described above to undertake the activities of confirming strategic positioning, determining scale of change in product function and/or form and establishing product portfolio priorities.

Whether the firm opts to adopt a conventional or an entrepreneurial new product development orientation, the golden rule at this stage is to seek to maximise the number of product ideas (Crawford 1994). These typically include traditional sources such as customers, intermediaries, the sales force, employees from all areas of the organisation, the R&D department and suppliers, and identifying weaknesses in competitors' products. Those organisations which operate in a market where customers and/or suppliers are relationship orientated are also able to draw on these external sources for additional ideas. This is in contrast to organisations operating in transactionally orientated market sectors that are often forced to develop products with limited assistance from other members of their market system.

Organisations may seek to extend the breadth of their search for ideas by exploiting sources such as markets in other countries, forming links with research institutions and monitoring scientific breakthroughs in areas outside the mainstream technology being utilised within their industrial sector. Such practices are probably most prevalent in sectors of industry where long-term success is critically dependent upon making a major technological advance and then protecting this new knowledge with patents (such as biotechnology and telecommunications).

In recent years, writers such as Buzan (1993) have cautioned that the logical, positivist education most people receive in Western nations may be causing the excessive production of 'left brain thinkers' whose mindset is biased towards conventional solutions. This type of person typically favours systematic investigation of problems and the formulation of a solution through a step-by-step analysis of a situation. It is argued that what is required within many organisations is more intuitive or 'right brain thinkers', because such persons, by using an open-minded, often multi-faceted exploratory problem-solving approach, often generate ideas capable of challenging established conventions. This view of alternative thinking styles has, over recent years, resulted in the introduction of a diverse range of techniques for enhancing employee creativity (for example, mind mapping, lateral thinking and brainstorming (Buzan 1993)).

CONVENTIONAL NEW PRODUCT MANAGEMENT

Large, conventional Western firms, concerned about sustaining their quoted share price, tend to be risk adverse organisations. Given the potential high costs associated with a new product failure, it is hardly surprising to find that many of these firms have adopted a linear control model of the type shown in Figure 6.6. As the costs associated with development increase at almost an exponential rate while the product is being progressed through to launch, then clearly the earlier the firm reaches a project termination decision, the greater the savings that will be made. The attraction of these linear models is that they are capable of identifying what might be commercially very risky ideas early into the development process, prior to significant funds being expended. It should be recognised, however, that these types of system are essentially negative control systems; that is, their utilisation is not designed to maximise success, but to minimise the possibility of failure.

A clear risk that accompanies the use of this type of control orientation is that a project termination decision may be made purely because an idea under consideration is concerned with technologies and/or market sectors of which

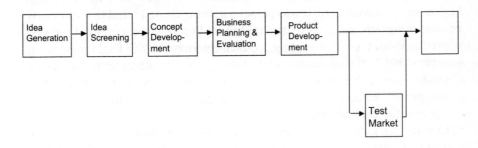

Figure 6.6 A traditional linear new product process management model

the firm has minimal prior experience. As a consequence, a 'drop error' can be made and the firm forgoes a very significant source of incremental revenue (for example, IBM apparently declined the offer to become involved in the photocopying technology which subsequently formed the basis for the creation of the Xerox corporation).

In many cases, the conventional firm reinforces the probability that a highly entrepreneurial ideas will not be progressed by using an idea screening process stage. This involves a form of scoring system in which all ideas are rated against factors that represent a perspective concerning a vision of the future based upon many prior years of cumulative trading experience (for example, market size, market growth trends, intensity of competition, and so on). As long as future market conditions continue to mirror the past, then such systems can be reasonably effective. However, where the future can be expected to be radically at variance with the past, then these types of control systems can have disastrous consequences. This scenario appears to the case for the Apple corporation following the decision to fire Steve Job and its subsequent attempt to market the company's product range as if it were a hi-tech version of a popular canned drink.

Concept testing is intended to validate the appeal of a new idea among potential customers. The potential risk is that if the idea is somewhat radical, customers will not immediately perceive any real product benefit and will indicate a low level of purchase intent. Such was the case with the Sony Walkman: apparently, customers did not immediately perceive the benefit of being offered a small tape recorder which had only a play-back capability. The only reason the concept was not terminated at this stage was that the chairman of Sony had faith in the product and overrode objections of more junior managers who felt that the project should not be progressed.

Even assuming that a new idea survives the concept testing stage, the next hurdle is to prove to senior management that the product has the potential to generate an adequate return on investment. At the end of the 1970s, when Western marketers were often promoted on the basis of their skill at controlling expenses and manipulating balance sheets as a route for sustaining high return on investment, it was perhaps not surprising to find that most new product programmes emphasised cost reduction as a conventional path by which to extend the life of existing products. Evidence of this frightening trend was provided in the research undertaken by the consulting firm Booz Allen Hamilton (see Table 6.1), which found that the majority of new product development efforts in American corporations was directed towards improving the profitability of existing products.

Despite the fact that this study was widely communicated to Western industry at the beginning of the 1980s, even by the end of the decade, following years of Western firms losing market share to their more entrepreneurial counterparts from Pacific Rim nations, research comparing the European operations of American, Japanese and UK firms demonstrated that huge cultural differences still existed concerning the management of innovation (Wong et al. 1988).

Table 6:1 New product resource allocation within US industry

Proportion of Resources (%)	Nature of Project Activity
11	Cost reduction for existing products
7	Repositioning of existing products
26	Improving the performance of existing products
26	Product line extensions for existing products
20	Products new to the firm
20	Products new to the world

Source: Booz Allen Hamilton (1982).

The study by Wong et al. (1988) measured the attitudes of British managers working for US, Japanese and UK-owned corporations. It revealed that managers in UK firms are still expected to avoid risk by focusing on short-term profit generation, concentrating on cost reduction and operating in the bottom, price orientated, end of a market. In contrast, their counterparts in Japanese firms are expected to take a longer-term view, and to build share by using innovative, entrepreneurial approaches to develop and launch superior product performance capable of providing market leadership in the highly profitable middle and/or top end of market sectors.

BREAKING WITH INNOVATION MANAGEMENT CONVENTIONS

Entrepreneurial firms have always tended to believe that innovation should be driven by the need to meet customer aspirations, not the financial community's insatiable demand for year-on-year stable increases in overall profitability. More recently, however, more and more Western firms in consumer goods markets such as electronics and domestic appliances are apparently now willing to introduce next-generation products that cannibalise their own existing products. It would appear that even the most conventional of the multinationals have now accepted the critical importance of placing the sustaining of a higher level of innovation within their organisations ahead of maximising current-year shareholder dividends.

The other aspect of convention breaking within the large firm sector has been the re-visiting of the classic stage gate process described in Figure 6.6 and to recognise that this essentially linear system can lead to rigid and inflexible decision making within the organisation. Cooper (1994) has proposed that greater creativity within the stage gate process can be achieved by permitting progression to the next stage in the development, even though certain issues may remain unresolved and thus still require further investigation. What essentially drives Cooper's new vision is a fact repeatedly validated by Japanese corporations: the organisation must find ways of reducing the time taken from idea generation through to product launch. In an increasingly competitive world, when seeking to reduce 'time to market', managers will have to balance the risks of not proceeding to the next phase until key information becomes available against being pre-empted by a more entrepreneurially orientated competitor.

These latter organisations have often achieved significant reductions in product development times by adopting a concept known as concurrent engineering. Although now a widely accepted concept within modern management thinking, Dickson's (1995) study of conventional high-growth, high-profit companies concluded that senior managers in conventionally orientated firms are still not able effectively to manage the change in mindset required if one is to successfully change the firm from a sequential to a concurrent engineering approach. Identified problems include excessive emphasis on thorough testing of the validity of new manufacturing processes prior to adoption, the demand for highly accurate cost estimation and, because of concerns over confidentiality, waiting too long before involving suppliers and/or customers in the development process.

Until very recently, another convention found in many fast moving consumer goods (FMCG) companies was for newly promoted brand managers' first assignment to be the management of a new product. The more entrepreneurially orientated organisations, however, have for some years realised that assigning the least experienced managers to new product development means that projects critically important to the firm's future are being placed in the hands of individuals with the least level of managerial experience. Such individuals thus perform poorly when required to overcome any major problems which might emerge during the product development process.

Given the poor track record for innovation within the FMCG sector, increasingly even the most conventional of firms are beginning to revise their management practices and move towards the models that have been in use for many years among their more entrepreneurial competitors. In most cases this will involve the creation of a new department to manage major product innovation projects. Staffed with highly experienced managers, the new department is typically independent of the established products marketing operation, acquires access to resources across the entire organisation by the creation of cross-functional teams, and reports directly to the main board of the company.

Entrepreneurial firms have also demonstrated that a critical element within this alternative approach is to ensure that new products are no longer seen to be aligned with any single department, but are now the responsibility of all employees within the organisation. This increases the breadth of sources from which ideas can be drawn, and avoids development delays because all departments are recognised as having a critical role to play in the management of innovation. Furthermore, because emphasis is placed on effective interdepartmental communication, inappropriate decisions are avoided which might cause problems at a later date.

MINIMISING FAILURE

A number of authors have undertaken research to identify factors influencing the success and failure of new products. Unfortunately, none of these writers has apparently attempted to delineate differences in success or failure factors between conventional versus entrepreneurial organisations. Nevertheless, it does seem reasonable to assume that within the very large-scale cross-sectional and longitudinal studies of Canadian firms undertaken by the most prolific writer in this area, Professor Cooper (1975, 1986, 1988, 1990), a high proportion of entrepreneurial firms were included within his sample frames. It thus seems reasonable to suggest that his predictive assessment of the key factors influencing the successful probable performance of a new product is equally applicable no matter what management style is adopted by organisations.

Cooper's conclusions, which are now available in the form of a scenario evaluation software tool known as Newprod, are that key innovation success is a result of the following key factors:

- *Product superiority/quality*, in relation to the issue of how product features, benefits, uniqueness and/or overall quality contribute to competitive advantage
- *Economic value*, in terms of offering greater value than existing product(s)
- *Overall fit*, in terms of the product development project being compatible with the organisation's existing areas of production and marketing expertise
- *Technological compatibility*, in terms of the product being compatible with the organisation's existing areas of technological capability

- *Familiarity to firm,* in terms of whether the firm can draw upon existing expertise or will be forced to learn completely new operational skills
- *Market opportunity,* in terms of nature of market need, size of market and market growth trend
- *Competitive situation,* in terms of how easy it will be to penetrate the market and cope with any competitive threats
- *Defined opportunity,* in relation to whether the product fits into a well defined category as opposed to being a truly innovative idea providing the basis for a completely new market sector
- *Project definition,* in terms of how well the product development project is defined and understood within the organisation.

BUILDING AN ENTREPRENEURIAL CULTURE

Over the last 20 years, as more research has been undertaken on the factors influencing the performance of firms, some theorists have suggested that senior managers need to pay greater attention to the nature of the prevailing culture within their organisations. Unfortunately, these various writers rarely appear to agree on exactly what is meant by the term 'culture'. For the purposes of the following discussion, it is assumed that culture is a reflection of the dominant attitudes and values exhibited by the majority of the workforce.

The survival of large, multinational FMCG companies is often dependent upon their ability to offer superior value, standardised goods across a diverse range of transactionally orientated markets around the world. It is perhaps understandable, therefore, that many of these firms find that the most effective operational culture is that based on closely defined employee job roles, permitting minimal variation in personnel policies between departments and using detailed, performance indicator-type monitoring systems to identify financial variances rapidly.

The risk with highly regimented internal environments is that employees cease to exhibit creativity and flexibility in responding to new situations. This is not a problem as long as the organisation is able to sustain growth while retaining a conservative-transactional marketing style. However, many firms have found that as markets have become more competitive, there is a need to become more entrepreneurial, and implementing a culture shift of this magnitude is no easy task.

Perhaps one way of comprehending the scale of change required to become a truly entrepreneurial organisation is to observe prevailing practices within the Minnesota Mining and Manufacturing corporation. More commonly known as 3M, this firm has an amazingly diverse product portfolio ranging across market sectors which include antistatic videotape, translucent dental braces, synthetic ligaments for damaged knees, reflective coatings for warning signs, industrial abrasives and heart–lung machines. In 1988, 32 per cent of 3M's $10.6 billion annual turnover came from products it had introduced since 1982.

The cornerstone of 3M's success is its retention of an entrepreneurial culture directed towards new ways of delivering customer satisfaction. Rigid operating policies are kept to a minimum, salaries are tied to the success of new products, and employees are encouraged to be inventive. The 25 per cent rule requires that a quarter of a division's sales must come from products introduced within the last five years. Meeting the 25 per cent rule is a crucial yardstick at bonus time, so managers are forced to take innovation seriously. Any barriers to success, such as 'turf fights' between departments, are kept to a minimum, and the 'not invented here' syndrome is actively discouraged. Divisions are kept small – on average, about $200 million turnover – and there are now more than 40 divisions within the corporation.

At 3M, staying close to the customer is an ingrained cultural trait. Researchers, marketers and manufacturing personnel are actively encouraged to spend time in the field, and customers are routinely invited to join brainstorming sessions organised by 3M. Once an employee comes up with an idea, he or she is encouraged to form a multi-disciplinary action team to progress the new concept through to market launch. The success of a product is accompanied by promotion for the originator. At the $5 million sales level, the individual becomes a project manager; at $20–$30 million, a department manager; and once annual sales approach $75 million, the individual becomes a division manager. To give people thinking time, there is a 15 per cent rule which permits virtually anybody to spend up to 15 per cent of his or her working week engaged in an activity of his or her choosing, as long as this is associated with product development or improvement.

In 1983, some employees complained that worthwhile projects were going unnoticed because guaranteed free time did not mean that necessary resources would be made available. To overcome this criticism, 3M created the 'Genesis Grant' which gives inventors up to $50,000 in funding to progress projects beyond the idea identification stage. A panel of experts reviews the grant applications and, on average, over 100 new projects are funded every year. In total, 3M's investment in R&D regularly exceeds 6 per cent of sales, which is twice the level of spending among the other top 50 corporations in the US.

Despite 3M's divisional structure, the company seeks to encourage interchange of technology. Experts on abrasives, for example, cooperated with technologists from the non-woven fibres group to create the Scot-Brite scrubbing sponge. This type of interdivisional cooperation, when linked to all the other elements associated with creating an entrepreneurial culture, is the reason why 3M has created a trading entity which continues to excel in delivering customer satisfaction based upon 'out-innovating' competition on a global scale.

ORGANISATIONAL STYLE AND THE FOCUS OF INNOVATION

Major new-to-the-world innovation typically occurs because a highly entrepreneurial individual and/or organisation decides to break free from existing customer satisfaction conventions and to offer a radically new solution. This type of innovation is somewhat difficult to achieve in large firms serving established markets because internal orientation is towards discovering new ways of improving the quality/value mix for existing products through emphasis on process-orientated innovation. In view of this situation, therefore, it is critical for a firm to understand whether its marketing style is compatible with its innovation management aspirations.

As illustrated by the Innovation Ownership Matrix in Figure 6.7 (Chaston 1999), once a new-to-the-world concept has been launched, there are two possible lifecycle pathways which can occur. Which pathway becomes a dominant influence within an industrial sector will be determined by the two factors of product technology complexity and market penetration. In those cases where the technological complexity is relatively low (for example, in most consumer non-durable goods and service markets), as the product gains acceptance within a market, the originating entrepreneurial-transactional firm(s) usually faces the choice of (i) retaining ownership through the late growth/maturity stages of the product lifecycle by revising its corporate operational style, or (ii) accepting that, over time, product ownership will shift into the hands of conservative-transactional firms that are more competent at producing standardised products offering a superior price/quality/value combination. Whether the new product originator changes style, or ownership moves to other firms, the focus of innovation within the market sector will tend to shift away from product performance towards being focused on using upgraded process technologies to enhance product value further (for example, exploiting economies of scale to drive down prices; simplifying manufacturing processes to reduce costs; offering customers greater choice by expanding the breadth of the product line).

In many of today's industrial markets, once a scientific breakthrough has been made, the complexity of technology is of a scale that requires the entrepreneurial originator to form partnerships with other organisations in order to be successful. This step is necessary to gain access to the additional expertise

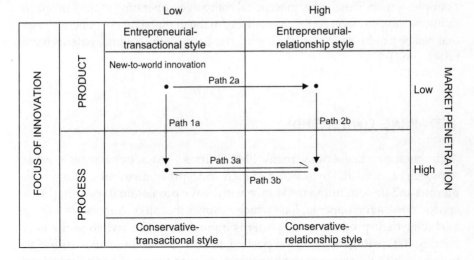

Figure 6.7 An Innovation Ownership Matrix

Source: adapted from Chaston (1999).

required to create a product which offers genuine performance benefits to the customer. A recent example of this scenario is the Internet which, originally created as a data interchange system for American scientists, only became a truly commercial proposition following the involvement of specialist software firms in Silicon Valley, California. Here again, however, as demonstrated by Netscape and Microsoft's growing dominance of the Internet software market, once a new product begins to achieve high market penetration, the entrepreneurial-relationship orientated developers will have to change style or accept loss of ownership to firms more able to deliver standardised, low-cost product propositions.

Once a product has entered the late growth/maturity phase of the lifecycle, as shown in Figure 6.7, effective process innovation may involve switching between transactional and relationship marketing styles. It is posited that Path 3a may occur because members of a supply chain recognise that it is necessary to work in much closer partnership with others in order to exploit new technologies. For example, Japanese car manufacturers, seeking to improve the performance of their products further have demonstrated the benefits of forming R&D partnerships with their component suppliers.

Path 3b in Figure 6.7 also suggests that once a technology is widely understood and price becomes the dominant influencer in the purchase decision, firms that are extremely competent at conservative-transactional

123

process innovation may become the major players in a market sector (for example, certain French pharmaceutical companies, operating in the European public health provision sector, specialising in the manufacture of generic drugs that can be produced at a much lower price because the original patents have now lapsed).

RETAINING OWNERSHIP

A common practice among many FMCG firms is to adopt a mass market approach of immediately seeking to gain widespread distribution for a new product and underpinning the launch with heavy promotional spending. This approach has a fundamental flaw which assumes that all customers are willing to change their product usage patterns immediately and switch to the new offering. Yet, as Rogers (1983) has posited, there exists an 'innovation diffusion process' which he proposes can be characterised as a normal curve containing five adopter groups exhibiting the following very different purchase behaviours.

1. *Innovators* – venturesome individuals who are so willing to try new ideas that they are often prepared to accept that the product is so new that performance may be less than perfect.
2. *Early adopters* – opinion leaders within their industrial and/or personal social groups, who are willing to try new ideas ahead of others, but make careful assessment of potential risk before placing an order.
3. *Early majority* – people who try new ideas ahead of the majority, but typically delay initial purchase until information from early adopters indicates that the new product is meeting claims made by the supplier.
4. *Late majority* – people who tend to be sceptical about new ideas and avoid purchase until there is clear evidence that the new product is successful.
5. *Laggards* – traditionalists who are suspicious of change and will delay purchase until the new product has been on the market for a significant period of time.

The speed with which a new product gains market acceptance and is adopted by the five different customer types on the diffusion curve is influenced by a whole range of factors that the marketer will need to understand in order to design a successful market launch. These factors include:

*   relative product advantage
*   compatibility

- product complexity
- product divisibility (that is, the degree to which the product can be tried on a limited basis)
- communicability (that is, the degree to which the benefit claims can be easily described to potential users).

The influence of these factors is relatively small in the case of an easily understood consumer product. Consequently, in only a very short period of time, a new product of this type will usually gain widespread acceptance within the market (for example, the move from dishwasher detergent powder to detergent tablets). As described by Figure 6.8, however, producers of technically complex products usually face a much harder task in gaining acceptance of their product; in many cases, the major differences in buyer behaviour between the various customer groups on the innovation diffusion curve will demand completely different marketing strategies.

Entrepreneurial-transactional firms tend to draw upon the latest technological breakthroughs in their sector as the basis for developing new-to-the-world propositions. The majority of their customers are researchers working in scientific institutions, R&D laboratories, or quality control departments within manufacturing firms who are also deeply

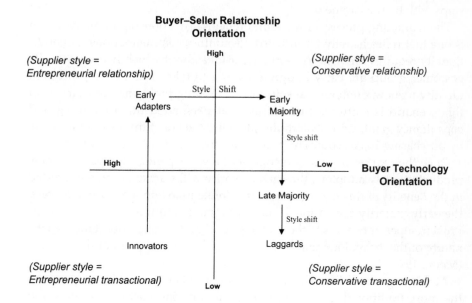

Figure 6.8　A hi-tech customer adoption model

Source: adapted from Chaston (1999).

fascinated by the exploitation of the latest technology and for whom moving forward the frontiers of knowledge is often more important than purchase of a reliable product with proven applications. Management of the marketing process is often undertaken by the firm's researchers who operate in a world where customers find out about its new product expertise through word-of-mouth recommendations within the same sector of industry or academia.

New ideas based upon the latest technology often require the involvement of the customer in assisting the supplier firm with the development of a truly new, effective product. Thus, if the original inventor wishes to retain ownership of the proposition as the market evolves and develops, he or she will probably need to shift marketing style to become more entrepreneurial-relationship orientated. This style shift will then permit the successful formation of innovation partnerships with like-minded customers so that together they can develop a new product offering genuinely superior performance.

In many cases the entrepreneurial-transactional owner/manager within the supplier firm, having provided a solution to a customer problem, is more interested in moving on to a new project than in seeking to gain a high volume of sales for his or her previous new product idea. As a result, it is not unusual for the further development of the product concept to pass into the hands of entrepreneurial firms that are orientated towards working in close partnerships with their customers.

The marketing process of the entrepreneurial-relationship orientated firm is one that relies heavily upon word-of-mouth recommendations, but additionally requires the firm to have a clear idea about which firms among its customer group are early adopters willing to take risks in the process of identifying new, often radical solutions to existing problems. An example of this scenario is software firm Lotus, that persuaded the accounting and consultancy giant, Price Waterhouse, to enter the era of the 'electronic office' by purchasing 10,000 copies of its then unproven Lotus Notes product.

Once the market begins to recognise the widespread adoption of a new product by early adopters, the early majority will start to become interested in the benefits of this latest innovation. Unlike innovators or early adopters, the early majority take a much more pragmatic attitude to new products. Proven, superior benefits to the user are significantly more important than the nature of the technology that has permitted the development of the product (Moore 1991).

At this stage in the life of the product, the supplier will need to begin to use the more traditional marketing tools of identifying customer targets and formulating promotional campaigns to communicate new benefits, and must be prepared to commence the battle of convincing the market that the new product is clearly capable of outperforming existing products. The market expansion task is made significantly easier if the supplier has an in-depth knowledge of the customer. This is why, at this point on the PLC curve, unless the entrepreneurial-relationship firms are willing to change their marketing orientation, their role in the life of the product often passes into the hands of conservative-relationship firms. These organisations are often larger firms who have typically monitored the progress of any new innovation, and when they feel that the majority of the market is willing to adopt the new product, they will enter the sector offering a specific solution targeted at customers known to be dissatisfied with the performance of existing products.

An example of this dissatisfaction scenario is provided by Oracle, which carefully monitored the growing concerns that its customers were exhibiting over the fact that many new database software products were designed to operate on specific hardware platforms. This meant that it was often impossible to integrate different information systems effectively within their organisations. Oracle's solution was to launch a database system which was compatible with most hardware systems, thereby allowing its customers to begin creating fully integrated management information systems.

The late majority is usually completely uninterested in technological advances. Instead, they are influenced by the fact that the product has proven capabilities, is widely used within their market sector and is realistically priced relative to existing products. Servicing this type of customer is best undertaken by larger firms who can exploit scale in their manufacturing operations, have a marketing operation capable of implementing large-scale promotional campaigns and a distribution operation able to service a diversity of market channels. Typically, these are the skills found within conservative-transactional marketing operations, and a current example of this scenario is provided by Canon's increasingly global domination of the laser printer market.

Laggards are only really motivated by proven solutions available at low prices. The strong price orientation across this group of customers means that their needs are best served by very large, conservative-transactional firms that specialise in producing and distributing a large volume of goods at highly competitive prices (for example, the Korean electronics firms that now dominate the domestic VCR market).

REFERENCES

Booz Allen Hamilton (1982) *New Products for the 80s*, Booz Allen Hamilton, New York.

Buzan, T. (1993), *The Mindmap Book*, BBC Publications, London.

Chaston, I. (1999), *New Marketing Strategies*, Sage Publications, London.

Christensen, C.M. (1997), *The Innovator's Dilemma: When New Technologies Cause Great Firms to Fail*, Harvard University Press, Boston, MA.

Cooper, R.G. (1975), 'Why new industrial products fail', *Industrial Marketing Management*, Vol. 4, pp. 315–26.

Cooper, R.G. (1986), *Winning at New Products*, Wesley, Reading, MA.

Cooper, R.G. (1988), 'The new product process: a decision guide for managers', *Journal of Marketing Management*, Vol. 3, No. 3, pp. 235–55.

Cooper, R.G. (1990), 'Stage-gate systems: a new tool for managing new products', *Business Horizons*, Vol. 33, No. 3, pp. 44–54.

Cooper, R.G. (1994), 'Third-generation new product processes', *Journal of Product Innovation Management*, Vol. 11, pp. 3–14.

Crawford, C.M. (1994), *New Products Management*, fourth edition, Irwin, Burr Ridge, IL.

Dickson, P. (1995), 'Managing design in small high-growth companies', *Journal of Product Innovation Management*, Vol. 12, pp. 406–14.

Doyle, P. (1998), *Marketing Management and Strategy*, Prentice Hall, Hertfordshire.

Freedman, D.H. (1997), 'Sonic boom', *Inc. Magazine*, Goldhirsh Group, Boston, MA, p. 36.

Heldey, B. (1977), 'Strategy and the business portfolio', *Long Range Planning*, February, pp. 1–14.

Moore, G.A. (1991), *Crossing the Chasm*, HarperBusiness, New York.

Richman, T. (1989), 'Growth strategies: cart tricks', *Inc. Magazine*, Goldhirsh Group, Boston, MA, p. 138.

Rogers, M. (1983), *Diffusion of Innovation*, The Free Press, New York.

Slywotzky, A.J. (1996), *Value Migration: How to Think Several Moves Ahead of the Competition*, Harvard Business School Press, Boston, MA.

Wiersema, F. (1996), *Customer Intimacy: Pick your Partners, Shape your Culture, Win Together*, HarperCollins, London.

Wong, V., Saunders, J. and Doyle, P. (1988), 'The quality of British marketing', *Marketing Management*, Vol. 4, pp. 32–46.

TIME AND PROCESS-BASED ENTREPRENEURSHIP

The perceptive marketer realises that many of the opportunities for delivering greater customer satisfaction can only be achieved by the entire organisation focusing upon new approaches that can influence factors such as build quality, delivery time and low prices. In the mid-1980s, Western marketers realised that their frighteningly aggressive counterparts from the Pacific Rim had decided to break yet another convention; they radically reduced the time taken to complete standard manufacturing processes. The issue which first attracted consideration by the Japanese was the global convention that, to minimise costs, firms should (a) schedule long runs of a single product, and (b) use economic order quantity (EOQ) models to ensure that the firm always has sufficient buffer stocks to handle unexpected order surges from customers.

The Japanese perspective was that, although this manufacturing industry convention could theoretically optimise production costs, any savings in unit manufacturing costs are more than offset by the concurrent massive investment in working capital required to fund cash outflows for raw materials for on hand, work in progress and inventoried finished goods. Their ultimate solution was to reject the concept of long runs of individual products based upon specified EOQs and to investigate the potential for scheduling production only to match on-hand orders from customers. Their outstanding success has subsequently become better known as the Just In Time (JIT) manu-facturing philosophy, and by the 1990s had become the new convention for firms wishing to be considered 'world class' organisations. Essentially, to be effective, JIT demands a commitment to the following.

1. Careful monitoring of customer order patterns.
2. Suppliers who can respond very rapidly and have the capability cost effectively to deliver only sufficient raw materials for the next scheduled production run.

3. Manufacturing operations in which machine tool set-up time is minimised.
4. A highly proactive, responsive workforce.
5. Logistics systems capable of delivering smaller order quantities economically to customers.
6. 'Real time' information capture systems capable of diagnosing the cause of any emerging procurement, production scheduling or delivery problems immediately (Storey 1994).

One extremely radical example of applying JIT to every aspect of business operations has been provided by Honda who, by the end of the 1980s, had managed to reduce the cycle time of concept identification to market launch for its next generation of vehicles to the amazingly short time-span of only 30 months. This could be contrasted starkly with the then cycle time at Mercedes-Benz of seven years. The implication of this scenario was that in the time taken by a Western firm to develop and launch a new vehicle, Japanese car manufacturers could market three generations of new car designs. If this was not enough of a threat, Honda subsequently announced its aim of reducing development cycle time further from 30 to 18 months.

A TIME-BASED ENTREPRENEUR

Located in Fountain Valley, California, Kingston Technology succeeds by developing and shipping new products faster than the competition (Welles 1992). In the world of computing, many manufacturers produce standard machines which have insufficient memory to undertake the tasks for which they were designed. Kingston solved this problem for the machine user by designing and manufacturing memory, processor and storage upgrades for PCs, laptops, laser printers and workstations. When a major brand launches a new computer product range, Kingston aims immediately to produce an upgrade that will make these new products capable of operating the latest available software. The company then sells the upgrade to distributors and re-sellers of computer equipment.

Kingston was founded in 1987 by David Sun and John Tu when there was a shortage of a certain type of chip used in memory upgrades. They realised that they could alter another chip which was in ample supply to produce a similar product. In the late 1980s, most computers operated using their own proprietary system, each requiring its own own unique memory, which meant that Kingston had the opportunity to offer an extensive range of memory upgrades.

The underlying entrepreneurial rationale for Kingston's success is speed of response. In many cases, it is able to develop and ship a new upgrade within a week of identifying demand for the product. However, relying merely on fast innovation is only half the story; the company also aims to ship all orders on the day they are received. This compares with a typical order response time for most of their competitors of four to six weeks. Additionally, these competitors usually test only 5 per cent of components before shipping, whereas, to avoid creating operating problems for the customer, 100 per cent of components at Kingston are checked before shipment.

To achieve such rapid order cycle response times, the company is critically dependent upon its suppliers. To cement these relationships, Kingston believes in forming long-term partnerships with vendors who are selected on their ability to offer consistent on-time deliveries and high quality standards. In some cases, where the supplier is very small, Kingston will assist its cashflow by pre-paying on orders placed with that vendor.

TIME AND PROCESS MANAGEMENT

Not unsurprisingly, perhaps, the Japanese entrepreneurial challenge to global manufacturing conventions sparked a flurry of writings concerning the critical need for Western firms to adopt time reduction as a fundamental element across all of their organisations' strategies, policies and processes. One of the first management theorists to recognise the critical importance of time and process management was Davis (1987). He pointed out that in the world of business, the concept of time is undergoing a radical transition. In the industrial age, the established convention was a 9-to-5 business day, whereas, in a post-industrial society, the customer is now seeking 24-hour service, 7 days a week, 365 days a year.

Davis believes that this change in customer demand necessitates the entre-preneurial marketer carefully studying every aspect of internal operations, from product conceptualisation through to customer post-purchase consumption. He reports that marginal reductions in time (that is 10–20 per cent) can be accomplished simply by improving efficiency. However, a major reduction (50–100 per cent) usually requires a willingness to challenge every convention across the entire procurement, production, distribution and delivery cycle. He therefore proposes that firms should adopt the entre-preneurial vision of *zero-based time* which has the ultimate goal of never keeping the customer waiting.

Similar views have also been expressed by Tucker (1991). He, too, believes that the number one driving force for challenging market conventions is to revise organisational processes to accelerate the speed with which the organisation can respond to customer needs. He suggests that the following eight steps permit exploitation of the 'speed imperative'.

1. Assess the importance of speed to the customer.
2. Challenge every time-based convention that exists within the organisation.
3. Involve customers both in identifying their waiting time dissatisfaction and in generating ideas to reduce response times.
4. Continuously monitor time savings achieved as new initiatives are implemented, with the goal of eventually identifying new, incremental actions to reduce response times further.
5. Clearly promote the nature of your speed imperative philosophy to the market.
6. Reflect the costs of outstanding speed in the pricing of products and services.
7. Reward employees for finding new, entrepreneurial ways of saving time.
8. Having achieved high speed response, build this achievement into your customer guarantee system.

Tom Peters echoed similar views in a 1990 article in which he suggested a number of 'must dos' for companies planning to compete on the basis of faster response times. He recommended that, to challenge conventions, a firm must be willing to carry out the following five steps.

1. Decentralise and share information across the entire workforce.
2. Flatten the organisational structure both to improve information flows and the speed of decision making.
3. Redesign all business processes.
4. Measure and celebrate time-saving initiatives.
5. Empower employees such that they have the freedom to respond immediately to situations without first having to gain the approval of their immediate superior.

Barden corporation, UK

An example of adopting a time-driven operational strategy is provided by the Barden corporation, based in Plymouth, England. This UK firm specialises in the manufacture of precision bearings. Since the early 1990s, it has been owned by the massive German engineering firm, FAG, Schweinfurt. At the beginning of the 1990s, Barden UK was in the enviable situation of being positioned at the top end of the precision bearings market with an outstanding reputation for both product quality and technical customer support from pre-purchase through to the provision of post-purchase, after-sales service. Within its sector of the global bearings industry, the convention prevailing for many years is that the complexities of designing and machining precision bearings means that customers may have to wait anywhere between 14 and 52 weeks for their product to be delivered.

In seeking to strengthen its position as a global leader further, Barden adopted the highly entrepreneurial attitude of seeking to reduce delivery times from weeks down to a maximum of five days. An in-depth analysis of existing manufacturing procedures immediately led to the identification of the need for a more effective 'line-of-site' cellular manufacturing system, in which raw materials entered at one end and the finished product flowed out of the system a few days later, without the occurrence of any work-in-progress delays.

To achieve this aim, the first obstacle encountered was that the firm had too many layers of management and that shopfloor workers had no real decision making authority to resolve production problems immediately as they arose. Barden therefore moved to delayer the firm, and at the same time created a highly flexible, multi-skilled workforce. The other identified obstacle in the manufacturing process was that significant periods of time were being lost while machines were being re-set prior to the shopfloor workers being able to move on to producing a different product.

In order both to communicate the critical importance of reducing machine set-up times and to prove to a somewhat sceptical management team that this was feasible, the specialist bearings Divisional Group Managing Director undertook to solve this problem for what was considered to be the most difficult machine tool in the company. Within three weeks, this individual had reduced set-up from 6.5 hours down to 14 minutes and 5 seconds. Having achieved this goal, he then sent copies of the video he had made of the project to all employees within the specialist bearings group around the world.

At Barden UK, following receipt of the video and a very clear accompanying management directive, it took only a year to reduce set-up times to the point where 80 per cent of all machine settings could be changed in not more than 30 minutes. Of significant interest was the source of inputs to achieve this highly credible performance. Only 25 per cent came from better organisation of paperwork flows and 25 per cent from improved engineering practices. The most important source of entrepreneurial ideas, representing 50 per cent of the solution, came from the machine setters on the shopfloor. The impact of breaking the sector's convention on delivery times is evidenced by the fact that, over a three-year period, Barden UK's sales rose from £8 million to over £24 million as customers increasingly opted to purchase from a supplier capable of delivering products within five days instead of the industry standard convention of many weeks.

THE NEED FOR CONTROL

Although it may seem intuitively appealing to stimulate the entire workforce to think more entrepreneurially, the experience at the Donnelly corporation highlights the need for adopting a somewhat cautious approach on occasion (Jones 1999). The firm is a large American car parts manufacturer that, in the 1980s, was encountering problems in trying to meet increasing pressure from its customers to upgrade quality and reduce delivery times further. In the early 1990s, the firm instituted a programme to 'empower' the workforce based on the concept of encouraging teams independently to develop new entrepreneurial solutions. The outcome was in-plant chaos. For example, workers on one shift would adjust machines to increase yield which then resulted in quality problems for workers on subsequent shifts. The company also experimented with an unsupervised approach to continous improvement schemes based on the Japanese *kaizen* philosophy.

By the mid-1990s, Donnelly realised that, although exploiting the entrepreneurial skills of its employees was a valuable tool with which to identify new, more innovative working practices, the company also desperately needed to inject some semblance of order into the activity. Its solution was to appoint two former Toyota managers to oversee all new initiatives. The 5,000 employees are still encouraged to experiment, but ideas for change cannot be implemented without permission. This means that once a new idea is identified, management then assesses viability and only after very careful testing is the idea introduced on a company-wide basis. Furthermore, clear standards are defined for each change and actual performance is then carefully monitored in order to ensure that every entrepreneurial idea is actually delivering the level of benefit predicted.

PROCESS RE-ENGINEERING

Two American management consultants who have championed the critical need to find ways to introduce the concept of breaking with current time and process management conventions in Western industry have been Hammer and Champy. From the experience gained from working with many large, highly conventional organisations, they have coined the phrase 're-engineering the corporation' (Hammer and Champy 1993).

Hammer and Champy describe their philosophy as one where, for a company, 'it means tossing aside old systems and starting over. It involves going back to the beginning and inventing a better way to do work.' The underlying principle of undertaking a searching review of operations during which no activity is sacred is further emphasised in their definition that '[r]e-engineering is the fundamental rethinking and radical redesign of business processes to achieve dramatic improvements in critical contemporary measures of performance, such as cost, quality, service and speed'.

Hammer and Champy's opinion is that the prevailing Western industrial model rests on the basic premise that workers have few skills and little time or capacity for training. This inevitably leads to the conclusion that jobs and tasks assigned to workers must be kept simple. This philosophy is, of course, supportive of the earlier writings of the founding father of economics, Adam Smith, and the champion of scientific management, Alfred Taylor. They both argued that people work more efficiently when they have one easily understood task to perform.

However, as industrial processes have become more complex during the twentieth century, it has been necessary to develop complex information and decision making processes to weld together the multitude of jobs within a large organisation associated with order generation and the delivery of large volumes of output. Thus, the conventional industrial model in existence for the majority of the twentieth century, and one which, until very recently, has huge rewards for both nations and shareholders, is that of mass production.

Proponents of re-engineering argue that mass production models unfortunately have now evolved to the point where they do not permit organisations to respond to the contemporary concurrent market demands for quality, service, flexibility and low costs. Hammer (1995) has now gained extensive experience of facilitating major re-engineering projects across a diverse range of industrial sectors. He concludes that there are a number of recurring themes and characteristics which can be expected to be encountered while implementing the process. These include the following.

1. The convention that several jobs undertaken by various specialists within the organisation is the most cost-effective approach is no longer valid, and combining tasks into a single role that can be undertaken by one person is the best way forward (for example, an insurance company which previously had numerous people reviewing and checking different aspects of an application for life cover that revises this process by upskilling individuals to act autonomously in processing the customer's application).

2. The convention that the most effective structures are those based around vertical hierarchies in which workers 'work', but, if any decisions have to be made, these should passed upwards to managers because they are the only ones with the necessary breadth of knowledge to fulfil this task. What typically happens during re-engineering is that the organisation is

delayered and workers are given authority to make decisions on issues that impact directly on their own performance.

3. The convention that actions must be taken in a natural, logical order. An excellent example of this philosophy was provided by the linear new products management control model presented earlier in Chapter 6. One of the key reasons for Honda's ability to reduce 'time to market' was its willingness to act entrepreneurially; to break with convention and initiate tasks further downstream in the model before earlier phases have been completed. Another example of this philosophy is provided by Honda's willingness to ignore the industry convention that new machine tools should not be ordered until the prototype new car has been thoroughly tested. Although this latter approach minimises risk, it also results in a significant delay before manufacturing of the new model can commence. Thus, Honda's solution was to place orders with machine tool suppliers much earlier in the project, such as at the idea generation or concept evaluation phase.

4. The convention that to maximise profitability by exploiting economies of scale, the market should be offered a single, standard product or service. A more entrepreneurial philosophy is to recognise that customers have highly variable needs and that, where possible, attempts should be made to satisfy this requirement for diversity. The benefits of being prepared to respond flexibly to real market conditions are exemplified by Dell's willingness to scrap the computer industry convention that all customers will be offered the same product. Dell has established the world's largest computer direct marketing operation by permitting customers at the time of order to request a specification for their new PC which has operating features individually customised to their specific product usage needs.

5. The convention that specific tasks must be undertaken by specialist centralised departments (for example, that all purchasing – even down to the smallest of items, such as paper clips – must be done by a Head Office procurement department). The reality, of course, is that any savings made through volume discounts are then totally amortised by the costs associated with keeping track of the order/delivery cycle paperwork, managing the logistics of distribution and allocating costs to remote units located some distance from Head Office.

6. The convention that all activities must be closely checked and controlled – for example, the insistence that, prior to any travel, all employees should receive written authorisation and that, upon subsequent submission of travel claims, these must be approved by the immediate line manager, audited by the department's accounting team and then re-audited by the Head Office accounting group prior to expenses being paid. Another aspect of this 'check and control' culture is often prevalent in

procurement. The department seeking to make a purchase has to make out an order request; this is passed to accounting for checking, then passed to procurement, which issues an order, and the supplier is then required to provide duplicate delivery notes for the department requiring the item, plus the accounting and procurement departments. Upon arrival at the company, the supplier then has to wait while a detailed inspection is made to ensure that the goods accurately meet the details described both on the original order form and on the delivery note.

THE IMPORTANCE OF TECHNOLOGY

It is frequently the case that being able to break with convention in the production of goods is made feasible only through the advent of new, affordable technologies. In many cases the reason for technology becoming affordable is the increased availability of powerful specialist microchips. One example of this trend is in the area of robotic visioning systems (Brown 1998). The problem in the past has been that robots had the capability to handle data from only two dimensions which meant that the machines could not exhibit any form of depth perception.

In the last few years, as microchip costs have fallen, robotic systems have been developed which can handle data from three dimensions, so the machines can be programmed to undertake unconventional production and quality management tasks. The Gulf Stream States Paper corporation, for example, has a robotic system which decides how each log passing through its mill should be cut. The machine uses a laser system to analyse each log. The data generated by the laser measurements permits determination of the best mix of plank sizes which should be produced in order to maximise the value of the wood and minimise waste.

Similar technology has been introduced into the Mercedes-Benz plant in Alabama in the US. A critical problem facing car manufacturers is achieving consistency in car body assembly. The traditional approach is regularly to take sample cars from the line and inspect them manually. When a problem such as a poorly fitting door is identified, only then can action be taken to resolve the matter. At the Mercedes-Benz Alabama plant, a machine has been installed at the end of the production line with 38 laser cameras that can check all key measurements in 45 seconds. Every car can now be inspected, which also means that assembly line faults can be detected instantly and immediate action can be taken to resolve the fit problems on the assembly line.

However, a potential problem with robots is that it takes a very long time to develop the software through which they are programmed to undertake their assigned task. Programming the robot on the production line means putting the machine in place and then carefully analysing every element of motion. In the case of a complex activity this can take weeks, during which time the company's production line cannot be used for normal production.

Having recognised this problem, an Israeli company, Tecnomatix, had the entrepreneurial idea of simulating the motions required of the robot on a computer workstation (Ross 1999). This is possible because manufacturers now use CAD systems to design their products, and the ready-made files from the CAD system can be installed in the simulator to provide the basis for defining the necessary actions required of the robot engaged in installing the component. Then, if it becomes clear that the robot cannot handle the installation process, there is the option of either redesigning the component or reprogramming the robot. Known as 'off-line programming', Tecnomatix can now install the pre-trained robot on a real production line in approximately 48 hours, thereby virtually eradicating the downtime associated with the more traditional approach to the on-line programming of robots.

IS RE-ENGINEERING ENTREPRENEURIAL?

During the early 1990s, re-engineering (or process re-engineering) has become increasingly popular with Western firms in both the manufacturing and the service sectors. As popularity infers widespread acceptance bordering upon standard, normal behaviour, it seems reasonable to pose the question, 'Has re-engineering moved from being an entrepreneurial to a conventional business practice?'

One way of addressing this question is to review two cases that were widely cited during the early days of re-engineering – IBM Credit and Ford. At IBM Credit, when a salesperson called in a request for financing a customer's purchase of a computer, the approval process took on average at least six days. The risk associated with this delay was that the customer might find another source of financing, or, even worse, select a computer from another, more responsive vendor.

After a number of failed conventional attempts to resolve the problem, two senior IBM Credit managers decided to follow the approval process personally through the five steps of writing up the application, checking customer creditworthiness, preparing the lending contract, determining the appropriate interest rate on the loan, and issuing a formal customer quote. They learned that the whole process could be completed not in six days, but in 90 minutes. The outcome was that IBM Credit decided to break with convention and to replace the various specialists who were responsible for each phase of the application with a single generalist who managed the entire process without turning to other staff for approvals.

Ford, having acquired a 25 per cent stake in Mazda, observed that this latter organisation had only five people working in its accounts payable department. This contrasted with Ford which had over 500 people performing the same tasks. By analysing the current workflows, Ford realised that its system of 'checking and control' had resulted in a multi-copy purchase order approach, a goods inwards form and an invoice submitted by the vendor. Within the accounts payable department, payment against invoice would not occur until a Ford employee (a) had copies of all documents and (b) was happy that there was a precise match of information across all documents. Under its new re-engineered regime, when a purchase order is issued, this same information is entered into a computerised database. At the time of delivery, the shipping clerk checks goods inwards against the database. If there is a match, the goods are accepted and the computer automatically authorises issuance of a cheque to the vendor. When order and shipment do not correspond, the goods are refused by Ford. The result is that Ford now requires only 125 people in its vendor payment operation (Hammer and Champy 1993).

In both examples, the two firms have broken with convention for a specific activity and hence it can be considered that a specific department and/or group of departments have acted in an entrepreneurial fashion. Other large firms that might learn of such cases may then act to revise their own operations along similar lines. However, it can be argued that this is not an entrepreneurial response by the latter organisations because all they are doing is merely reacting to the fact that within their industrial sector, a new convention has been established.

The other issue is whether implementation of a re-engineering project infers that a firm has changed from a conventional to an entrepreneurial organisation. Certainly Hammer's (1995) description of the attributes of individuals who make good candidates for leading a re-engineering project are those one would expect to be exhibited by an effective entrepreneur (that is, a holistic perspective, creativity, enthusiasm, restlessness, optimism, persistence, tact, being a team player and having a high level of communication skills). However, a large proportion of the available case material seems to infer that many companies adopt a temporary operating philosophy to re-engineering projects, in which they identify a problem, form a project team and implement a solution which usually represents a break with longstanding internal conventions. In many cases, however, the project (a) is confined only to a small number of departments, and (b) an apparent 'Chinese wall' is created to ensure that the activities do not spill over into those parts of the organisation not directly impacted by the identified problem.

In view of these observations, it does appear that re-engineering is usually associated with the following attributes.

1. The process can be expected to be encountered within conventional organisations facing a problem that cannot be resolved by applying standard solutions.
2. The scale of the activity may involve the entire organisation, but in many cases will be confined to a specific area of organisational activity.
3. Once the re-engineering team has completed its task, the team is dissolved and the individuals return to their permanent job assignments.
4. If the new solution is publicised, other conventional firms will recognise the merits of the approach and move to initiate similar changes in their operations. Thus the re-engineered operating philosophy soon becomes the new convention within an industrial sector.

On the basis of the above analysis, it is proposed that, in fact, re-engineering is in many cases an ephemeral phenomenon invoked by conventional firms when traditional solutions are no longer viable. For example, it seems unlikely that either IBM Credit or Ford became fundamentally different organisations as a result of the changes they made in certain aspects of their financial administration procedures. Thus, although the re-engineered solution may represent a dramatic change in business practice, essentially this change is one which results only in the establishment of a revised convention. As such, therefore, it can probably be concluded that re-engineering should usually be perceived as a very effective mechanism with which to introduce entrepreneurial thinking temporarily into large, conventional organisations. Nevertheless, over the longer term one must still expect that the underlying traditional, more conventional, long-imbedded culture will continue to prevail.

However, this conclusion should not be accepted as being valid in all scenarios, for it possible that if an organisation wants to sustain a permanent culture shift in which employees are striving continually to revise conventions, then this can often be achieved by the appointment of an entrepreneurial, visionary new Chief Executive with the drive and enthusiasm to re-engineer the entire organisation from being conventional to becoming more entrepreneurial in outlook. A classic example illustrating this possibility is the appointment of John Egan as the new Managing Director of Jaguar cars in the 1980s. Through both his tireless enthusiasm and a whole series of ruthless removal of conventions he recognised as being severely damaging to build quality, Egan took a sick company and re-established its reputation as a leading producer of premium-quality, high-performance cars. Interestingly, however, following his departure after Ford's acquisition of Jaguar, it did appear that the firm soon began to slip backwards to become a somewhat more conventional organisation. It is only recently that the firm has appeared to come alive again and to have re-acquired the capability to launch the standard of innovative new designs the world has come to expect of the Jaguar brand.

RE-ENGINEERING A PERMANENT STYLE SHIFT

Established ten years ago, Solutions Ltd is a disguised example of a small firm which, through re-engineering, has achieved a complete style shift that has permitted a radical market repositioning. Its founder, Steve Giles, was the manager of a design and print production studio within a large company. His employer went into receivership and, being in his early fifties, Giles recognised that finding a similar job in another organisation would be virtually impossible.

Having heard that the receivers were willing to dispose of the studio equipment at a nominal price, Giles decided to use this opportunity to establish his own design studio. For the first five years, the company specialised in the design and production of point of sale (POS) materials such as in-store display cards and end-aisle 'dump bins' for small manufacturing firms. The conventional processes found in virtually every small design studio involved in serving this market are described in Figure 7.1. It can be seen that the process is complicated, labour intensive and because Giles, similar to his competition, lacked the equipment to undertake the forming, cutting, bending and folding of complicated designs, these activities had to be subcontracted out to another firm.

One of the problems Solutions Ltd faced by operating as a regional supplier at the bottom end of the POS market was that there were numerous other small competitors located in the same area, and consequently the market was extremely price-competitive. Hence, after a few years, Giles recognised that to build a highly profitable business he would have to break with sector convention and cease to be a small regional supplier to SME sector firms. He decided that he would attempt to find a way of becoming a provider of POS materials to large national/multinational firms that were more interested in high-quality, innovative solutions to their merchandising problems, and as a result, were less likely to make purchase decisions purely based upon lowest quoted price.

In discussions that the author had some years later with Giles, he admitted that for the first time in his life he could not draw upon previous industrial experience and just attempt to scale up the operation by buying the printing machinery found in larger firms in the industry. Fortunately, because the print industry over the last few years has embraced IT for developing new ways of managing the design and production of print materials, Giles had become deeply fascinated by the use of desktop publishing systems as a hobby using Apple Macintosh technology. He decided to start with a blank piece of paper and attempt to design a studio operation that utilised computer technology to generate the quality of POS materials demanded by national firms. He also

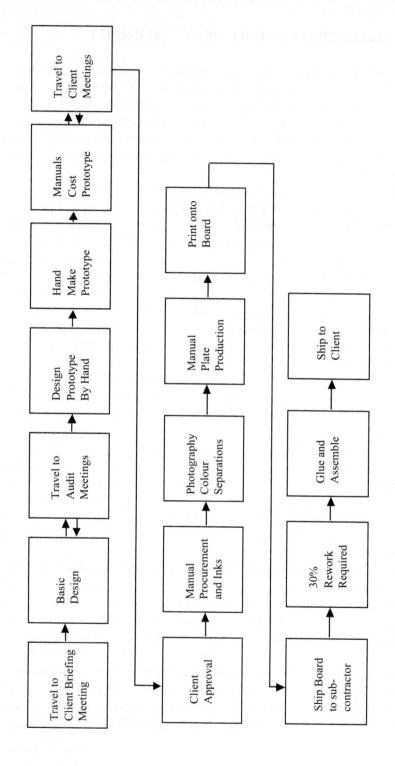

Figure 7.1 Original process flow model at Solutions Ltd

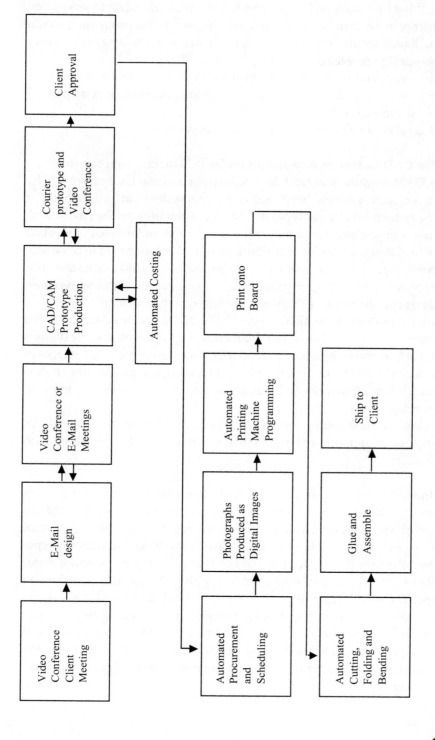

Figure 7.2 Revised process model at Solutions Ltd to serve national customers

realised that he would probably never achieve the scale advantages enjoyed by larger printers, and hence decided that the only viable positioning would have to based around rapid response, flexibility and a willingness to solve complex design problems.

Although it has taken almost five years of careful investment in new technologies, Solutions Ltd has now evolved a production process system of the type shown in Figure 7.2.

Listed below are the critical elements in this system.

1.   The CAD system for designing complex POS materials on-screen.
2.   A CAM machine that can take CAD output and use the data robotically to cut, score, fold and bend cardboard. This system can be used both for the generation of prototypes in a matter of minutes (in the past, it took two or three days using a manual approach) and for the batch production of final designs. This latter attribute permitted Solutions Ltd to cease subcontracting the manufacture of complex materials. The benefits from this move were a lowering of production costs, improved customer response times and the virtual abolition of product quality problems.
3.   An integrated system digital network (ISDN) telephone system for video conferencing with clients, rapidly forwarding copies of possible designs for online review by the client, and the online transfer of visual images in a digital form from photographers/photographic production studios which can automatically be scanned into the company's automated printing system.
4.   A sophisticated costing system which permits almost instant pricing once the design and required production quantities have been finalised with the client.

Although there are similarities at first glance between the two process models shown in Figures 7.1 and 7.2, in application terms, Solutions Ltd can offer high-speed response, can rapidly develop solutions to complex problems and can guaranteed on-time delivery. The benefit of radically repositioning the firm is evidenced by the fact that the company is now a major supplier to major multinationals, not just in the UK, but also elsewhere in Europe. The other major difference, which is obvious only by visiting the plant, is the clear commitment of staff at all levels to finding new ways of exploiting IT to enhance all aspects of the firm's operation. This is evidenced by the impressive number of R&D projects in progress to develop new entrepreneurial approaches for designing and manufacturing highly innovative POS concepts.

RE-ENGINEERING ALTERNATIVES

On the basis of the various writings and cases described in this chapter, it seems reasonable to suggest that organisations face a number of alternative possible responses in considering the use of reengineering to assist future performance. It is proposed in Figure 7.3, that the starting point for any discussions must be:

(a) to undertake a detailed review of existing processes across the entire organisation
(b) to determine the process conventions used by the majority of firms within a sector, and
(c) to benchmark the organisation against sectoral 'norms' for each process.

Only having acquired this information is the organisation really able to effectively debate the issue of whether the concept of entrepreneurial re-engineering has any potential application for enhancing future performance.

For an organisation that has already exceeded process performance standards within a sector, then re-engineering probably has no real relevance and available time would better spent on other, more productive, entrepreneurial activities. The majority of firms will probably identify one or two areas of their operations where a re-engineering project would be beneficial. In this scenario, the firm will usually form a temporary team that will complete its work by adopting an ephemeral entrepreneurial orientation. Within a few months the project will be completed and the staff, in reverting to their previous job roles, will probably return to behaving in a more conventional way. The same overall organisational style will thus be retained and the firm's market position will remain unchanged. In terms of overall performance, however, the outcome of the re-engineering project is that one or more revisions to operational processes that have been adopted will lead to an improvement in overall organisational performance.

Where it is decided that a large-scale entrepreneurial re-engineering programme is necessary in order to reposition the firm totally in the marketplace, the firm faces the choice of whether the existing organisational style should be retained or whether a significant style shift would be advisable. Whichever path is selected, in both cases a highly entrepreneurial orientation will be required to achieve fundamental revisions across one or more highly critical areas of organisational process.

If no change in overall organisational style is selected as the best way to proceed, it is very likely that a special team, led by an entrepreneurially minded senior manager, will have to be formed. This team will clearly have to be seen to have board-level authority delegated to it across all stages of the

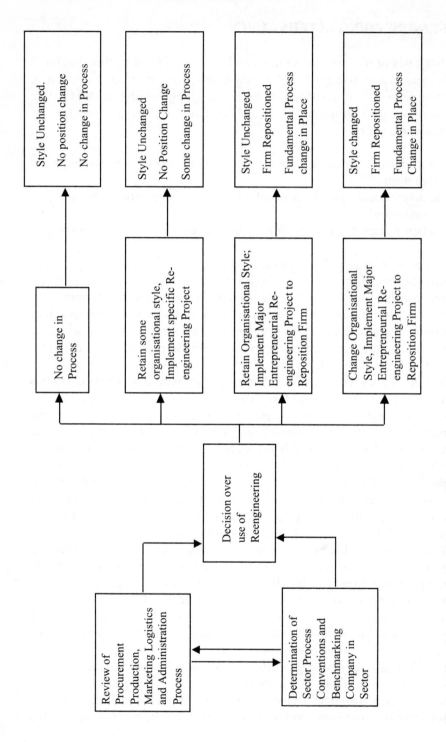

Figure 7.3 A process re-engineering planning and outcome flow model

project, from identifying the process revisions through to implementation and total completion. At the end of the project, which may take two or three years to implement, it will be extremely difficult to reintegrate the team back into their previous job roles. During the project, careful consideration will thus have to be given to the precise nature of the future roles these people will be offered. In very large organisations, it is frequently the case that team members are promoted to more senior positions and assigned the task of introducing fundamental process changes across their new areas of responsibility.

Possibly the most difficult decision to reach is whether to make a fundamental change in organisational style as a key component within a large-scale re-engineering project to reposition the firm in the marketplace. In small firms, this can usually only be achieved if the owner/manager is willing to lead the project or alternatively, is willing to promote a subordinate – respected by the entire workforce – into the position of Managing Director. The usual outcome in this latter situation is that the owner/manager moves into the newly created post of Chairman. This should then be a signal to the workforce that, over the medium term, he or she will either be retiring or intending to take a much less active role in the future management of the company.

In the somewhat unusual case that the board of a large organisation decides on a fundamental organisational style shift while using entrepreneurial re-engineering to reposition the firm, it will usually seek to appoint a new Managing Director to head up the entire process. Such a change is necessary in order to communicate to the entire workforce that ongoing, fundamental organisational change is on the agenda for the foreseeable future. An example of this type of radical move was provided in the 1980s by the large UK multi-national firm, ICI. The board recognised that there was a need to move away from the bulk chemical commodity business and to reposition the firm as a major player in the higher margin, specialist products sector of the firm's industry. To lead this fundamental shift, the board appointed the highly flamboyant John Harvey Jones, who certainly projected a public aura very different from that ever exhibited by any previous ICI Managing Director.

MASS CUSTOMISATION

As firms have acquired experience of using new technologies to achieve the aim of becoming more flexible and responsive, the more entrepreneurial manufacturers are beginning to see an opportunity to move away from mass production and towards mass customisation (Schonfeld 1998). This idea has been made feasible by a whole range of technological advances, including robots, bar-code scanners to track component flows and databases which contain detailed information on varying customer needs.

ENTREPRENEURIAL MARKETING

The leading exponent of mass customisation is possibly Dell Computers which, through direct marketing, has created close relationships with customers and assembles products only upon receipt of an order. A critical element in the firm's success is the use of technology to manage inventories. When an order is received, the firm uses sophisticated software to analyse customer needs, schedule production and contact suppliers for parts needed to meet the computer configeration requested by the customer.

Other firms are following this example. The Mattell corporation has launched a website that permits children to order a customised Barbie doll by offering 6,000 different permutations of skin tone, hairdo, clothing and accessories. The firm refers to the concept as 'customer personalisation'. Another entrepreneurial example is provided by the Tokyo-based firm, Paris Miki, which makes spectacles. Using special software, it designs lenses and a frame that conform to the shape of a customer's face. The customer can then review the design on a computer monitor and, having made his or her product selection, the company grinds the lenses and produces the customised frames. Another successful mass customiser is Chemstation, based in Dayton, Ohio. The firm produces over 1,700 industrial soap formulas. The company analyses the cleaning needs of each industrial customer and then formulates a specific cleanser. This is then delivered to the customer's premises in reusable containers. The impact of Chemstation's efforts is that the firm enjoys a customer loyalty level of over 95 per cent.

RESPONDING ENTREPRENEURIALLY TO TOUGH TIMES

Many of the entrepreneurial actions initiated by Japanese manufacturers occurred during the country's rapid economic expansion in the 1980s. The 1990s downturn in the Japanese economy, accompanied by declining business confidence and problems with the banking system, caused the more entre-preneurial firms to reconsider their methods of managing their production operations (Kano and Rao 1995).

In the face of domestic customers seeking lower-priced goods, the response of the more entrepreneurial firms has been to examine new ways for de-engineering products as a route through which to both reduce costs and increase employee productivity. To achieve this objective, the firms have moved from examining ways of improving production processes to re-examining the way that products are designed. The Yokogawa corporation, for example, produces recorders that are used in process industries to track variables such as temperature, pressure and flow rates. To reduce costs, they identified numerous small ways that changes could be made to the product at the design stage. They developed a new die-casting method which allowed the plastic cover to be produced as a single piece. In the past, this same box required 31 separate components. Additionally, the recorder's knobs were redesigned, cutting materials costs by 30 per cent and assembly time by 45 per cent.

In some cases, the change to a more simplified manufacturing philosophy can be achieved only by gaining the support of customers. Nippondenso employed highly sophisticated robots to produce over 13,000 different types of car dashboard instrument panels. Their 'expense reduction' programme highlighted the poor productivity associated with this extreme level of manufacturing diversity and, having persuaded Toyota and Honda to accept change, Nippondenso has reduced component diversity by over 40 per cent.

Essentially these Japanese firms appear to have initiated a new manufacturing philosophy based around 'the pursuit of excellence in simplicity'. However, this philosophy shift has not gone unnoticed by their American competitors. The General Electric (GE) corporation, for example, has started to instigate similar programmes and is achieving equivalent results. The team working on GE's CF6 jet engine, for example, identified ways of eliminating 24 brackets, 33 feet of cable, 24 tubes and 70 fasteners. As a result, the new version of the engine is 81 pounds lighter, resulting in an operating cost-saving of $150 per hour.

WHO WANTS TO BE AN ENTREPRENEUR?

In Western academic literature there tends to be a bias towards believing that entrepreneurship will, and should, be located within the marketing operation (Murray 1981). This view has been challenged by Foxall and Minkes (1998), who have concluded that entrepreneurial behaviour can be located anywhere within the organisation. However, even these authors conclude that innovative behaviour is less likely to encountered among staff who are 'internally' orientated, such as cost accountants and production managers.

This perspective is clearly not supported by the case materials on management practices related to innovation, TQM and JIT programmes among Japanese firms, because it appears that the entire workforce is engaged in examining how the challenging of industrial sector conventions might contribute towards further enhancing organisational performance. These Japanese scenarios seem to fit more easily with Drucker's (1985, p. 25) perception of entrepreneurship: that managers should seek to stimulate entrepreneurial behaviour across all areas of the organisation by fostering the philosophy that all employees have the potential to 'search for change, respond to it, and exploit it as an opportunity'.

For large organisations that decide to encourage a new entrepreneurial spirit, possibly the best place to start is to encourage all employees to develop an orientation towards seeking to break the time and process managing conventions that currently act as barriers to productivity within their task role. A major attraction to using time and process issues as the starting point in invoking a more entrepreneurial spirit is that virtually every employee has extensive experience of barriers that exist to optimising their own personal productivity. In order to ensure that convention breaking is a constructive activity, however, initiation of this type of project should probably be preceded by some form of basic training in areas such as problem analysis, creative thinking, solution generation, decision making, interacting with others and project management. Once this phase of skills development has been completed, employees should be encouraged to analyse their day-to-day activities with the objective of identifying where the speed and effectiveness of their task roles could be improved by challenging conventions.

In many cases, the first convention barriers that tend to be identified are those associated with internal administrative rules concerning minimal delegated authority to take action. For example, service technicians find that the time taken to repair machinery is lengthened because they are required to obtain written authority from their line supervisor before procurement is willing to issue the replacement machine parts that they need. Employees should be encouraged, however, to widen and deepen their perceptions of task role by activities such as visiting other departments to discover (a) how output from their job role impacts on others, and (b) whether other departments have already discovered an entrepreneurial idea that can be imported back into their own department. The three golden 'Ds' found to assist such activities are:

1. *dehumanise* by replacing human involvement with some form of automation
2. *delegate* by having the task undertaken by a subordinate or an external supplier
3. *delete* by removing those elements of the task that are unnecessary.

Once a stronger employee entrepreneurial orientation begins to be reflected in changing internal work practices, the next stage is to let the workforce loose on all aspects of the organisation's interaction with the external business environment. Have them analyse their contribution to all aspects of serving customer needs by walking through every phase of the customer experience, from pre-purchase enquiry through to post-purchase service. Similarly, by turning employee thinking through 180 degrees, have the workforce also examine the relationships they have with suppliers. In both cases the battle cry should be: 'By changing the rules, how can we do this faster, how can we do this better?'

One of the possibly reasons that many firms have not sought to exploit the time and process dimension of entrepreneurship is the idea promoted in academic literature that the degree to which an organisation adopts an entrepreneurial orientation depends upon the environment in which the organisation operates. Such views can cause managers to believe that they should worry about being entrepreneurial only if their organisation is facing rapidly changing environments, such as the IT and telecommunications sectors in which technology is undergoing dramatic change. Furthermore, because many managers prefer to avoid the added burden associated with change management, individuals who operate in more stable market environments often conclude that the academic literature provides justification for not seeking to challenge conventions. As demonstrated by the repeated success of Japanese corporations in coming from nowhere to attain market leadership, it is often in apparently very stable markets that organisations face the greatest risk of losing ground to competition, because management has become too comfortable and acts to sustain and reinforce current sectoral conventions. Clearly, one way of avoiding falling into this trap is for all organisations to promote an internal culture where saving time and operating smarter is a primary driving force across all aspects of both internal operations and interfacing with the external environment.

REFERENCES

Brown, S. (1998), 'Giving more jobs to electronic eyes', *Fortune Magazine*, 16 February, pp. 49–50.

Davis, S.M. (1987), *Future Perfect*, Addison-Wesley, Reading, MA.

Drucker, P.F. (1985), *Innovation and Entrepreneurship*, Heinemann, London.

Foxall, G.R. and Minkes, A.L. (1998), 'Beyond marketing: the location of entrepreneurship in the modern corporation', in Hills, G.E. and Miles, M.P. (eds), *Research at the Marketing/Entrepreneurship Interface*, University of Illinois at Chicago, pp. 377–91.

Hammer, M. (1995), *The Reengineering Revolution: The Handbook*, HarperBusiness, New York.

Hammer, M. and Champy, J. (1993), *Reengineering the Corporation: A Manifesto for Business Revolution*, Brealey Publishing, London.

Jones, T.Y. (1999), 'Looking for nirvana', *Forbes Magazine*, 8 March p. 15.

Kano, C. and Rao, R.M. (1995), 'New management secrets from Japan', *Fortune Magazine*, 27 November, pp. 45–52.

Murray, J.A. (1981), 'Marketing is home for the entrepreneurial process', *Industrial Marketing Management*, Vol. 10, No. 2, pp. 93–9.

Ross, P.E. (1999), 'Virtual robots', *Forbes Magazine*, 8 March, p. 32.

Storey, J. (1994), *New Wave Manufacturing Strategies*, P. Chapman, London.

Schonfeld, E. (1998), 'The customised, digitized, have-it-your-way economy', *Fortune Magazine*, 28 September, pp. 31–6.

Tucker, R.B. (1991), *Managing the Future: Ten Driving Forces of Change for the 90s*, Putnam, New York.

Welles, E.O. (1992), 'Built on speed', *Inc. Magazine*, Goldhirsh Group, Boston, MA, p. 82.

8

LARGE-FIRM
ENTREPRENEURSHIP

INTRODUCTION

One of the UK's largest defence contractors recently revised its mission statement to include the word 'entrepreneurial'. When questioned about how the employees were expected to interpret this change, the response of a senior manager was that the action was aimed at reminding staff of the importance of adopting a more innovative orientation in the future fulfilment of their assigned job roles. Upon being asked whether, in being more entrepreneurial, employees should seek to challenge conventions, the senior manager was somewhat horrified by the thought that this might occur. As he explained, the company's primary customer is the UK Ministry of Defence, and the one well known trait of the military is its deep suspicion of unconventional ideas. He illustrated this fact by pointing out that down through the ages, virtually every major change in warfare technology (the torpedo, the tank, the aeroplane, the submarine, the jet engine, and so on) was initially treated with deep suspicion by the military establishment. Usually the only reason that acceptance eventually occurred was that individuals from private sector firms and/or relatively junior officers were willing to challenge entrenched traditions and sought, often at great personal risk to their careers, to prove that a radically new, unconventional idea had dramatic potential for altering the future face of warfare.

Thus, although the word 'entrepreneurial' has been incorporated into the mission statement of the defence firm, apparently what is really meant by this phrase is the need for the employees to apply conventional forms of innovation to assist in the future delivery of greater customer satisfaction. The corporate desire to avoid offering unconventional propositions that might upset the customer is, however, not unique to the defence industry. As demonstrated by Christensen's (1997) study of innovation, in many cases the reason why large firms continue to seek to improve existing products is that major customers would react adversely to a major supplier proposing a major product change based upon radical revisions in core technology.

A frequently articulated view in academic literature is that the failure of large companies to be innovative can be attributed to a failure to recognise impending, fundamental changes in sector technology (for example, in the electronics industry, the move through the different technologies of valves, transistors, integrated circuits and very large scale integrated (VLSI) circuits). The implication of this view is that leading companies are frequently poorly managed, and therefore blind to new opportunities. However, Christensen posits the alternative perspective that in many cases, leading companies are aware of new technologies, but their key customers are resistant to change and concurrently continue to press for further improvements based on existing conventional technology.

One example cited by Christensen is the Winchester disk drive industry. The first 14-inch disk drives were designed for use in mainframe computers. Once introduced into the market, customers expressed the desire to purchase improved disk drives capable of storing and retrieving more and more information. This was achieved through the actions of replacing particulate oxide disks and ferrite heads with thin-film technology and magneto-resistive heads. An unconventional change in the late 1970s, was the development of the smaller 8-inch drive. This product lacked the storage capacity offered by 14-inch drives and was rejected by mainframe computer manufacturers. Thus, the new entrants into the 8-inch disk drive market, such as Shugart Associates, Priam and Quantum, were forced to turn to the newly emerging microcomputer manufacturers who were more interested in reducing the size of their systems and were prepared to forgo the lower data storage capacity offered by these smaller drives. By the time the 14-inch producers realised that they should not only continue to meet the demands of their mainframe customers, but also develop a smaller drive for the microcomputer market, it was too late – the latter market was now owned by the early entrants in this sector.

In 1980, Seagate Technology introduced a 5.25-inch disk drive and the whole cycle of customer rejection and search for new markets was repeated. It found that the smaller product was of no interest to microcomputer manufacturers but, by trial and error, Seagate found that its new market was with the early producers of the desktop PC. Interestingly, at a later date Seagate did develop a 3.5-inch disk drive, but its customers, such as IBM, were not interested in this smaller drive because it did not offer the same low cost per megabyte that could be achieved with 5.25-inch drives. Seagate therefore postponed its entry into this market sector. Other firms, however, such as Connors Peripherals, developed a new market by selling 3.5-inch drives to the early producers of portables and laptop machines who were more interested in further miniaturisation of drives that increased data storage capability.

Another, similar scenario identified by Christensen is that of the mechanical excavator market. The original market was for large steam shovels used in mining, quarrying and large-scale civil engineering projects. Most of the key manufacturers were able to make the transition safely from steam to gasoline power in the 1920s because this change was acceptable to their existing customers. However, all of these excavator firms continued to build machines that used cable-actuated systems to operate the shovel head. The first hydraulic excavator was developed in the UK in 1947, and similar products soon emerged among a number of American firms. However, the limited power of the early hydraulic systems, their poor shovel reach and the inability of their machines to rotate through a full 360 degrees, did mean that they were no match for the conventional cable-actuated products. As a result, these new entrants were forced to think entrepreneurially and to identify a new customer group. Their solution was to sell their excavators as attachments for small industrial and agricultural tractors to be used in activities such as digging narrow ditches, where there is insufficient room to operate a large, conventional excavator. Nevertheless, as hydraulic technology improved over time these firms were subsequently able to compete in the traditional markets previously dominated by the manufacturers of cable-actuated machines.

ENTREPRENEURIAL IDENTIFICATION OF NEW CUSTOMERS

Slywotzky (1996) is another American researcher who has studied the changing fortunes of corporations. He concludes that success can often be attributed to those firms recognising that customer patterns of need are undergoing fundamental change and move before their competition does. The managerial approach that Slywotzky recommends is to recognise that factors such as regulation, commoditisation, new technologies, new supply sources made possible by new technology and the falling costs of production can all have an impact on customer decision making. By carefully analysing these factors it is often then possible to evolve new, unconventional business designs to exploit these new, emerging market opportunities.

One example of identifying a trend and revising business design is provided by Ray Kroc, the founder of McDonald's. He realised in the 1950s that the American middle classes were migrating from the cities to the suburbs. A visit to the McDonald brothers' restaurants in California caused him to observe how to provide rapid service and competitively priced food. He acquired the franchising rights to McDonald's and, unlike other franchisors who merely worried about selling franchises, Kroc adopted the unconventional approach of concentrating on both the franchisee and the end consumer (that is, the rapidly rising number of new suburban households). By creating a manufacturing orientation across every aspect of the food delivery process, from procurement through to in-store preparation, he was able to offer the promise that whenever and wherever the end customer entered a McDonald's outlet, he or she could expect to be offered consistently decent quality, rapidly prepared, low-cost food (Love 1986).

Most examples of an entrepreneurial shift in response to changing customer needs usually involve a large firm only ever making one significant revision to its conventional business design. However, an exception to this scenario that Slywotzky (1996) has identified is the American pharmaceutical company, Merck. In the 1950s, this firm, similar to its competitors, operated on the conventional business design of investing huge sums of money to develop new breakthrough drugs which, because of 17 years of exclusivity provided by the American patent laws, would guarantee the company many years of highly profitable sales. By the late 1970s, the cost of developing new drugs had risen dramatically. Furthermore, tragedies such as thalidomide – the sleeping pill which was found to create birth defects – meant that government regulatory authorities were now requiring the drugs industry to exhibit a much greater level of proven due diligence in its research programmes. Merck's response was to perceive that in addition to the medical profession, they had another new customer – the American FDA. Hence the company instigated the unconventional step of inviting the FDA reviewers into the new drug development process at a very early stage and also sought their guidance in the definition of appropriate R&D activities. The result of Merck's entrepreneurial decision was that in 1986 it achieved approval for a new drug in only 11 months. This was at a time when other firms were having to wait more than 30 months.

In the late 1980s, the exponentially rising costs for health care in the US led to the emergence of new entities known as Health Maintenance Organisations (HMOs) and Pharmacy Benefit Managers (PBMs) who offered major employers and the medical insurance companies the service of minimising the cost of medical treatment. Again, Merck realised, ahead of competition, that the traditional purchasers, the doctors, were being replaced by bulk buyers such as HMOs and PBMs. Merck's entrepreneurial solution was to redesign its selling operation, moving away from the conventional one-to-one contact with doctors and redirecting efforts to offer highly sophisticated drug cost-optimisation services to these new bulk buyers.

STAYING AHEAD IN THE RACE

One of the dilemmas facing the large firm that achieves a reputation for consistently acting entrepreneurially and indentifying new market opportunities is that after a while, its competitors begin carefully to analyse every move the lead firm makes, because they realise that the latest unconventional action will rapidly lead to the creation of a new sector convention. Although senior management of the entrepreneurial firm may receive a major ego boost from repeatedly being featured in business magazines such as *Forbes* and *Fortune*, the downside in this scenario is that the competition can usually be expected to redesign their business operations in order rapidly to follow the lead firm in exploiting any newly identified market opportunity.

This situation is probably most prevalent in service sector industries, because even large firms find it quite difficult, having found a new market segment, to then construct entry barriers to keep the competition out. Possibly the only way to survive is to ensure that the firm continues to employ visionary senior managers who are more forward thinking than their counterparts elsewhere in the same industrial sector. By drawing upon the creativity of such individuals, the organisation can always remain one step ahead of the competition.

One of the most enduring examples of 'staying ahead in the race' is provided by the San Francisco-based brokerage house headed by Charles Schwab. In the late 1980s, this firm realised that as private citizens gained experience in investing in the stock market, it had less and less need for the services available from the conventional stockbroking firms. Schwab's solution was that, by offering market access without providing any investment counselling support, they could charge a much lower commission on trades (*Business Week*, 19 December 1994). However, within only a few years, other brokerage houses recognised that the Schwab philosophy was the way ahead and redesigned their operations to reflect this market change. In response, Schwab sought to find new ways of providing increased trading functionality to individual investors. In 1989, for example, the company introduced automated telephone touchpad trading and, in 1993, launched StreetSmart for Windows, a software package that allows its customers to trade via a modem. This was followed in 1994 by Custom Broker, a telephone, fax and paging service for active traders. These entrepreneurial ideas were accompanied by the launch of OneSource which gave investors direct access to many hundreds of no-load funds run by the country's top money managers (Wayne 1994). Following this success, Schwab has now entered the world of online trading in which the consumer, sitting comfortably at home, can use the Internet to buy and sell shares at a cost over 60 per cent lower than that which he or she would have incurred by trading through a traditional brokerage house. Schwab is not only the current market leader in the provision of an Internet share trading service; some observers are also suggesting that this move may eventually revolutionise the stockbroking business completely.

INTERNAL BARRIERS TO ENTREPRENEURIAL PROCESS

Within a large corporation that has, over the years, successfully established a business based on managing sector conventions more effectively than the competition, it is little wonder that an employee seeking to persuade management to accept a radical, unconventional change in operational philosophy can expect to encounter severe resistance to such ideas. The firm, in weighing up the appeal of an unconventional idea, will need carefully to assess the potential impact on existing products, the degree to which capital assets might be rendered obsolete, the potential impact on the workforce and the possible response of shareholders.

In addition to these apparently rational forms of analysis, the entrepreneurial employee can also expect to encounter another range of potential obstacles to having his or her ideas accepted (Quinn 1985). One possible barrier is that some senior executives in large companies have insufficient contact with current market thinking, and therefore cannot really appreciate the potential appeal of offering customers an unconventional product solution. Since risk perception is inversely related to familiarity and experience, another possible obstacle is that financially orientated senior managers are likely to perceive radical changes in technology as being extremely risky. Additionally, these types of senior managers usually prefer the organisation to exhibit a relatively calm behaviour pattern, and their common perception of entrepreneurs is that these are people who are troublemakers and are not prepared to be good 'team players'. Finally, these senior managers face pressure from the financial community to sustain a steady increase in year-on-year profits and dividends. They thus tend to have an averse reaction to radical change because they realise that this might endanger achievement of the near-term profit targets specified in the company's annual report to shareholders.

Another potential obstacle confronting the entrepreneurial employee is that the established culture in most large firms is orientated towards a strong preference for gradual, conventional innovation because this can be managed easily and monitored using project evaluation routines and timing (PERT) planning models with project progress being regularly revalidated through market research. Entrepreneurial projects, on the other hand, are much less controllable, make unexpected demands on scarce resources and can rarely be evaluated effectively other than by launching the new product. Additionally, in most large firms, under the banner of 'efficiency', very rigid control procedures exist involving numerous approvals and audits of expenditure variance. Entrepreneurial projects rarely fit comfortably within such control systems, and this situation can often lead to pressures from the finance department to terminate such projects, because they are exhibiting insufficient evidence that the respective management teams have everything under control.

THE IMPORTANCE OF LEADERSHIP

In the hands of Tom Watson and Tom Watson Jr, IBM was a highly entrepreneurial organisation which could, without question, claim that it brought the business world into the IT age. Like so many firms whose actions create the conventions that others follow, IBM's own organisational behaviours became so conventional that all momentum for growth disappeared. Re-awakening such a slumbering giant is no easy task, and certainly not one which was initially of any interest to the current President, Lou Gerstner (Morris and McGowan 1997).

In looking at Gerstner's career at firms such as RJR Nabisco and American Express, most people would not immediately perceive him as an entrepreneur. However, if one examines his approach to smashing conventions at IBM, then it does seem that the label of entrepreneurial leader is applicable. While his initial actions of cutting costs, laying off employees and restructuring have all of the attributes associated with conventional, classicist management theories, the entrepreneurial dimension of his actions lay in his willingness, in the face of fierce resistance inside the corporation, to take the firm back to its innovative roots as the world's leading IT management company. This has been achieved by ensuring that both customers and employees clearly understand that the future focus of IBM is to assist large companies to survive in a networked world. Under Gerstner's leadership, IBM now focuses on devising its customers' technology strategies, building and running their systems and ultimately becoming the repository of knowledge on integrating computer systems across entire industrial sectors.

In order to deliver the new strategy, Gerstner has also been forced to act internally to challenge conventions that were impairing the organisation's ability to respond rapidly to new opportunities. Gone is a comfortable, congenial internal environment in which executives tried to avoid upsetting each other and time was wasted gaining everybody's approval before even the most minor of decisions could be implemented. Gerstner has injected a new sense of urgency and honesty which has been a major factor in assisting IBM to regain a market image for rapid and effective response to changing customer needs.

Another example of strong entrepreneurial leadership is provided by Donald Schneider, the owner of a $2.5 billion privately owned trucking and logistics company based in Green Bay, Wisconsin (Bermann 1998). The American trucking industry – a highly competitive, price orientated sector of the American economy – is not renowned for its entrepreneurial behaviour. However, this did not seem to bother Donald Schneider, who has introduced a whole series of innovations to achieve his goal of building the nation's largest truckload carrier. One of his innovations was to settle for sole suppliers of key aspects of the operation instead of following the industry convention of continually shopping around for the best deal. Sole suppliers are selected on the basis of their commitment to offering a good price and priority service. For example, Goodyear provides all of the company's tyres and the Wabash corporation fulfils all of the firm's requirements for trailers.

When deregulation came into the industry, Schneider recognised the importance of not adopting a confrontational approach to working with the Teamsters Union. Instead, he created one company to which all union drivers were contracted and another company for non-union drivers. Today, virtually all of the Schneider drivers are non-union but he has managed this transition without the acrimony that has occurred elsewhere in the trucking industry.

When the industry became extremely price competitive in the 1980s, Schneider avoided participation in industry price wars by focusing on on-time delivery. He installed satellite tracking systems to link each truck to both the customer and the company's Head Office. As a result of this entrepreneurial approach to what is a somewhat conventional sector of the American economy, Schneider has become the primary supplier to major corporations such as Procter & Gamble, Sears and Chrysler, all of whom draw upon his expertise when seeking to optimise their massive logistics operations further.

However, entrepreneurial leaders can sometimes emerge from somewhat unexpected sources. Such is the case of Gary Loveman, an associate professor from Harvard Business School, who took leave of absence to become Chief Operating Officer of Harrah's Entertainments. This company operates a chain of 20 casinos (Lubove 1998). Loveman was recruited by Harrah's Chairman, Philip Satre, who realised that a fresh approach was required in order to sustain the company's performance in an industrial sector where revenue was no longer growing. Loveman's perception of the problem was that the casino industry myopically focuses its attention on the efficient operation of casinos, and that customers are given minimal consideration in the formulation of operating policies. His entrepreneurial solution for achieving business growth was to redirect Harrah's marketing strategy towards becoming much more closely involved with its customers. This he achieved by acquiring detailed information on customer behaviour including such issues as their superstitions and entertainment preferences. By exploiting this knowledge to demonstrate the company's commitment to its customers, complemented by conventional marketing tools such as discount vouchers, Harrah's has already achieved a much higher level of customer loyalty than any of its competitors.

Slywotzky et al. (1997) have argued that the common feature of successful leaders who break with convention is that they and their organisations have recognised ahead of the competition that the rules of the game in their market sector have changed. In many cases this is because the intensity of competition between firms, all using the business model accepted as convention within a sector, means that all organisations have achieved high levels of efficiency and the only solution is to compete for greater market share by lowering price. At the same time, customers have become well informed and are quite prepared to shop around for the best possible deal.

To break out of this spiral of ever-declining profits, firms must be prepared to break with convention and reinvent their business design on a regular basis. Mirroring the examples described above, Slywotzky et al. argue that the visionary leader must force the organisation to pose the following questions.

1. What is important to the customer?
2. Where can the firm make profit?
3. How can the firm gain market share in that market space where profits can be made?

In support of the validity of their simple formula for the successful reinvention of the organisations, they point to examples such as:

1. Jack Welch, who led the move to adapt GE's business design to sustain profitability in an industrial sector where other firms have faced margin erosion, and
2. Nicholas Hayek's successful launch of the Swatch brand as a route by which to rebuild the Swiss watch industry.

MANAGING ENTREPRENEURIAL PROCESS

Many large firms acknowledge that their more entrepreneurial employees can often encounter problems in gaining acceptance for their ideas. How firms react to this situation will often depend upon the degree of importance that senior management place on exploiting entrepreneurial projects in terms of potential contribution to future revenue. On the continuum concerning the degree to which large firms utilise entrepreneurship for achieving long-term strategic goals, at one extreme are the organisations that have a successful, major, conventional core business, and for whom current market trends would suggest that no real perturbations can be expected to occur within the external environment in the foreseeable future. Under these circumstances, such firms often support individual employees who wish to participate in 'random acts of entrepreneurship'. This usually involves accepting that, as long as employees fulfil their assigned conventional job roles, they are free to pursue their own ideas as long as this makes minimal demands upon the organisation's available resources. Tom Peters (1989) describes this approach as promoting a 'small start in small markets' philosophy. The perceived advantages are failures can immediately be terminated and ineffective ideas can rapidly be improved through inexpensive modification. Additionally, a very active small start programme permits the firm to gain experience across a whole new range of markets and/or production technologies. To prove the benefits of small starts, Peters points to the General Motors scheme which led to the soft bumper system for the Corvette; the 'friendly fender' for the Fiero; fibreglass wheels, fibreglass springs and fibreglass bumpers.

A somewhat more impactful approach to entrepreneurship may be exhibited by conventional firms who are beginning to perceive that, either now or within only a few years, their market position may be impacted by fundamental sectoral change. The more astute senior managers realise that any attempt to initiate a major entrepreneurial move inside the current conventional organisational structure and culture will probably be stifled by one or more of the obstacles to process described earlier. Possibly the most effective solution to this problem is to utilise 'reintegrative entrepreneurship'. This involves spinning-off an entrepreneurial development team that works independently of the firm's mainstream activities, and many cases are based at an autonomous site located some distance from the firm's other operations. With this approach to entrepreneurship, the assumption is that, at a later date, and once the entrepreneurial project has begun to have market impact, the product concept will be reintegrated back into the firm's mainstream operations. In some cases, if the entrepreneurial project is very successful, the unconventional solution may become the organisation's new conventional core business in the long-term.

An example of this approach is provided by IBM's eventually successful move from the mainframe/minicomputer sectors of the computer industry into the PC market. Recognising the vital importance of rapidly launching a successful product, the company created an autonomous organisation based in Boca Raton, Florida, far away from the New York State headquarters. This new product development team immediately broke some basic IBM core conventions: they were willing to outsource the development of the processor chip to Intel and the operating system to a then tiny company called Microsoft. In making these decisions, the team actually provided the foundations upon which both Intel and Microsoft have subsequently built their almost impregnable leadership positions within today's IT industry. In fact, some industry experts have argued that in making these decision not to develop the chip and operating system in-house, IBM gave away the huge profits that are generated in the upstream components of the PC industry supply chain. Whatever the validity of this opinion, there is little doubt that had the team at Boca Raton not acted in this way, IBM would never have been able to enter the world PC market successfully.

In those cases where an organisation perceives that by sustaining a conventional strategy, business failure will be a certain outcome, then one possible solution is to accept that a fundamental entrepreneurial organisational re-orientation is needed in order to achieve a radical repositioning of the firm's core operations. Given the critical importance of projects of this type, it is usually the case that all activities from planning through to implementation are executed under the direct control of senior management. This type of line authority is necessary to ensure that the project team encounters no obstacles from more conventional staff who feel threatened by growing evidence of internal change that is likely to have a dramatic impact on their future job roles.

On the basis of the high number of corporate giants that have fallen in the last 100 years – either from leadership to an 'also ran' position, or have disappeared completely (for example, the UK motorcycle firms Triumph and Norton who are mere shadows of their previously glorious selves, and the demise of the American global carrier Pan Am) – it can probably be concluded that 'entrepreneurial strategic repositioning' is a somewhat rare event. However, one well documented example is provided by the American chip manufacturer, Intel (Burgleman 1994). The firm was founded by exploiting pioneering work on metal-on-silicon technology, and in 1969, produced the world's first dynamic random access memory (DRAM) integrated circuits.

Intel enjoyed a number of years as a global leader in the electronics industry, but in the late 1970s both revenue and profit margins began to decline in the face of increasingly intense competition from Japanese semiconductor producers. Fortunately, however, having developed the original microprocessor for a Japanese calculator company, Intel's far-sighted engineering team persuaded the company to purchase the patent for the microprocessor. During the 1970s, IBM's decision to choose Intel's 8088 microprocessor for its new PC, combined with the fortuitous aspect of the company's accounting system which allocated investment capital on the basis of product line profitability, caused Intel's entrepreneurial R&D staff to apply unconventional thinking which eventually moved the firm into a world leadership position in terms of its understanding of the design and manufacture of microprocessors. Once employees at all levels within the company began to accept that microprocessors, not DRAM circuits, were the way of the future, it became relatively easy for senior management to reposition the company by exiting the high-volume/minimal-profit DRAM business and focus solely upon the high-volume/high-profit world of microprocessors. The firm's success in implementing a total repositioning is demonstrated by (a) the current performance of the company's Pentium, Pentium II and Pentium III range of chips in world markets, and (b) the somewhat questionable decision of the American Federal Trade Commission (FTC) in 1988 that Intel, similar to

Microsoft, had now become so huge that the firm might be exhibiting evidence of unfair trading practices in seeking to retain its dominance of the world microprocessor market.

THE EMERGENCE OF THE TECHNOLOGY ENTREPRENEURS

The fastest-growing major corporations over the last 20 years have tended to be founded by entrepreneurs whose knowledge of technology has caused them to build companies based on completing changing the world in which we live. Possibly the most famous entrepreneur is Bill Gates of Microsoft, who, from the day he founded his business empire, continually articulated that his goal was to 'put a computer on every desk and in every home in America'. Bill Gates is not alone in visioning new applications for IT and establishing a hugely successful corporation. Another example is provided by Marc Andreessen, the individual who was excited by the potential he could see was offered by one emerging technology, the Internet (Tetzeli and Puri 1996). Only four years out of college, he and Eddy Bina wrote the first version of Mosaic, the browser which made the World Wide Web accessible. After this first success he then went into partnership with Jim Clarke to found Netscape. Like many of the technology entrepreneurs, Andreessen's role in Netscape is to act as a catalyst and stimulate employees into developing and implementing new ideas. Although he can rightfully be seen as the founder of the business, he reports to the Chief Executive Officer, Jim Barksdale. This latter individual concentrates on guiding the business to optimise financial performance, leaving Andreessen free to manage the role of being the organisation's entrepreneurial visionary.

The entrepreneurial act which made this new company so successful was simplicity itself. The company gave away free copies of its easy-to-use net browser, Netscape Navigator, as a result, the software rapidly found its way on to 45 million PCs around the world. A key reason why Netscape was so successful was that the firm had broken with sector convention by developing a Web browser which would run on any operating system. This situation apparently disturbed Microsoft because, if software developers began to write applications which were compatible with Navigator, this would cause the browser to become a universal platform – thereby creating a situation in which the characteristics of any underlying operating system such as Windows would be irrelevant (Eddy 1999). To add further fuel to the fire, Microsoft was preparing to launch the latest version of its own operating system, Windows 95. The scene was now set for a major battle between two entrepreneurially orientated organisations, each seeking to dominate the technology conventions that underpin the IT industry. The subsequent events are a key component of the evidence used in the US Department of Justice's antitrust suit against Microsoft.

On 7 December 1995, Microsoft announced that it had developed its own browser, the Internet Explorer, which would be given away to customers. Even though Explorer was available at no charge while Netscape Navigator was then being sold for $39, most users appeared to perceive the latter software as significantly superior to the Microsoft offering. Additionally, at this time the majority of Internet service providers – through whom most users gain access to the World Wide Web – were using Netscape software. The exception was America Online (AOL) which had its own proprietary product and was seeking to purchase a better browser. While Netscape sought to sell its browser to AOL, Microsoft's counter-offer was to supply Explorer free. Furthermore, in return for signing an exclusive deal, AOL would be given space on the Windows 95 product. It is alleged that Microsoft's next move was to approach other Internet service providers, offering packages which went well beyond offering just a free browser.

In 1998, Microsoft announced its next unconventional act: to integrate Explorer 4 into its Windows operating system in preparation for the launch of Windows 98. Furthermore, Microsoft offered large discounts on licensing fees to computer manufacturers to encourage them to bundle together the two programmes. This appears to have been the last straw for Netscape; it announced that from then on its browser, renamed Communicator, would be given away free while the firm would now focus on marketing other software products and services.

Another technology entrepreneur with the ability to envision new opportunities in the world of IT is Michael Saylor, the founder of Microstrategy (Urresta 1997). In comparison to the Netscape story, the company's speciality, relational online analytical processing (ROLAP), seems at first glance to be a somewhat mundane and unexciting business. The underlying purpose of the technology is to provide the capability to analyse huge datasets. For example, ROLAP is a vital ingredient in permitting large firms to integrate their diverse databases such as customer records, transactions, invoices, warehouse records and shipping information. Having brought these datasets together, the company's employees can then all use this information to more effectively undertake their assigned job roles more effectively and, possibly even more importantly, to interact with others inside the organisation. These same databases can also be accessed by the organisation's customers and suppliers as part of the process of further optimising the performance of entire supply chain.

Having acquired the reputation of being the leading firm for assisting corporations in undertaking what is known as 'data warehousing', Saylor's vision is to exploit Microstrategy's competences further in the development of large databases to the point that they are accessible to the general public. Saylor sees a future where the World Wide Web will give us a dial tone similar to that of the telephone and we will be able to ask any database to respond to questions regarding topics as diverse as the best hotel in a given location or where to get treatment for a specific medical complaint.

ORGANISATIONAL STRUCTURE

In 1961, Burns and Stalker suggested that the organically structured organisation, characterised by attributes such as flexibility, informality and authority vested in situational expertise, is a very appropriate environment in which to foster innovation. Conversely, they argued that innovative behaviour was likely to be stifled in mechanistic organisations because of the influence of factors such as administrative system rigidity, formalised operating procedures and adherence to bureaucratic values (Burns and Stalker 1961). However, it is not clear from their writings whether they were observing firms involved in conventional or unconventional innovation activities.

The increasing intensity of global competition has caused both conventional and entrepreneurial organisations to seek new ways of improving the speed and flexibility of response to rapidly changing market circumstances. Reich (1983) argues that this new environment demands a revision in organisational work practices. Kanter's (1983) survival strategy for dealing with increasingly turbulent market conditions is to abandon rigid segmentalist structures and move towards integrative systems. These concepts were subsequently popularised by Peters (1989), who argued that the basic building block used by excellent organisations to achieve global competitive advantage is the creation of organic structures based on employees organising into self-managed teams.

One of the few studies that has attempted to determine a quantitative relationship between firm structure and performance is that of Covin and Slevin (1989). They argued that, based on earlier studies by individuals such as Khandwalla (1977) and Miller (1983), no examination of the suitability of organisational structure can be divorced from the influence of top management's entrepreneurial orientation. On the basis of these and other written sources concerning the fit between style and structure, Covin and Slevin evolved the hypothesis that 'in organically orientated firms, increases in management's entrepreneurial orientation will positively increase performance; in mechanistically structured firms, increases in management's entrepreneurial orientation will negatively influence performance'.

Covin and Slevin further argued that the need for congruency between style and structure leads to the existence of the following types of firm.

1. Efficient-bureaucratic firms that exhibit a conservative (that is, non-entre-preneurial) management style and have a mechanistic structure. These firms are successful because they operate in environments in which customers require standardised, uniform products or services.
2. Unstructured-unadventurous firms that exhibit a conservative style and have an organic structure. These firms have the ability to respond quickly to opportunities, but are not particularly efficient in providing the standardised, uniform output required by their customers.
3. Pseudo-entrepreneurial firms that exhibit an entrepreneurial manage-ment style and have a mechanistic structure. These firms are ineffective because their rigid, inflexible structure is a barrier to being truly entre-preneurial.
4. Effective-entrepreneurial firms that exhibit an entrepreneurial manage-ment style and have an organic structure. These firms are effective because their organic structure enhances communication and minimises bureaucratic barriers to innovation.

Perhaps not unsurprisingly, given the potentially somewhat negative conno-tations associated with the terms 'pseudo-entrepreneurial' and 'unstructured-unadventurous', Covin and Slevin concluded that an organic structure would make a positive contribution to those firms exhibiting an entrepreneurial management style, whereas a conservative firm would be well advised to retain a mechanistic structure. Slevin and Covin subsequently proposed that successful firms are those that manage to move back and forth between the two congruent style/structure states of efficient-bureaucratic and effective-entrepreneurial (Slevin and Covin 1990). They cite the example of a computer firm that proactively develops a new product and then, as sales grow, and to sustain product quality and fulfil delivery dates, the organisation is forced to become conservative and mechanistic. As sales subsequently begin to show signs of flattening, the firm cycles back into an effective-entrepreneur-ial state in order to manage the development of its next generation of products successfully.

However, other researchers have encountered difficulties in validating the Covin–Slevin concept in other countries and/or sectors of industry. The author, for example, in a study of UK manufacturing firms (Chaston 1997), did find that the highest level of sales growth is most likely to be achieved in those firms that are entrepreneurial and organic in structure. However, validating the other aspect of the Covin–Slevin model, that high performance can only come from firms operating with a conservative style accompanied by mechanistic structure, or an entrepreneurial style and an organic structure, did not prove possible. In the case of UK firms, the research results suggested (a) that a conservative style/mechanistic organisation can expect to achieve the lowest overall performance of any of the four possible types of firm, and (b) that relatively high levels of performance can also be achieved either by being entrepreneurial and mechanistically structured or by remaining conservative but adopting a more organic structure.

In view of these findings it seems that blindly accepting the view that only entrepreneurial firms should be organically structured may be somewhat unwise. A possibly much safer approach is to follow Hamel and Prahalad's (1994) advice that, in selecting an appropriate structure, the starting point is first to define a strategy for the future and then to decide which core competences are critical to achieving specified performance goals. Having determined these issues, the firm can then examine whether an organic or a mechanistic structure would the most effective for delivering the organisation's future vision.

Mintzberg (1979, 1988) has also questioned acceptance of the generalisation that organic structures are the most effective form for implementing entrepreneurial strategies in large organisations. Although he accepts the validity of the concept in the case of unpredictable, dynamic environments, he argues that for complex environments (for example, a hi-tech research organisation or a factory manufacturing complex prototypes), what is preferable is an 'adhocracy'. He reasons that, to manage conventional complex core activities, the firm will probably need to use techniques such as division of labour, extensive differentiation between operating units and well defined operating policies to support formalised behaviour patterns. To break away from this pattern and act entrepreneneurially will probably not be achieved merely by establishing an autonomous, organic project team. The complex nature of the new product and/or technology development problem will require sophisticated coordination of the activities of specialist areas of expertise drawn from across the entire organisation.

Mintzberg has proposed that there are two forms of adhocracy: operating adhocracies, which will be found in those situations where the organisation is seeking effectively to coordinate the activities of multi-disciplinary teams engaged in solving complex problems on behalf of clients (consultancy firms and advertising agencies, for example), and administrative adhocracies, where the firm is engaged in undertaking a project to serve itself (such as bringing a new technology on-stream) and needs to link together the entrepreneurial project and the organisation's conventional core activities.

Once the operating adhocracy has completed the assigned task, it is often the case that the team's unconventional solution is found to have additional applications within the core business. Thus, over time, and if no further ongoing large-scale entrepreneurial activities are perceived as necessary, the adhocracy is usually absorbed back into the organisation's bureaucratic processes. Administrative adhocracies, because of the complexity of the problems being resolved, tend to have a much longer life. This is usually due to the fact that senior management perceives significant benefits for the firm in continuing to sustain a high level of entrepreneurial behaviour. Management thus communicates its support overtly for a policy which prohibits staff based in mainstream conventional operations from attempting to take over and conventionalise the activities of their more entrepreneurial counterparts within the organisation.

REFERENCES

Bermann, P. (1998), 'The big orange machine', *Forbes Magazine*, 6 April, pp. 4–6.

Burgleman, R.A. (1994), 'Fading memories: a process theory for strategic business exit in dynamic environments', *Administrative Science Quarterly*, Vol. 39, pp. 24–56.

Burns, T. and Stalker, G.M. (1961), *The Management of Innovation*, Tavistock Institute, London.

Business Week (1994), 'The Schwab revolution', 19 December, p. 89.

Chaston, I. (1997), 'Organisational performance: interaction of entrepreneurial style and organisational structure', *European Journal of Marketing*, Vol. 31, No. 11/12, pp. 32–43.

Chaston, I. (1993), *Customer-focused Marketing*, McGraw-Hill, Maidenhead.

Christensen, C.M. (1997), *The Innovator's Dilemma: When New Technologies Cause Great Firms to Fail*, Harvard Business School Press, Boston, MA.

Covin, J.G. and Slevin, D.P. (1989), 'Strategic behaviour of small firms in hostile and benign environments', *Strategic Management Journal*, Vol. 10, pp. 75–87.

Eddy, P. (1999), 'The selfish giants', *Sunday Times Magazine* (London), 14 March, pp. 43–8.

Hamel, G. and Prahalad, G.K. (1994), *Competing for the Future*, Harvard Business School Press, Boston, MA.

Kanter, R.M. (1983), *The Change Masters: Corporate Entrepreneurs at Work*, Unwin, London.

Khandwalla, P.N. (1977), *The Design of Organisations*, Harcourt Brace, New York.

Love, J.F. (1986), *McDonald's: Behind the Arches*, Bantam Books, New York.

Lubove, S. (1998), 'The odd couple', *Forbes Magazine*, 7 January, p. 22.

Miller, D. (1983), 'The correlates of entrepreneurship in 3 types of firms', *Management Science*, Vol. 29, pp. 770–91.

Mintzberg, H. (1979), *The Structuring of Organisations*, Prentice Hall, New York.

Mintzberg, H. (1988), *Mintzberg on Management: Inside our Strange World of Organisations*, The Free Press, New York.

Morris, B. and McGowan, J. (1997), 'He's smart, he's not nice, but he's saving Big Blue', *Fortune Magazine*, 14 April, pp. 21–6.

Peters, T. (1989), *Thriving on Chaos: Handbook for a Management Revolution*, Macmillan, London.

Quinn, J.B. (1985), 'Managing innovation: controlled Chaos', *Harvard Business Review*, May–June, pp. 56–63.

Reich, R.B. (1983), *The Next American Frontier*, Times Books, New York.

Slevin, D.P. and Covin, J.G. (1990), 'Juggling entrepreneurial style and organisational structure – how to get your act together', *Sloan Management Review*, Winter, pp. 43–53.

Slywotzky, A.J. (1996), *Value Migration: How to Think Several Moves Ahead of the Competition*, Harvard Business School Press, Boston, MA.

Slywotzky, A.J., Morrison, D.J. and Andelman, B. (1997), *The Profit Zone*, Corporate Decisions Inc., New York.

Tetzeli, R. and Puri, S. (1996), What's it really like to be Marc Andreessen?, *Fortune Magazine*, 12 September, pp. 34–5.

Urresta, L. (1997), 'Now I know how a real visionary sounds', *Fortune Magazine*, 9 September, pp. 51–2.

Wayne, L. (1994), 'The next giant in mutual funds?', *New York Times*, 20 March, Section 3, pp. 8–9.

9

SMALL-FIRM ENTREPRENEURSHIP

INTRODUCTION

In the period immediately following World War II, the large multinational corporations dominated Western economies. Beginning in the early 1970s, however, these organisations, in the face of increasing Pacific Rim competition, began to implement actions such as delayering to improve flexibility, downsizing to improve productivity and relocating assembly operations offshore to lower labour-cost areas of the world. The eventual outcome has been that the small firms sector has replaced large firms as the primary source of employment in most Western nations. Within the European Union, for example, over 60 per cent of the workforce is employed in the SME sector, with over 90 per cent of such jobs being in firms employing less that ten persons.

As governments came to recognise the critical importance of the small firms sector, they began to allocate a larger and larger proportion of their economic development budgets to funding a diverse range of SME research and support service initiatives. As reflected in recent years by the ever-increasing number of departments of entrepreneurship which are being opened in universities around the world, academics have also not been slow in realising the need for their institutions also to become more heavily involved in the provision of services to the small firms sector.

Unfortunately, even to this day some academics appear to believe that the only difference between large and small firms is that the former have more zeros on the numbers in their balance sheets. As a result, such individuals frequently undertake research projects seeking to demonstrate how the latest trend in large-firm management thinking will also be extremely valuable in assisting the performance of SME sector organisations. Their research methodology tends to be that of the traditional positivist, large- scale surveys that typically generate the result that there is little evidence of the latest management concept yet being adopted by small firms. The standard conclusion is that there is a need to promote the latest concept across the small firms sector. In some cases, their message is heard by governments who then fund a new initiative designed to persuade owner/managers to adopt this new, latest management philosophy.

In the UK, for example, after large firms discovered the benefits of TQM in the 1980s, the government was persuaded of the need for small firms to upgrade their ability to manage customer relations more effectively by embracing the concepts associated with the management of quality. The solution was to promote the merits to small firms of becoming registered under some form of accreditation scheme, such as BS5750 or ISO 9000. The UK consultancy fraternity clearly made massive financial gains from being hired to deliver this initiative. Unfortunately, subsequent research has demonstrated that for many small firms, management of quality through accreditation was at best likely to have minimal impact on improving market performance and, at worst, could increase operating costs to the point where the firm was placed at a competitive disadvantage against other businesses that had not sought to install a quality accreditation system.

Fortunately, over the last few years both governments and academics are at last beginning to listen to the wiser, more experienced small-firm researchers when they relay the message that small firms cannot be treated as downscaled versions of multinational corporations. Thus, in the UK for example, following years of effort by individuals such as Professors Curran, Gibb and Storey, the need to evolve management concepts that are directly relevant and applicable to the SME sector is finally being accepted both by government agencies developing new support schemes and by academics in their design of teaching research programmes.

Listed below are our important areas of difference that need to be registered with those individuals and organisations seeking to work in the SME sector.

1. Although all large firms tend to have similar aims and objectives, such as achieving market leadership and an adequate return for their shareholders, the motivations which drive owner/managers are often very different. Some owner/managers, for example, have a lifestyle aim of wishing to create a business that leaves them free to play golf or go sailing on at least two days a week. Others are concerned with enjoying a comfortable retirement and spend their time organising a directors' pension scheme based around the creation of tax efficient capital asset, sale and leaseback schemes. There is yet another group of individuals who specialise in purchasing poorly run businesses at a knockdown price, upgrading the management team, installing effective control systems and, once the business begins to recover, selling the enterprise for a massive profit.

2. There is a need to avoid making the common error of assuming that the entire small-firms sector can be considered as a homogeneous entity

within which one can apply the same standard management paradigms to all situations. Even today, regretfully, this error is still to be found in some government support initiatives (such as many new business start-up schemes) and the 'introduction to entrepreneurship' educational programmes delivered by some universities. In reality, however, there are huge variations in the nature of the management processes across the SME sector in relation both to the size of the small firm (for example, a micro-enterprise consisting of three employees is clearly a very different proposition, even when compared to a firm employing 15 individuals) and the sector of the economy in which the small firm operates (a small hotel in the leisure industry versus a manufacturing firm producing hi-tech sub-components for the aerospace industry, for example).

3. It is not uncommon to hear the view articulated by both academics and support agency personnel that most small firms are orientated towards implementing a growth strategy which can lead to the creation of new job opportunities. This perspective probably explains why so many departments of entrepreneurship within universities now offer management of growth programmes, and within Europe there is a plethora of government schemes making funds available to stimulate small-firm expansion. However, if one talks to the average owner/manager, it soon becomes apparent that in fact, most are 'growth adverse', but their reasons for adopting this position are diverse. For example, some owner/managers do not want the added HRM responsibilities that would accompany any expansion of their business. Others recognise that they lack the skills necessary to provide the quality of leadership necessary to implement a growth strategy effectively. In some other cases, the owner/manager accepts that his or her business has never really developed a genuine competitive advantage, and thus any further growth could probably only be achieved through the highly risky action of becoming more price competitive.

4. Another common misconception is that the majority of small firms are entrepreneurial. In fact, as demonstrated (a) by the highly conventional nature of most new business start-ups (for example, landscape gardening, industrial cleaning, house painting, and so on) and (b) by the strong appeal of entering the sector through the purchase of a conventional franchise (such as fast food, retailing, printing services), the vast majority of small firms seek to avoid the highly risky business of challenging prevailing market conventions.

The risk adverse attitude of many owner/managers has probably been reinforced over the years by these individuals being exposed to tragic tales of entrepreneurial failure, such as that recently provided by the UK company,

Walker Windsails Ltd. This business was founded by an entrepreneurial husband and wife team in 1981 to develop airfoils as cost-effective, supplementary propulsion systems for commercial vessels. Marketing efforts were not very successful and only one system was ever fitted to a merchant ship. In the late 1980s, the company decided to enter the leisure market by developing yachts powered by airfoils instead of conventional sails. Over £13 million of equity capital was raised from 6,500 small investors and plans were announced for the production of 134 boats per year by 1999. In July 1998, having never really been able to gain a foothold in the leisure market, the firm went into receivership. The comment of the owners at this juncture was that the business 'was torpedoed by dissenting shareholders'. The response of one of these shareholders was that 'it was impossible to retain faith in a production company run by a husband and wife team' (Plymouth *Evening Herald*, 4 August 1998).

ENTREPRENEURIAL GROWTH

There exists an extensive body of academic literature concerning the factors influencing the market performance of small firms. Much of this can be classified under the three major headings of organisational development, functional management skills and sectoral economics. A common element in the organisational development school of thought is to examine the relationship between the goals of the entrepreneur and the objectives of the organisation (Steinmetz 1969). In many instances, the discussion of relationships assumes that once initial market penetration has been achieved and sales begin to grow very rapidly, this will be accompanied by a need to a move from an entrepreneurial to a 'professional' management style. However, given the current debate on the needs of larger organisations to move in the opposite direction and become more entrepreneurial (for example, Slevin and Covin 1990), some doubts must exist about whether this growth model philosophy should be offered as a normative theory by which to guide the activities of SME sector owner/managers.

The functional management school emphasises the need for the smaller firm to adopt a more formalised approach to activities such as strategic planning and the installation of effective control systems (Brock and Evans 1989). Although this rational decision making approach has received extensive coverage in the literature, there is still only limited evidence to support the view that clear links exist between the acquisition of classicist marketing management competences and the subsequent growth rate of the firm (Carland et al. 1989).

Sectoral studies usually seek to identify factors of influence within an industrial system as the basis for predicting potential for growth. Researchers have often been able to demonstrate clear relationships between the performance of OEMs and growth rates of small business subcontractors in sectors such as the car, computer and consumer electronics industries (for example, Storey et al. 1987). Overall, however, these studies do not appear to provide the basis for a generalised predictive model for the management of SME sector organisations (Doctor et al. 1989).

These three schools of thought have all made significant contributions to the evolution of theoretical paradigms for the understanding of management processes within smaller firms. Unfortunately, they also appear to share the common weakness that it is difficult to apply these various concepts to evolve a predictive model for determining how small firms should best manage the marketing process in order to fully exploit the potential for growth which may confront the small firm (Gibb and Davies 1990). One possible alternative solution is to adopt the holistic view that common key characteristic among firms that succeed in achieving growth in their market share is their ability to develop appropriate internal competences (Chaston and Mangles 1997).

In order to identify internal competences which might influence the market performance of small firms, Chaston and Mangles undertook a review of the literature which revealed four studies where the researchers had sought to examine conventional versus entrepreneurial behaviour, had based their studies on an extensive sample frame, had used methodology evolved through careful pilot testing, and had presented their data in a quantitative form that permitted some degree of statistical validation of the findings. The findings from these projects (summarised in Table 9.1) were used to evolve a visual descriptive model of how entrepreneurial small firms can achieve and sustain market growth (see Figure 9.1).

The entry point into the proposed model is for the business to identify a market niche that can be occupied by offering an unconventional product or service proposition (for example, the New Zealand yacht sail manufacturer that, instead of offering a range of standard products, has used a CAD/CAM system to create sails that are designed to cope with the prevailing climatic conditions yachtsmen can expect to encounter in any specific region of the world). The next stage in the process is to evolve a business plan. It is not suggested that this be achieved by following the classic strategic management approach found in many small-firms textbooks which recommend a detailed and extensive analysis of both external and external business conditions to provide the basis for evolving a detailed specification of planned actions. In the real world, many firms will not have access to the extensive data sources necessary to undertake such an analysis. Furthermore, many entrepreneurs can rarely be persuaded to divert more than a minimal amount of time away from managing their firm's day-to-day operations to become involved in detailed planning exercises. Nevertheless, the existence of a plan is critical both for ensuring that all employees understand the future direction proposed for the business and for supporting any negotiations which may occur with sources of external finance.

Table 9:1 Summary of findings concerning characteristics exhibited by SME sector growth firms

A: COOPERS & LYBRAND (1994)
- Perceive their markets as intensively competitive.
- Are flexible decision makers.
- Seek leadership through offering superior quality in a niche market.
- Deliver superior pre-/post-sales service.
- Use technology-driven solutions to achieve a superiority position.
- Emphasise fast, frequent launch of new/improved products and draw upon external sources of knowledge to assist these activities.
- Emphasise application of technology and techniques such as cross-functional teams, process re-engineering, to optimise productivity.
- Recognise the need to invest in continual development of their employees.
- Rely mainly on internal profits to fund future investments.

B: CRANFIELD STUDY (Burns 1994)
- Seek niches and exploit superior performance to differentiate themselves from competition.
- Operate in markets where there is only an average-to-low intensity of competition.
- Utilise clearly defined strategies and business plans to guide future activities.
- Rely mainly internally generated funds to finance future investment.

C: GERMAN VERSUS UK FIRMS (Brickau 1994)
- German firms emphasise acquisition of detailed knowledge of external factors capable of influencing performance.
- German firms can clearly specify their competitive advantages.
- German firms seek niches exploited through a superiority positioning.
- German firms use strategies and plans to guide future performance.
- German firms concurrently seek to improve products through innovation and enhance productivity through adoption of new process technologies.
- German firms fund investment mainly from internal fund generation.

D: NEW ZEALAND EXPORT FIRMS (Tradenz 1990)
- Emphasis on R&D to achieve continuous innovation and gain control of unique technologies.
- Orientation towards achieving 'world class' superiority is specialist niches.
- Use structured plans based upon extensive information search to guide future performance.
- Exhibit a very entrepreneurial management style and encourage employee-based decision making.
- Strong commitment to using superior quality coupled with high productivity as a path to achieving competitive advantage.

The small-firms literature often contains reference to the view that entrepreneurial small firms face immense difficulties in raising finance. A closer investigation of these claims, however, often reveals that the firms encoun-

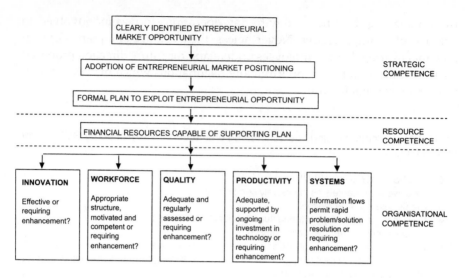

Figure 9.1 A competence model of a growth orientated entrepreneurial firm

tering such problems have been under-capitalised from the outset and/or the owner/manager lacks the necessary financial management skills required to ensure an appropriate balance between ongoing trading activities and the working capital position. Additionally, it is usually the case that successful entrepreneurial small firms, after having initially funded the business through borrowing and/or raising equity through a venture capitalist, from then on rely mainly on internally generated profits to support future market expansion plans.

However, it is necessary to recognise that entrepreneurial small firms can face a problem if seeking to raise a relatively small amount of equity capital (for example, £10,000–£100,000). This is due the fact that institutional investors tend to be interested only in propositions requiring an equity injection of at least £500,000. In recent years, owner/managers seeking relatively small amounts of equity capital are increasingly finding that this level of funding is more likely to be acquired by approaching private investors. Additionally, in both the US and Europe, this sector of the market has been expanded through the creation of lending networks known as the 'Business Angels' scheme. Even today, however, some types of entrepreneurial propositions can still expect difficulties when seeking their first injection of equity capital. In the UK, for example, this situation currently confronts firms in the hi-tech sector and/or those owned by individuals from ethnic minorities.

For the entrepreneurial firm that has identified an appropriate niche, evolved a plan and structured the business to ensure access to sufficient funds for supporting future trading objectives, Figure 9.1 proposes that there are five areas of business activity requiring effective management if the entrepreneurial firm is to be successful:

- new product development
- HRM practices
- employee productivity
- management of quality
- information management.

Of these, the one that is probably of most interest to the highly active, 'serial' entrepreneur, is the continued development and launch of new products. In fact, in some cases, the drive to improve continually on the past often results in this type of owner/manager racing ahead to make existing products obsolete long before the firm has maximised the potential income that might be derived from this source if only the existing product line had not be replaced by further acts of innovation. This type of small-firm behaviour is likely to occur most commonly in the IT industry. One will often encounter owner/managers and their 'techie' employees during their traditional Friday afternoon bonding sessions – centred on munching pizzas and drinking Cola – happily deciding to 'junk' a recently launched, potentially highly successful piece of software because they now see a more technically challenging way of solving an even wider range of problems than those for which the earlier system had originally been developed.

Although the majority of entrepreneurial firms tend to adopt a somewhat more conservative attitude to the rapidity with which new products are developed and launched, it is necessary to register that the importance of acquiring a high level of competence in managing product innovation does vary by industrial sector. Research on the model shown in Figure 9.1, for example, suggests that in both hi-tech and manufacturing firms, new product innovation is extremely critical; whereas in the service sector, other variables such as quality and information management competences have considerably more impact on the successful implementation of a high growth rate strategy (Chaston 1997).

It is often the case that highly successful entrepreneurs are so single-mindedly driven by the desire to achieve market recognition for their endeavours that they have a tendency to ignore the need concurrently to establish an appropriate internal working environment, capable of optimising both employee motivation and job satisfaction. As demonstrated by its success in markets such as Japan and China, New Zealand contains more highly entrepreneurial firms as a proportion of the total small firm population than possibly any other country in the world. It therefore seems to be more than a coincidence that within these firms, one frequently encounters owner/managers who exhibit a management style orientated towards involving the entire workforce fully in all key decisions and who place heavy emphasis on the continued development of all employees as a critical component in sustaining the ongoing success of their organisations.

Most entrepreneurial small firms tend to operate in premium-price/premium-quality sectors of markets and hence, in theory, probably need to be less concerned about employee productivity than competitors positioned at the bottom end of the market. However, such attitudes can be dangerous where the firm is based in a high labour-cost country while endeavouring to compete in world markets. This is the situation confronting small firms in Germany, a country that has totally embraced the principles of the EU's Social Charter and, as a result, faces some of the highest direct and indirect labour costs in the world. The solution to this problem for small German firms is continuously to seek new ways of investing in new capital equipment through which to further reduce the labour input content of the manufacturing processes (Brickau 1994).

Many entrepreneurial manufacturing firms are founded by engineers who gain their greatest satisfaction from modifying and revising their production processes. Although driven more by a fascination with how unconventional approaches can improve on longstanding sectoral conventions than any real desire significantly to influence production costs, the outcome is that entrepreneurial engineers frequently introduce new operating procedures that can dramatically increase employee productivity. An example of this scenario is provided by a UK firm, Rigibore Ltd, that produces the drill bits for machine tools used in high precision engineering companies. The conventional way of designing a new drill bit, which can take several weeks to meet the customer's drilling specification, is to make lengthy calculations, generate the design drawings manually and finally to have a specialist machine setter calibrate the machine for manufacturing the new design. Rigibore has developed a proprietary CAD/CAM system that permits total automation of the process from design through to manufacture. The firm can now produce a new drill bit in hours, which provides an amazing employee productivity advantage over its more conventional competitors – who still take several weeks to complete the same task.

Since the Pacific Rim nations made the rest of world painfully aware that quality is a very successful weapon with which to gain global advantage, there has been an explosion of interest in re-establishing adequate standards of quality in large and small firms sectors of Western nations. Unfortunately, a significant proportion of the guidance issued by quality experts is concerned with creating internal systems designed to ensure that the firm consistently achieves the minimum quality standards expected by the customer. Entrepreneurs, on the other hand, have long realised that to use some aspect of quality of service as a source of competitive advantage can only succeed if the firm finds a way of greatly exceeding customer expectations.

A example of this philosophy is provided by a Devon-based entrepreneur who runs a financial brokerage in the UK used-car market. He was aware that the largest problem facing car dealerships was locating finance for customers who, for reasons such as uncertain income and/or poor credit history, are not considered to be an acceptable risk by the large national finance companies. Previously, the conventional way the dealer resolved this problem was to ring the smaller finance houses and wait, often for several days, while these firms manually assessed the level of credit risk. During this waiting period it was not unusual for the dealer to discover that the potential customer had bought a car from another dealer, who, on this occasion, had been lucky enough to get a faster quote on an appropriate hire purchase agreement.

In his search for a solution, the Devon entrepreneur discovered a finance house in the US which specialised in high-risk finance by breaking with the convention of manually analysing high-risk propositions and developing an online credit, automated computer-based assessment system that could generate a lending decision in minutes. He approached this firm, and, learning that it was considering entering the UK market, negotiated a licence to act as its sole distributor for the South West of England. For car dealers whose service response expectation for a high-risk lending proposition was several days, having access to a service providing a decision in a matter of minutes is a highly attractive proposition. As a result, within 12 months of market launch, the new financial brokerage service achieved a sales turnover in excess of £750,000 per annum.

A characteristic of the small-firms sector is the generally poor level of financial literacy and apparent aversion of owner/managers to being concerned with close supervision of day-to-day details. Of course, this is why so many small firms get into financial difficulties, because they usually lack any form of management accounting system and rely on their year-end audit to reveal any financial problems. As a result, they have no understanding of how, by regularly accessing their firm's sources of financial information, they could be provided with an internal early warning of an impending problem that could destroy the business (for example, reviewing debtors levels on a daily basis and, having identified any overdue debts, moving to collect monies owed and thereby being in a better position to respond to demands from creditors that either their outstanding invoice must be paid or they will cancel delivery of critically important raw materials needed to fulfil a priority order from key customers).

With the recent advent of extremely low-cost PC-based accounting and project management systems, it is likely that this situation of too many owner/managers making insufficient use of financial control systems to monitor performance can be expected to undergo change within the foreseeable future. Nevertheless, at the present it is still quite unusual to find examples of firms who have adopted an entrepreneurial approach to the use of information systems as a route by which to achieve competitive advantage.

An exception is provided by the disguised example of a full service advertising and public relations agency located in the South West of England. The founder, who resigned from a large London agency to fulfil his ambition of establishing his own agency, started his new enterprise in the usual way: for the first year, he operating from an office based in his house. As the business expanded, it was relocated to an office in a nearby town and, within only a few years, billings had exceeded £750,000 per annum. Unfortunately as is often the case in the advertising industry, revenue growth was not accompanied by an equivalent increase in profitability.

Analysing the situation, the owner/manager identified the two problems impacting profitability: (i) unexpected cost increases on existing contracts due to last-minute changes requested by clients and/or poor project management practices by agency staff, and (ii) pitching for new accounts without prior careful assessment of the nature of the probable mix of new business attracted to the agency (that is, design work, printing, buying advertising space, advising on promotional strategies and managing publicity campaigns), often resulting in the setting of an inadequate annual service fee. After discussing the problem with friends at his old London agency, he decided that the solution was to install a computer-based management information and decision support system. Unfortunately, he soon discovered that no standard software was available and that to purchase a customised system would be extremely expensive. His solutions response was to ask the accountancy practice providing his company's annual audit services to create a manual management accounting and standard costing system that served as a foundation upon which to begin building a computer-based decision support system.

In addition to transferring the management accounting and costing system on to the prototype system, the owner/manager used his business contacts to acquire detailed benchmarking data on all aspects of the process of delivering a diversified portfolio of promotional services to clients. Some of the key features he is incorporating into the new system provide the capability to undertake the following tasks.

1. Any member of staff can access the system to obtain a real-time statement of time and material costs versus budget for a client assignment.
2. If clients wish to change an assignment specification, the agency can immediately determine whether this can be accommodated within the existing budget for the specific project.

3.   During client meetings concerning discussions about a new project, staff can use laptops fitted with modems to access the main office system, even from remote locations, and thereby instantaneously provide the client with a provisional estimated cost for the new project.

4.   Prior to pitching for new business, staff can examine the probable mix of services required by the prospective client and decide on an appropriate service fee that will generate an adequate level of profit on the potential new proposition.

Although at the time of writing the system is still under development, feedback from staff indicates that it has significantly improved their under-standing of the profit implications of making project management mistakes. Even more importantly, both existing and new clients have expressed the view that they have a strong preference for working with the agency because of its unconventional approach, compared to others in the advertising agency business, of exhibiting a highly professional approach to the management of activities such as providing rapid quotes, staying on budget, fulfilling any detailed cost breakdowns that might be requested by the clients' accounting departments and being able to provide instant feedback on the cost implica-tions, if any, of requesting changes to in-progress projects.

THE ENTREPRENEURIAL PERSONALITY AND PERSONAL CHARACTERISTICS

The dominant influence of owner/managers in terms of their control over the managerial processes utilised within their small firms has understandably caused researchers to focus on the issue of whether these individuals exhibit certain unique characteristics which set them apart from other types of manager. Drawing upon the earlier Schumpeterian definition, Fry (1993) proposes that 'an entrepreneur is an individual who launches a venture and/or significantly improves it through innovative means'. However, in the context of the concept of entrepreneurship presented in this text, when examining the issue of the characteristics of entrepreneurs, it is felt that a more accurate definition would be: 'A small business entrepreneur is an individual who launches an unconventional venture and/or significantly improves it through unconventional innovative means.'

The subject that has received possibly the greatest academic attention is the impact of an entrepreneurial personality on the market performance of small firms. Brockhaus and Horowitz (1985) identified a number of psychological characteristics associated with the decision to become an entrepreneur.

1. *A need for achievement*, in the context of wishing to be successful as a business person. It is necessary to register, however, that this trait may vary in strength between different cultures around the world.

2. A tendency to have *an internal locus of control*, reflected in the entrepreneur's belief that any important event occuring in the business is a result of his or her behaviour. Research would suggest, however, that this trait is not unique to entrepreneurs, being found also among managers in other, non-entrepreneurial situations.

3. *A propensity to take risks*. Here, again, the research evidence is somewhat contradictory. Some studies suggest that entrepreneurs have a propensity to take high risks, whereas other research has concluded that many entrepreneurs are either moderate risk takers or, at the extreme, are 'risk adverse'.

4. *Creativity and an aptitude for problem solving*. Again, research tends to generate conflicting results. Some writers feel that entrepreneurs are extremely effective as creative problem solvers. The available evidence, however, would suggest that this is not a unique characteristic because it will also be encountered in managers working in large, conventional organisations.

5. *A high tolerance of ambiguity*, in terms of accepting that uncertainty is a normal part of business life. Even though entrepreneurs may give the impression of having everything under control, in fact they are often willing to accept less than perfect information and make decisions even when they have access only to very limited amounts of data. This can be contrasted with managers in large organisations who tend to want access to significant quantities of data prior to taking any action, in order to be in a position to make a well informed decision.

6. *Personal values system*. Brockhaus and Horowitz concluded from their review of the literature that 'results seem to support the perception of the entrepreneur as a concrete thinker who is concerned with the immediate problems and operations of the business. However, as the organisation grows, the entrepreneur has to adjust his interpretation of the world to deal with its increasing complexity.' Again, however, on the issue of personal values, Sexton and Bowman (1985) have concluded from their research that this is not a trait that can be used to distinguish entrepreneurs from managers in other types of business.

In an attempt to resolve this debate, Chell et al. (1991) have argued that there is a need to distinguish between the small business owner/manager and the small business entrepreneur, which can be achieved by adopting a taxonomy of classifying owner/managers into four categories:

1. Entrepreneur
2. Quasi-Entrepreneur

3.   Administrator
4.   Caretaker.

Furthermore, these authors feel that instead of seeking simply to identify psychological characteristics, it is also necessary to determine how identified traits manifest themselves as modes of behaviour in particular circumstances. This view, in fact, echoes that of Bamburger (1983), who believes that to understand an owner/manager's personality it is necessary to study this in the context of the leadership style exhibited and the organisational form that this individual has created.

Other writers have sought to understand whether the personal characteristics of entrepreneurs also have influence over their success or failure in business. Numerous studies have been undertaken on issues such as social background, gender, educational background, age and ethnicity. Similar to the topic of personality, here, again, results tend to be somewhat contradictory. It thus appears that one should be very careful in concluding that an individual exhibiting a specific personal characteristics is more or less likely to succeed as an entrepreneur (Fry 1993).

One distinguishing feature which does appear to be effective in identifying certain specific traits among entrepreneurs is that of commitment to high growth. It would appear that a significant proportion of entrepreneurs with clear aspirations to own high-growth businesses tend to come from middle-class backgrounds, have received a good education and have gained experience of small business from working in their family's existing, successful small firm. In researching the issue of the growth orientated entrepreneur, Ginn and Sexton (1990) found that this type of individual is willing to delegate much of the day-to-day operations to others, stays close enough to the business to maintain overall control, but tends to spend the majority of his or her time crafting strategy and policy.

ACHIEVING SCALE

One of the most critical constraints facing small firms is that their size often means they are unable to achieve scale sufficient to effectively implement entrepreneurial market expansion strategies. Following a number of studies on how entrepreneurial firms in Northern Italy form alliances (or 'business networks') in order to service large international customers traditionally adverse to purchasing products from very small organisations, entrepreneurial SME sector firms around the world are increasingly adopting the concept of business networking as a path by which to achieve market scale. The following are illustrative examples of ways in which firms have used networking as a path towards expansion of market share.

- Ten landscape gardening firms interested in the opportunities available in the construction of golf courses realised that, by acting individually, none of them would be considered of a size sufficient to be awarded major contracts in overseas markets such as the US, so they formed a consortium.
- A group of small appliance and telecommunication retailers grouped together to share marketing planning and promotional costs. As a network they were able to obtain a contract to market the best-selling modular telephone, whereas, acting individually, none of them would have been considered of a size sufficient to be granted the agency.
- Eleven textile manufacturers producing different products formed a network called 'CD-line'. While continuing to operate independently in their traditional markets, the consortium has been able to enter Germany, marketing a complete range of image clothing for employees in large corporations such as banks and car manufacturers.
- Four furniture companies collaborated in the design of a new range of furniture for the Netherlands market and jointly resourced the opening of an export sales office to market the range in that country.
- Three furniture firms formed a network to supply all the equipment needs for the Winter Olympics in Lillehammer, Norway.
- Four producers of kitchen equipment formed a network to offer total system catering solutions for oil platforms in the North Sea.
- Four fish-farming equipment manufacturers together developed a complete range of products in order to begin offering total farm management system in overseas markets.

On the basis of these and other examples, it is appears that there are two dimensions associated with the formation and operation of entrepreneurial, small-firm marketing networks. One is the sharing of expertise/resources to manage more effectively the marketing processes directed at increasing sales to current customers, gaining access to larger customers in existing markets and/or entering completely new markets. The other dimension is the revision of the product offering, either through the combination of existing products to offer an enhanced proposition, or through the development of an entirely new range of products.

By combining these two dimensions, as demonstrated in Figure 9.2, one can generate the following nine different collaborative pathways from which firms can select the best option for enhancing their marketing operations.

Cell 1   Sales of existing products to existing customers are increased by a pooling of resources. (For example, a grouping of small furniture manufacturers to create a single sales force to represent all their products in the marketplace.)

Cell 2   The pooling of resources permits access to new customers for existing products. (For example, a group of cheese producers already distributing their products through local retailers can now gain access to national supermarket chains because together they can offer a full range of cheeses from a single source.)

Cell 3   Sales of existing products can be increased by the pooling of resources to permit entry into a new market. (For example, a group of component manufacturers in the leisure craft industry may pool promotional resources to develop new export markets.)

Cell 4   The pooling of resources allows an enhanced product to be offered to current customers. (For example, a group of accountants may draw upon their various areas of specialist expertise to offer a complete financial management services portfolio to their clients.)

Cell 5   The pooling of resources leads to the creation of an enhanced product proposition which can assist in gaining access to new customers. (For example, a group of specialist management trainers may pool their resources to create a 'complete training solution' package, which means that they would then be considered as viable potential suppliers to large multinational corporations.)

Cell 6   The pooling of resources to enhance an existing product permits entry into a new market. (For example, a group of specialist computer software designers, who normally work as subcontractors for system provider firms, may combine their skills to move into the systems provision market.)

Cell 7   The pooling of resources permits the creation of a new product marketed to existing customers. (For example, a group of hotels may create their own package holiday operation.)

Cell 8   The pooling of resources creates a new product for sale to new customers in an existing market. (For example, a group of fresh juice processors, that distribute their product through small retailers, may develop a new, longer shelf-life product, which means they could then market their output to national retail chains.)

Cell 9   The pooling of resources leads to the development of a new product to create access to new markets. (For example, a group of civil engineering firms, each specialising in specific aspects of construction, may pool resources to create a total project design and management system, which permits them to enter overseas markets offering a complete tourism infrastructure project management capability.)

Market Product	Existing Market(s)		New Market(s)
	Existing Customers	New Customers	New Customers
Existing Product	1 Sharing of market management resources to increase existing customer sales	2 Sharing resources to achieve scale effect to gain access to new customers	3 Sharing market management resources to execute new market entry strategy
Merged Product Line to Enhance Product Position	4 Increased sales to existing customers by offering an enhanced product proposition	5 Access to new customers through offering an enhanced product proposition	6 Gaining access to new markets through offering an enhanced product proposition
New Product	7 New sales to existing customers through launching new product	8 Gaining access to new customers by launching new product	9 Gaining access to new markets through offering new product

Figure 9.2 Alternative strategies for business networking

Source: adapted from Chaston (1999).

REFERENCES

Bamburger, I. (1983), 'Value systems, strategies and the performance of small firms', *European Small Business Journal*, Vol. 1, No. 4, pp. 25–39.

Brickau, R. (1994), 'Responding to the Single Market: a comparative study of UK and German food firms', Unpublished PhD dissertation, University of Plymouth, England.

Brock, W.A. and Evans, D.A. (1989), 'Small business economics', *Small Business Economics*, Vol. 1, No. 1, pp. 7–21.

Brockhaus, R.H. and Horowitz, P.S. (1985), 'The psychology of the entrepreneur', in Sexton, D.L. and Smilor, R.W. (eds), *The Art and Science of Entrepreneurship*, Ballinger, Cambridge, MA, pp. 25–48.

Burns, P. (1994), Keynote address, Proceedings of the 17th ISBA Sheffield Conference, ISBA, Leeds.

Carland, J.W., Carland, J.C. and Abbey, C. (1989), 'An assessment of the psychological determinants of planning in small business', *International Small Business Journal*, Vol. 7, No. 4, pp. 23–33.

Chaston, I. (1997), 'Organisational performance: interaction of entrepreneurial style and organisational structure', *European Journal of Marketing*, Vol. 31, No. 11/12, pp. 31–43.

Chaston, I. (1999), *New Marketing Strategies*, Sage, London.

Chaston, I. and Mangles, T. (1997), 'Competencies for growth in SME sector manufacturing firms', *Journal of Small Business Management*, Vol. 35, No. 1, pp. 15–24.

Chell, E., Haworth, J. and Bearley, S. (1991), *The Entrepreneurial Personality*, Routledge, London.

Coopers & Lybrand (1994), *Made in the UK: The Middle Market Survey*, Coopers & Lybrand, London.

Doctor, J., Van der Haorst, R. and Stokman, C. (1989), 'Innovation processes in small and medium-sized companies', *Entrepreneurship and Regional Development*, Vol. 1, No. 1, pp. 35–53.

Fry, F.L. (1993), *Entrepreneurship: A Planning Approach*, West Publishing, St Pail, MN.

Gibb, A.A. and Davies, L. (1990), 'In pursuit of a framework for the development of growth models of the small business', *International Small Business Journal*, Vol. 9, No. 1, pp. 15–31.

Ginn, C.W. and Sexton, D.L. (1990), 'A comparison of the personality type dimensions of the 1987 Inc. 500 Company Founders/CEOs with those of slower growth firms', *Journal of Business Venturing*, Vol. 5, pp. 313–26.

Plymouth *Evening Herald* (1998), 'Torpedoed', 4 August, p. 5.

Sexton, D.L. and Bowman, N.B. (1985), 'The entrepreneur: a capable executive and more', *Journal of Business Venturing*, Vol. 1, pp. 129–40.

Slevin, D.P. and Covin, J.G. (1990), 'Juggling entrepreneurial style and organisational structure – how to get your act together', *Sloan Management Review*, Winter, pp. 43–53.

Steinmetz, L. (1969), 'Critical stages of small business growth', *Business Horizons*, February, pp. 12–19.

Storey, D.J., Keasey, K., Watson, R. and Wynarczyk, P. (1987), *The Performance of Small Firms*, Croom Helm, London.

Tradenz (1990), *Export Manufacturing – Framework For Success*, New Zealand Trade Development Board, Wellington.

10

ENTREPRENEURIAL SERVICE MARKETING

INTRODUCTION

A characteristic of twentieth-century Western nation economies has been the increasing importance of service industries as a proportion of gross national product (GNP) and a source of employment. Various factors have contributed towards fuelling the growth of the service sector. In consumer markets, higher levels of affluence have permitted individuals to afford more expensive holidays, to participate in leisure pursuits and to delegate many household functions – such as cleaning and repairs – to external providers. These same individuals, along with industrial sector firms, are also purchasing techno-logically more complex products, which has spawned a whole new sector of industry offering specialist hi-tech support services in areas such as design, installation, maintenance and training.

There are at least two reasons why the service sector deserves special con-sideration in any study of entrepreneurship. First, in relation to new firm creation, the ratio of service to manufacturing business start-ups is in the region of five to one. To a large degree, this situation probably reflects the fact that launching a new service usually requires a much smaller capital investment than starting an equivalent-scale manufacturing business. Second, the service sector, as demonstrated by organisations such as the book company, Amazon, and the online stock trading company, Charles Schwab, are providing a large number of examples of how new, highly successful businesses can be established by challenging conventions.

STRATEGIC POSITIONING

As shown in Figure 10.1, similar to other industrial sectors discussed in this text, the service marketer has four alternative positions upon which to base a company's operations:

- price excellence
- transactional excellence
- performance excellence
- relationship excellence.

Very successful service firms tend to be those that are first to recognise a strategic opportunity, to initiate an entrepreneurial move ahead of competition and thereby to set a service standard which, in many cases, subsequently becomes the convention for the industry sector.

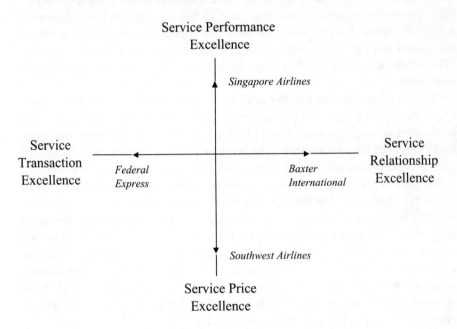

Figure 10.1 Alternative entrepreneurial service strategies

The example firms shown in Figure 10.1 are all organisations that have established the reputation of being willing to break with convention to beat competition successfully. The price excellence example in the Figure is Southwest Airlines. At the time the company was established, the industry convention in the US was based upon:

(a) the high fixed costs associated with operating a huge fleet of aircraft to provide national route coverage,

(b) delivering a reasonably high level of in-flight services, and

(c) a 'hub and spoke' configuration, whereby airlines fly passengers to a central hub to transfer them to their ongoing flights.

Herb Kelleher of Southwest Airlines decided to start an operation based in Houston that adopted a business design aimed at delivering a 'no-frills', low-price service positioning. Specific attention was given to minimising operating costs through using non-union labour which allowed for the introduction of unconventional and far more flexible working conditions. The company was also unwilling to pay the annual fees demanded of national reservation systems used by travel agents. Customers have to buy their tickets from the airline, carry their own bags and, if they want to eat, bring their own food with them. Furthermore, because the firm avoided operating out of congested airport hubs, planes could be turned round in 20 minutes. This allowed the company to offer more flights per day between cities than the competition.

The service transaction excellence example in Figure 10.1 is Federal Express. Over the years, this global parcel delivery service has introduced of whole series of new and unconventional ideas across areas such as work practices, and the use of new technology which has permitted the firm to achieve and retain market leadership in what is an intensely competitive service sector.

Superior service performance is exemplified by Singapore Airlines. While the conventional trend in this industry has been towards international carriers seeking to expand routes and introduce new ways of optimising operating efficiencies, Singapore Airlines has adopted the unconventional idea that passenger satisfaction should be the driving force determining the behaviour of its entire workforce. As a result, on the routes the airline flies, it consistently achieves superior ratings for service quality. The consequence is that the company enjoys an incredibly high level of passenger loyalty, which in turn ensures optimal utilisation of aircraft capacity.

The example in Figure 10.1 for service relationship excellence is the medical supplies company, Baxter International (Wiersma 1996). This company's marketing strategy is based upon the unconventional idea that, by working closely with customers and mutually sharing knowledge of medical procedures, Baxter can develop new ways of reducing the costs of health care. One product it has pioneered is the programmed buying and decision system (PBDS) programme which is an inventory control concept. The basis of this service is that Baxter supplies all of the items needed for a medical procedure in a single customised pack. These packs remove the need for hospitals to order, receive and assemble individual items to support each medical procedure, which in turn dramatically reduces the need for a vast stockholding of medical supplies.

SERVICE MARKETING PHILOSOPHY

As service markets became more competitive, many organisations, having recognised the need to modernise their marketing philosophies, employed transactionalist orientated managers from FCMG companies such as Procter & Gamble, General Foods and Nestlé. These individuals persuaded their new employers to adopt a highly conventional approach towards the management of the marketing process. This resulted in a major expansion of expenditure on various forms of mass marketing activity (for example, Western retail banks, in the 1970s and 1980s, investing in large-scale television campaigns and offering sales promotions to attract new customers and/or persuade existing customers to purchase a broader range of services).

In some cases, these purist, conventional FMCG approaches were extremely successful (for example, the global expansion of fast-food chains such as Burger King, Pizza Hut and Kentucky Fried Chicken). Other areas of the service sector, however, were not similarly rewarded. UK banks, for example, having expended millions in the 1980s on television advertising, found (a) that the proportion of total available consumers opening current accounts remained virtually unchanged, and (b) that many of their new customers were individuals who had been dissatisfied with their previous bank and had thus switched loyalties, but who continued to complain about the costs and/or quality of services being delivered by their new bank.

This mixture of success and failure within the service sector prompted both academics and practitioners to re-visit marketing theory. As a result, it became widely accepted that the marketing of services probably demands a whole new range of marketing conventions and operating principles (Cowell 1984). Initially, many of the writings on this topic focused on purist service marketing in sectors such as financial services and retailing. More recently, however, there has been a growing recognition that in many manufacturing sectors, firms can gain competitive advantage not by following the convention of marketing their capabilities to deliver a tangible core product, but through augmenting their offering with a portfolio of unconventional value added services.

For example, Quinn et al. (1990) have described how many of the firms at the top end of the pharmaceutical market have relied upon the use of unconventional value added services to survive in the face of competitive threats from price orientated, generic drug producers. Firms such as Glaxo and Merck have added value to their product line through service activities such as R&D, constructing legal and patent defences, rapidly progressing new drugs through the clinical clearances demanded by regulatory bodies, supporting clinicians in their use of new treatments, and offering advisory support on optimising the provision of health care by their customers, such as large hospitals and health authorities. These authors also argue that, as manufacturing becomes more universally automated, increasingly adding value does not come from the conventional behaviours associated with converting raw materials into finished goods, but in areas of service such as styling, perceived quality, product customisation, JIT distribution and post-purchase maintenance and repair services. Quinn et al. would argue, in fact, that the bastion of FMCG marketing, Procter & Gamble, is now a $15 billion service corporation that has achieved success by breaking with the sector convention of being perceived as branded goods operation and repositioning the organisation as offering superior services across the core areas of R&D, manufacturing and logistics management.

MANUFACTURING AS A SERVICE BUSINESS

Once all the major players in an industrial sector have a full understanding of the manufacturing technologies upon which their industry is based and all are buying from the same list of component suppliers, there is minimal opportunity available to differentiate products from competition. Under these circumstances, in order to remain profitable, the more far-sighted members of a sectoral supply chain will usually turn to seeking new unconventional ways of increasing the service component of their product offering (Hansell 1998).

This scenario is possibly best illustrated by the world of the PC, where essentially the box manufacturer is merely acting as an integrator of technology from chip producers such as Intel and operating systems from firms such as Microsoft. One of the first firms to recognise this trend was Dell Computers, whose entrepreneurial solution was to create a direct marketing operation that assembles a customised PC to meet the specification requested by the purchaser. As other firms sought to enter this market segment, Dell has continuously invested in new entrepreneurial manufacturing processes in order to concurrently reduce inventory levels and improve customer response times.

As the price war between PC manufacturers has intensified, other entrepreneurs have realised that they could exploit this situation by creating website trading operations to meet the needs of those customers to whom lowest possible price and minimal service was the basis for their purchase decision. For example, to compete in this market, Buycomp – based in Santa Ana in the US – has developed a software tool to monitor automatically competitor's online offerings and respond accordingly.

To survive in an increasingly competitive market, the major PC manufacturers have been forced to adopt a JIT management philosophy in order to remain profitable. Eventually, their desire to hold minimal stocks of either components or finished goods has opened up new service opportunities for intermediaries in the supply chain willing to take on the responsibility for final product assembly. One of the most entrepreneurial of these new assemblers is one of the world's largest computer distributors, Ingram Micro Inc.

This company has expanded its traditional wholesaling operation by setting up factories around the US to assemble computers on behalf of companies such as Compaq, IBM, Hewlett-Packard and Apple. In addition, by forming an alliance with the Solectron corporation, a components manufacturer, Ingram also assembles unbranded, 'white box' PCs which were previously built by specialist computer dealers. Now, these dealers can also exploit the world of JIT by contracting back into the supply chain to have Ingram produce boxes on to which the dealer's name is stamped at the time of shipment. Ingram can also arrange delivery to the final customer who, because he or she receives a box carrying the dealer's label, assumes that the product has been assembled by the dealer.

THE CHARACTERISTICS OF SERVICE GOODS

One the primary reasons for early writers positing the view that service marketers must break with traditional, branded goods conventions, was that service markets exhibit some very specific characteristics. One of these, intangibility, is encompassed by Kotler's (1997) definition: 'a service is any act or performance that one party can offer to another that is essentially intangible and does not result in the ownership of anything. Its production may or may not be tied to a physical product.'

However, it is necessary to recognise that the degree of intangibility will vary across product sectors. For example, at one extreme, service is a minor component of the product proposition (for example, a washing machine offered with free installation and three years' free repair and maintenance). At the other extreme, service may be the dominant or sole product component (for example, the preparation of a firm's annual accounts by an external auditor, or a session at an aromatherapy clinic).

The implication of intangibility does mean that a service, unlike physical products, cannot be seen, tasted, felt, heard or smelled before purchase. Thus, one of the tasks of the early service marketers was to develop mechanisms whereby customer uncertainty could be reduced. The solutions, which have now become conventions within the sector, typically include exploiting variables such as:

1. *place* – the physical setting around which the provision of services is delivered
2. *people* – those involved in working with the customer–organisation interface

3. *equipment* – being of the necessary standard to assist rapidly and efficiently in the service provision process.

An example of a conventional practice for managing the variables of place, people and equipment is provided by the UK car insurance industry. Until the mid-1980s, the industry handled these variables by having branches in all major towns, complemented by the activities of local brokers paid on a commission-only basis. The entrepreneurial firm Direct Line insurance recognised that the advent of computer-based, call-centre technology permitted it to service customer needs from a single location. The major lowering of operating costs associated with this unconventional idea also allowed the firm to charge much lower insurance premiums. By the end of the 1980s, the firm had achieved market leadership in the UK car insurance sector. Furthermore, in recognition of the operational advantages of the concept, most other members of the industry were then forced to close their branch networks and replace them with their own centralised call-centre operations.

A second characteristic of services is inseparability, because many services are produced and consumed simultaneously. The implication of this situation is that, for many service outcomes to occur, both the provider and the customer must be able to interact with each other.

A third characteristic of services is their variability which is caused both by differing customer needs and by the capabilities of employees within the provider organisation.

Unlike manufactured goods, which can be produced and inventoried for later use, a fourth characteristic of many services is that they are highly perishable. For example, an inability to sell every room in a hotel on a specific night means that a proportion of total revenue on this occasion has been lost for ever. Sasser (1976) has proposed a number of marketing strategies which, over time, have become the conventional responses for effectively matching supply and demand, and include the following.

- *Differential pricing*, to move demand away from peak to off-peak periods.
- *Alternative service provision*, to meet the varying needs of customers during peak periods.
- *Service modification*, to ensure that the needs of major purchasers receive priority during peak periods.
- *Demand management systems*, to permit the service provider rapidly to (a) identify current available capacity and (b) propose alternative solutions.
- *Temporary capacity expansion*, to enable the provider to increase its ability to respond to customer needs during peak periods.
- *Service sharing*, to enable a number of organisations to work together and be willing to cross-refer customers.
- *Customer participation*, to encourage customers to become self-providers.

An organisation's ability to manage these variables will clearly impact on customer perceptions of service quality. An example of a service provider that recognised that this opportunity could be exploited entrepreneurially by introducing new technology was American Airlines. Led by a technology visionary, Max Hopper, the company developed the service administration and booking reservation (SABRE) flight reservation system (Hopper 1990). The system was initially created so that American Airlines could track bookings and offer customers a more rapid response to their flight reservation enquiries. An added advantage of the system was that, by providing management with data concerning pricing, routing, staffing and other scheduling issues, the airline was able to deliver a much higher level of service quality. In fact, the system was so successful that marketing SABRE to other airlines has subsequently created a whole new revenue stream for the company.

CUSTOMER SATISFACTION AND SERVICE GAP THEORY

A number of writers have posited the theory that the objective of service satisfaction is to minimise the gap between customers' desires and actual experience (that is, the gap between what they hope will happen and what actually occurs). To permit service marketers to understand and manage service gaps required access to feasible techniques for the measurement and analysis of customer expectations and perceptions. This need was been met through the activities of Parasuraman et al. (1985, 1988; Zeithmal et al. 1990), who, from 1983 onwards, have implemented a carefully sequenced research project aimed at delivering an effective model for assessing the effectiveness and quality of the service provision process.

The first stage of their research was to identify some common variables with which to categorise customer expectations. By using focus groups, they identified the following five variables.

1. *Reliability* – the ability to perform the promised service dependably and accurately.
2. *Tangibles* – the images created by the appearance of physical facilities, equipment, personnel and communication materials.
3. *Responsiveness* – the willingness to help customers and to provide prompt service.
4. *Assurance* – by the process by which the knowledge, ability and courtesy of employees engenders customer trust and confidence in the service provider.

5.   *Empathy* – the feeling created by the caring, individualised attention that employees offer to the customer.

Having identified these generic expectations, Parasuraman et al. then went on to create the SERVQUAL model, which defined the following types of gap that could exist between expectations and perceptions.

Gap 1 – between the customer's expectations and the organisation's perceptions of customer need.

Gap 2 – between the organisation's perceptions and the definition of appropriate standards for the quality of service to be delivered.

Gap 3 – between the specified standards of service and the actual performance of the service provision process undertaken by the organisation's employees.

Gap 4 – between the actual service delivered and the nature of the service promise made in any communications with the customer.

Gap 5 – between customer expectations and perceptions created by the combined influence of Gaps 1–4; that is, the overall gap.

The magnitude and influence of the five service gaps can be measured using the SERVQUAL tool. The technique involves surveying customers to determine their expectations and perceptions by asking them to compare their perspectives on the desired service with their experience of the actual service received. Other gap dimensions are measured by surveying employee attitudes about various aspects of operations within their organisation (for example, the existence of quality standards, and mechanisms established for integrating all aspects of the service delivery process across the entire organisation).

The conventional firm's response to results from SERVQUAL-type research studies is to find ways of minimising the gap between customers' perceptions and their expectations. However, the entrepreneurial service firm recognises that the ultimate objective is to find ways of remove the gap completely. This will usually be achieved by implementing actions designed to ensure that the actual service experience exceeds customer expectations.

EXCEEDING CUSTOMER EXPECTATIONS

Closing Gap 1 – Edward Jones

Gap 1 involves gaining sufficient understanding of customer perceptions to enable the firm to act in a way that totally exceeds customer expectations.

Many people living in the small towns of rural America perceive the average stockbrokerage firm to be an organisation interested only in persuading customers to play the stock market regularly because this will maximise the commissions that can be generated. Edward Jones is a stockbroking firm that realised that if it could occupy the position of providing conservative advice on optimising long-term investments, this action would lead to the firm being perceived as one that exceeds customer expectations (Teitelbaum 1997).

To deliver this service strategy, the company's founder, John Bachmann, concentrated on opening a huge chain of single-broker offices in small towns and suburban areas of larger cities. The company's brokers are expected to recommend long-term investment strategies to their clients based on stable equities, highly rated bonds and good mutual funds. Brokers are granted wide freedom in all but one area of their service provision activities: the core value of offering conservative advice. Here the company carefully monitors each broker and, should an individual be seen to start switching a client's money between different funds, Head Office, through a satellite communication system, will immediately request the broker concerned to justify his or her actions.

Gap 2 – Starbucks

Once a firm comprehends the nature of customer expectations, one way of ensuring that these are always exceeded is to set operating standards well above those used by conventional competitors. Starbucks, a chain of coffee houses now operating in a number of countries around the world, started life in 1971 as a single gourmet coffee store in Seattle, Washington (Reese 1996). Initially, the business sold coffee beans and coffee-making equipment. Then, in 1973, it began roasting its own beans. When Howard Shultz joined the firm, he decided to branch out into coffee bars. The coffee supplies business was eventually sold off to one of the founders, while Starbucks focused on opening new coffee shops across the US.

The cornerstone upon which the company's success is founded is an obsession with brewing the best possible cup of coffee. To ensure that every store replicates the same high-quality product, the primary focus of the organisation is to set rigid standards that must be followed by all employees in relation to activities such as always purifying the water with Brita filters; never letting coffee sit on a hotplate for more than 20 minutes; using only milk steamed to at least 150 °F, but never to more than 170 °F; and ensuring that every cup of espresso must be pulled within 23 seconds.

To instil these standards into all employees, the company runs extensive training programmes during which participants are briefed in detail on every aspect of the Starbucks operation, from the correct way of opening coffee bags through to cleaning the milk wand on the coffee machine. During these sessions, employees are also educated about the world of coffee in order to enable them to hold informed conversations with their customers.

Gap 2 – Federal Express

Although setting and managing standards in operations such as Starbucks requires a deep organisational commitment to process, monitoring of actual versus specified levels of performance is a relatively simple task. However, the same situation does not prevail in a global parcel delivery business, where the organisation is seeking to monitor the performance of thousands of items moving between and within countries on a daily basis. The entrepreneurial service provider Federal Express has recognised that to sustain service standards under these circumstances requires a solution which has to be based on exploiting the latest advances in IT (Grossman 1993).

The core of their solution was the development of COSMOS IIB, which tracks items using real-time data. Monitoring commences when a courier first collects a package and continues through every stage in the distribution cycle. This is achieved using a hand-held SuperTracker computer which scan's the package's bar code. At the time of final delivery the courier undertakes the final scan to record safe receipt by the customer. SuperTracker automatically records the time and date of each scan and downloads the information to COSMOS IIB. Thus, when a customer contacts Federal Express to ask questions such as 'Where is my package?', 'What time was it collected?', or 'Who signed the delivery slip?', a customer service agent can provide an immediate response by accessing the COSMOS IIB database. The system also permits the organisation to gather and track employee performance across areas such as length of service call, speed of response and delivery time. To avoid a negative attitude among employees to the collation of such data, employees are encouraged to interrogate the database and utilise available information to determine how they might improve their performance in the future.

To further monitor and manage service standards, Federal Express has now given its major customers a system called Powerships. These are kits that store addresses and shipping data, print mailing slips and monitor package location. By integrating the customer more closely into Federal Express's data management system, the company has been able both to improve delivery times and to upgrade performance standards further across all aspects of the organisation's package delivery operations.

Gap 3 – The United States Automobile Association

An issue confronting organisations seeking to excel at exceeding customer expectations is how to organise both the workforce and work processes in such a way that the customer receives a rapid, yet apparently personalised, response to his or her demands for service. Writings on the issue of workforce capability are usually concerned with the topic of internal customer management, and this matter is discussed more fully later in the chapter.

Similar to the topic of managing standards, over recent years the service industry has, in seeking to improve internal capability, increasingly come to rely upon entrepreneurial applications of new technologies. The United States Automobile Association (USAA), a San Antonio insurance company, specialises in the provision of services to military personnel and their families. To upgrade its operation and to acquire the capability to personalise its contacts with customers, the company joined with IBM to create a computer imaging system that could eliminate all paper-based materials and could also offer the associated ability to track the physical progress of bulky customer files through the organisation's various departments (Teal 1991).

Employees are able to scan millions of pieces of incoming mail into electronic dossiers that are much easier to manage. The system even has the facility to record photographs from damage claims on to an optical disk, which means that this data can be retrieved for use in other documents. Furthermore, because telephone personnel can immediately call up a customer's file, they have all the necessary information in front of them when speaking with the customer. Despite rarely having face-to-face contact with its highly dispersed customer base, the company is perceived by its clients as an organisation that clearly cares, because it is deeply informed about its customers' personal insurance needs.

Gap 3 – IKEA

IKEA was originally a small, Swedish mail-order company. Over time it has evolved into a major retailer of home furnishings (Normann and Ramirez 1993). The aim of the company is to provide well designed furniture at low prices. The problem to be overcome was how to ensure a high level of in-store customer service while also seeking to minimise staff costs. IKEA's entrepreneurial solution was to involve the customer in the shopping process.

When customers enter the store they are given catalogues, tape measures, pens and notepaper. This allows them to fulfil many of the tasks undertaken by shop staff. Pushchairs are available for use in-store free of charge, and supervised child care is also available. After payment, carts are provided so that customers can transport their purchases to their car and if required, they can rent a roof-rack to transport larger purchases home. To reduce operating costs further, IKEA also exploits a now well established convention in the European furniture business of supplying goods in 'flat pack' form which the customer assembles at home. The only difference between IKEA and many of its competitors, however, is that IKEA has invested heavily in the development of assembly instructions which are simple and easy to understand.

Gap 4 – Car buying

All aspects of the interface between the customer and supplier communicate implicit or explicit statements about an organisation's service promise. These sources include advertising, salespersons' comments, switchboard operators responding to customer queries on any subject, and the physical facilities of the operation. Information provided by these sources influences the development of customers' expectations of the consequent quality of service they will receive from the supplier.

If one were to survey consumers, the market sector in which they would probably express the most discontent regarding expectations created by information provided and actual service received would be the car industry. In recent years, a number of entrepreneurial firms have recognised the credibility gap created by traditional car dealerships and have acted to exploit this opportunity (*Business Week*, 19 February 1996). The first moves were in relation to pricing information. Firms such as CompuServe's AutoNet have created Internet sites where the shopper can obtain detailed information on the alternative deals being offered by suppliers prior to starting an active search for a car. Even more assistance is provided by AutoByTel which operates a referral service to locate the best deal available to the customer.

These early moves are now being followed by the creation of superstore used-car chains that are redefining the physical environment in which the customer comes to shop. Companies such as CarMax ensure that their stores provide the same features consumers have come to expect in any shopping mall – amenities such as child care, coffee bars, touch-screen computers and huge inventories to maximise customer choice. All of these features are contributing to the communication of a service promise which reduces the credibility gap many people develop when visiting a traditional second-hand car dealership.

Gap 4 – Dell Computers

Possibly the entrepreneurial leader in ensuring that the information flow between customer and supplier acts to develop very positive customer expectations further is Dell Computers. From the first day the firm opened for business it recognised that direct marketing required an overwhelming commitment to maximising the effectiveness of the interface between the firm and the customer. The company was one of the first organisations to enter the world of Internet trading, and it rapidly realised that information management via this medium is critical in terms of influencing customer service expectations (Thurm 1998).

Over time, Dell has evolved a website than does much more than just take orders. Customers can access thousands of pages of information, tap into the technical guides used by Dell technicians, and also use the site to track the progress of their order from submission through to shipment. The firm has found that these types of service actually improve its selling efficiency. For example, the traditional purchaser makes five telephones calls before buying, whereas users of the Dell website browse and then place their order during their first telephone call. Additionally, Dell sales staff can interrogate the site to determine whether there is a need to follow up a customer's search activities with a one-to-one telephone conversation.

For corporate clients, Dell has now developed Premier Pages, in which the corporate customer can specify the creation of their own confidential home page. Employees of the customer who are seeking information on the product specifications their employer will permit when purchasing a new machine can then be directed to the home page. The Premier Page also has the capability of allowing the client to access databases showing what type of computers have been purchased by the client's company, where, and by whom they were ordered.

INTERNAL MARKETING

Ensuring that employees can respond to the diverse demands of customers in service markets does mean that, unlike many tangible goods situations, it is extremely difficult to separate the marketing activity from all the other functions of the firm. Furthermore, the nature of the buyer–seller interaction occuring at the production–consumption interface can have a significant impact on the customer's repeat buying decisions (for example, if a customer arrives at a restaurant to discover that a mistake has been made over a reservation and that his or her table is no longer available, the way in which the head waiter handles this problem will largely determine whether the customer can be placated or is 'lost for ever').

Eigler and Langeard (1997) have proposed that the following are three main categories of resource involved in the buyer–seller interaction.

1. *Contact personnel* – the employees interacting directly with the customer.
2. *Physical resources* – the human and technical resources used by the organisation in the production, delivery and consumption of the service offering.
3. *The customer* – the person forming a repeat-purchase loyalty decision based on the quality of service received to date.

Gronroos (1984) has proposed that managing these three variables is a marketing task that differs from conventional FMCG marketing because it involves using assets that are not usually part of the mainstream marketing operation, but instead draws from the entire production resources within the organisation. Gronroos has proposed that in service firms there exist three marketing tasks:

1. 'external marketing' (that is, the normal formal processes associated with the management of the four 'Ps': product, price, promotion and place)
2. 'interactive marketing' (that is, the activities occuring at the buyer–seller interface)
3. 'internal marketing' (that is, the activities associated with ensuring that every employee is (a) customer-conscious, and (b) committed to the philosophy that every aspect of his or her personal job role must be orientated towards achieving total customer satisfaction).

Given that errors at the buyer–seller interface and/or during the execution of the internal processes associated with service delivery can impact on customer satisfaction, there has been widespread debate on how best to manage the role of employees within service sector organisations. In two classic articles, Levitt (1972, 1976) eloquently argued for the adoption of a manufacturing orientation in the management of services. He believes that this approach is required because it allows for:

1. the simplification of tasks
2. the clear division of labour
3. the substitution of equipment and systems for employees
4. minimal decision making being required of the employees.

Early entrepreneurs in the fast-food chain industry, such as Ray Kroc of McDonald's, very effectively demonstrated the validity of Levitt's proposals. Even to this day within the McDonald's operation, operatives are taught how to greet customers and ask for their orders in a scripted way designed to suggest the purchase of additional items. Clearly defined procedures are laid down for assembling the order, placing them on the tray, positioning the tray on the counter and collecting the money. Meanwhile, in the 'back room', other operatives are executing tasks developed via the application of time and motion studies rapidly and efficiently to produce food of uniform quality. The net result is that this production line approach enables the company to operate an efficient, low-cost, high-volume food service operation that also delivers customer satisfaction.

The concept of the industralisation of service operations has not been without its critics. Such individuals argue that the approach is not only dehumanising, but also results in an inability to respond to heterogeneous customer needs because employees are forced to respond to all situations by adhering to rigid guidelines laid down in the organisation's operating policy manual. Zemke and Schaaf (1989) would argue that entrepreneurial service excellence is more likely to be achieved by 'empowerment', which involves encouraging and rewarding employees to exercise initiative and imagination. Similar views are expressed by Jan Carlzon (1987), the Chief Executive attributed with the successful turnaround of Scandinavian Airlines. He stated that, 'to free someone from the rigorous control by instructions, policies and orders, and to give that person freedom to take responsibility for his ideas, decisions and actions, is to release hidden resources that would otherwise remain inaccessible to both the individuals and the organisation'.

Bowen and Lawler (1992) have presented a somewhat more balanced view of the industrialisation versus employee empowerment service delivery debate. They point to the contrasting examples of two very successful American firms in the international package delivery business: the highly entrepreneurial Federal Express and its very conventional competitor, United Parcel Service (UPS). The Federal Express company motto, 'people, service and profits', is the foundation stone for an organisation built on self-managed teams and empowered employees as the mechanism with which to offer a flexible and creative service to customers with varying needs. In contrast, UPS, with its philosophy of 'best service at low rates', uses controls, rules, a detailed union contract and rigidly defined operational guidelines to guarantee that customers receive a reliable, low-cost service.

Bowen and Lawler suggest that the appropriateness of a service philosophy is a contingency issue: an industrialisation or empowerment orientation will be dependent upon the market in which the firm operates and the influence of overall corporate strategy on the selection of appropriate internal organisational processes. By building upon their views it is possible to define factors which may have an influence on determining which are likely to be the most effective service products and/or delivery processes for achieving the goal of customer satisfaction (Table 10.1).

Table 10:1   Factors influencing the service style decision

Factor	Range of response to factors	
Customer orientation	Transactional	Relationship
Service product need	Standard solutions	New, innovative solutions
Business environment	Predictable, stable	Changing, unstable
Service delivery technology	Simple	Complex
Firm's closeness to customer orientation	Low	High
Firm's service solution orientation	Established, well known	Applying new approaches
Average skills of workforce	Adequate for executing standard tasks	Capable of executing complex tasks
Managerial orientation	Directive	Delegators

Applying the factors of influence in Table 10.1 permits the suggestion that there are probably four alternative management styles which can be utilised by service organisations.

1. *Conventional-transactional service organisations*, which operate in stable markets where the customer wishes to obtain standard solutions without forming close relationships with the provider. Required services can usually be delivered by a relatively unskilled workforce and without resorting to the application of complex technologies (for example, a car wash business).

2. *Conventional-relationship service organisations*, which operate in changing markets where the customer wishes to form a close relationship with the provider as a way of obtaining standard solutions somewhat modified to suit their specific needs. Customisation may demand the application of complex technologies and/or involve creative inputs from a highly skilled workforce (for example, a distributor of IBM-specification PCs that offers customised computer installation, maintenance and IT training services).

3. *Entrepreneurial-transactional service organisations*, which operate in rapidly changing markets where the customer, although facing unique problems demanding a completely new solution, does not wish to form a strong close relationship with any one single provider. Solutions will demand the application of complex technologies and/or involve creative inputs from highly skilled specialists (for example, many of the major consulting firms that develop and then market concepts such as process re-engineering that require carefully researched new approaches in order to be suitable in a client specific situation).

4. *Entrepreneurial-relationship service organisations*, which operate in rapidly changing markets where the customer, seeking to resolve a unique problem demanding a completely new solution, does so by forming a strong, close relationships with a preferred service provider. Solutions will demand the application of complex technologies and/or involve creative inputs from highly skilled specialists working in a collaborative partnership with the client's own workforce (for example, computer software designers developing new risk management systems for international financial institutions involved in global currency and/or share trading).

It is proposed in Figure 10.2 that there are two dimensions associated with the four alternative management styles. One dimension is the degree to which employees are empowered to use creativity to revise the nature of the service delivery process. The other dimension is the degree to which employees are empowered to exercise imagination in the formulation of totally new forms of service. In the case of the conventional-transactional firm, employees are permitted little freedom in modifying either the form of service or the service delivery process. Customers of conventional-relationship firms are usually interested in their service provider optimising the service delivery process by

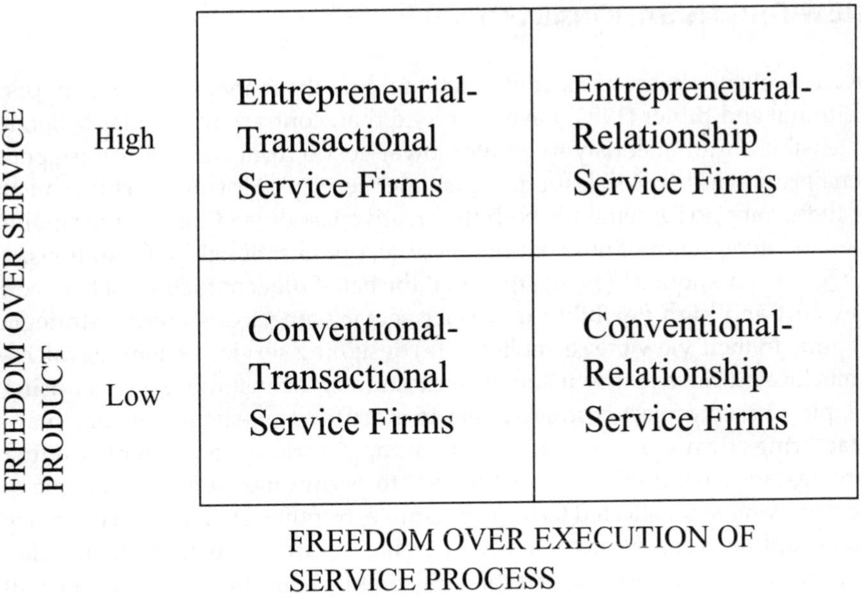

	High	Entrepreneurial-Transactional Service Firms	Entrepreneurial-Relationship Service Firms
	Low	Conventional-Transactional Service Firms	Conventional-Relationship Service Firms

FREEDOM OVER SERVICE PRODUCT

FREEDOM OVER EXECUTION OF SERVICE PROCESS

Figure 10.2   Alternative service positioning styles

205

being prepared to customise some aspects of what essentially is a standardised service (for example, a delivery service willing to modify the routing of its transportation fleet to ensure successful delivery of urgently needed spare parts to a remote location). Thus, to achieve this goal, the service provider employees should be permitted to exhibit personal initiative in overcoming any problems which might be encountered.

Entrepreneurial-transactional firms have clients that face a major problem, the resolution of which will probably require a new, radical approach. This can only be achieved if the provider is willing to delegate authority to its employees who are charged with the development of an appropriately innovative solution. As most contracts of this type contain fixed penalties for failure, the provider will, however, demand that staff adhere to clearly defined guidelines concerning all aspects of the project management process. This can be contrasted with the situation often confronting the entrepreneurial-relationship service firm. Here, the client and the provider both fully realise that collaborative 'blue sky' thinking by each other's employees is probably the only route to evolving a feasible solution; hence, the provider will seek to instil an attitude of employee empowerment in relation to both the generation and delivery of the most effective service solution that can be developed in the time available.

NEW ORGANISATIONAL FORMS

In an excellent review of the myths surrounding the management of services, Zeithmal and Bitner (1996) have proposed that, contrary to popular belief, it is feasible simultaneously to deliver lower cost outputs and maximise personalisation and customisation of customer services. However, achievement of these joint goals demands both the creative use of leading-edge technologies and acceptance of new, entrepreneurial, organisational configurations.

Quinn and Paquette (1990) argue that the belief that conflicts exist between low cost and high flexibility in service sector scenarios is merely strategic dogma. In their view the secret lies in (a) designing service systems as micro-units located close to the customer (for example, the insurance adviser using a laptop-based project-costing system to execute an on-site review of a manufacturing firm's needs for coverage appropriate to current trading circumstances) and (b) using technology to permit inexperienced people to perform very sophisticated tasks (for example, frontline staff in a travel agency using online reservation systems to create complex, customised holiday packages). In the process of achieving these goals, the organisation will probably recognise that new organisational forms are now demanded in order to optimise employee productivity.

One approach to the process of optimising productivity and reducing costs is simultaneously to exploit both technology and customer involvement. Hall-Kimbrell is an environmental services consulting business (Solomon 1989) that faced the problem of how to reduce costs of undertaking standard environmental audits for smaller clients. The client is now sent a videotape, covering the relevant environmental regulations, and an accompanying detailed questionnaire. Hall-Kimbrell analyses the survey data electronically and automatically generates a report specifying those areas where the client will need to take action in order to comply with the relevant regulations.

Computer-based information systems appear to mean that there is virtually no limit to the span of control between supervisor and operatives. This means that service organisations can safely consider moving to create 'infinitely flat' organisations, in which authority is delegated to the lowest possible level and all employees empowered to make the best possible decision to satisfy changing customer needs. Federal Express, for example, has over 42,000 employees in more than 300 cities world-wide, but has a maximum of only five organisational layers between operatives and senior management. Coordination of service provision activities is achieved by giving all employees access to the organisation's computerised management information systems.

As large international organisations such as accounting and consultancy firms offering complex client-specific services act to sustain localised customer contact by opening offices around the world, updating staff on technological advances – and thereby sustaining leading-edge service quality – becomes an ever-increasing problem. Fortunately, the advent of technologies such as Lotus Notes and video conferencing has enabled these organisations to re-orientate themselves into networked structures that use electronic media to ensure that the dispersed nodes of their service operation can remain in touch with each other continually. Quinn and Paquette (1990), for example, have described the entrepreneurial structure which has been developed by the leading consulting firm, Arthur Anderson & Co. The organisation uses the latest available technology to link together its 40,000 staff in over 200 different countries. One of the major benefits of this system is that an individual facing a difficult client problem can now use the organisation's electronic bulletin board to discover if any employee elsewhere in the world may have already evolved an effective solution.

Once an organisation has created such internal systems, it does not require much of a leap in entrepreneurial thinking to extend the system to service the needs of clients. Ernst & Young, for example, has created an online service for small firms that is capable of answering questions on issues such as how to train employees, what issues are associated with the issuance of a letter of credit and how one can track items through a continuous process manufacturing line (Cavanaugh 1996). E-mailed queries are screened electronically and routed to a 'knowledge provider' who is assigned the responsibility of responding within a specified time-period. The system also features a news clipping service and a Frequently Asked Questions database that can be accessed for more immediate information.

SMALL-FIRM NETWORKS

Service firms in the small business sector have traditionally faced the problem that they often lack sufficient breadth of expertise to compete with larger firms able to offer a complete service portfolio solution. Thus, one of the real attractions of structured networking is that small firms can enter into collaborative relationships with other like-minded organisations within their sector as a path by which to expand the range of services offered to their clients. An example of this philosophy is provided by a recently formed entrepreneurial small-business network, WEAR IT, based in the North East of England. The five small, specialist IT firms comprising this network are Omnicom, offering local area networks (LANs) consultancy; TGE, specialising in automated data protection; CIA, delivering specialist training across a broad range of commercial software systems; Treepax, offering client/server computing consultancy; RSD, that develops PC-based business solutions; and QIS, that has developed a interface management system. Although each has had some success in its respective market sectors, the new business network now permits them to enter the international market, offering a unique 'one-stop-shop' IT design, installation and operations service to large, multinational manufacturing and service organisations.

REFERENCES

Bowen, D.E. and Lawler, E.E. (1992), 'The empowerment of service workers: what, why, how and when', *Sloan Management Review*, Spring, pp. 31–9.

Business Week (1996), 'The revolution in the showroom', *Business Week Magazine*, 19 February, p. 17.

Carlzon, J. (1987), *Moments of Truth*, Ballinger, New York.

Cavanaugh, K. (1996), 'Big 6 to launch an on-line consulting service', *New York Times*, 31 May, p. 17.

Cowell, D. (1984), *The Marketing of Services*, Heinemann, London.

Eigler, P. and Langeard, E. (1977), 'Services as systems: marketing implications', in Eigler, P. and Langeard, E. (eds), *Marketing Consumer Services*, Marketing Science Institute, Cambridge, MA, pp. 89–91.

Gronroos, C. (1984), 'A service quality model and its marketing implications', *European Journal of Marketing*, Vol. 18, No. 4, pp. 36–44.

Grossman, L.M. (1993), 'Federal Express, UPS face off over computers', *Wall Street Journal*, 17 September, p. B1.

Hansell, S. (1998), 'Is this the factory of the future?', *New York Times*, 26 July, pp. 9–13.

Hopper, M. (1990), 'Rattling SABRE – new ways to compete on information', *Harvard Business Review*, May–June, pp. 118–25.

Kotler, P. (1997), *Marketing Management: Analysis, Planning, Implementation and Control*, ninth edition, Prentice Hall, Upper Saddle River, NJ.

Levitt, T. (1972), 'Production-line approach to service', *Harvard Business Review*, September–October, pp. 41–52.

Levitt, T. (1976), 'Industrialisation of services', *Harvard Business Review*, September–October, pp. 63–74.

Normann, D. and Ramirez, J. (1993), 'Trends in furniture retailing', *Retail Distribution Management*, Vol. 17, pp. 13–24.

Parasuraman, A., Zeithmal, V.A. and Berry, L.L. (1985), 'A conceptual model of service quality and its implications for future research', *Journal of Marketing*, Vol. 49, Fall, pp. 34–45.

Parasuraman, A., Zeithmal, V.A. and Berry, L.L. (1988), 'SERVQUAL: a multiple item scale for measuring consumer perceptions of service quality', *Journal of Retailing*, Vol. 64, No. 1, pp. 12–23.

Quinn, J.B., Doorley, T.L. and Paquette, P.C. (1990), 'Technology in services: rethinking strategic focus', *Sloan Management Review*, Winter, pp. 79–87.

Quinn, J.B. and Paquette, P.C. (1990), 'Technology in services: creating organisational revolutions', *Sloan Management Review*, Winter, pp. 67–78.

Reese, J. (1996), 'Starbucks: inside the coffee cult', *Fortune Magazine*, 9 December, pp. 34–6.

Sasser, W.E. (1976), 'Match supply and demand in service industries', *Harvard Business Review*, November–December, pp. 133–40.

Soloman, S.D. (1989), 'Growth strategies: cleaning up', *Inc. Magazine*, Goldhirsh Group, Boston, MA, p. 137.

Teal, T. (1991), 'Service comes first: an interview with USAA's Robert McDermott', *Harvard Business Review*, September–October, pp. 56–61.

Teitelbaum, R. (1997), 'The Wal-Mart of Wall Street', *Fortune Magazine*, 13 October, pp. 22–4.

Thurm, S. (1998), 'Leading the PC pack', *Wall Street Journal*, 7 December, p. 4.

Wiersma, F. (1996), *Customer Intimacy*, HarperCollins, London.

Zeithmal, V.A. and Bitner, M.J. (1996), *Services Marketing*, McGraw-Hill, New York.

Zeithmal, V.A., Parasuraman, A. and Berry, L.L. (1990), *Delivering Quality Service: Balancing Customer Perceptions and Expectations*, The Free Press, New York.

Zemke, R. and Schaaf, (1989), *The Service Edge: 101 Companies that Profit from Customer Care*, New American Library, New York.

11
ENTREPRENEURIAL PUBLIC SECTOR SERVICE PROVISION

INTRODUCTION

The origins of the Western public sector organisations are rooted in the urban-isation of society that accompanied the Industrial Revolution. As population density increased in the towns that sprang up around new industries, the resultant insanitary conditions soon led to major public health problems. As few industrialists felt that they were responsible for the living conditions of their workers, governments and municipalities were forced to work together in the provision of infrastructure such as roads, clean water, sewage treatment and hospitals.

After World War II, the majority of the electorate were willing to accept the imposition of large scale taxation to support the ideological concept that the entire population of the nation had the right to expect equality of treatment in areas such as education, housing and health care. These rights were encap-sulated in the creation of the welfare state, which led to a massive expansion in the number of public sector bodies providing a diverse range of socially necessary services.

The deep trauma created by high levels of unemployment during the depression of the 1930s also resulted in many governments favouring the Keynesian idea that they should become involved in economic policies likely to maximise the number of people in work. Therefore, as well as using the infrastructures created to manage the welfare state as a source of employment, governments also acted to protect jobs by nationalising key industries such as steel, coal and the railways. In those cases where an industrial sector was unsuited to nationalisation (agriculture, for example), governments implemented actions such as the creation of trade boards to guarantee prices, tariff barriers to protect domestic firms from overseas competition and export subsidies to stimulate the achievement of a positive balance of payments.

By the 1970s, the utopian dream of full employment and 'cradle-to-grave' social care was developing into a political nightmare. The post-war expansion of public services had been made affordable by a period of unprecedented economic growth. However, as Western economies experienced a downturn during the OPEC oil crisis and inflation rates soared, governments found that the cost of supporting public sector services, nationalised industries and price guarantee schemes was greater than their ability to fund these operations through taxation. Furthermore, their solution of increased public sector borrowing further fueled the rate of inflation.

The inflation problem was compounded by the strength of the public sector unions who understandably were demanding wage increases to sustain the earning power of the members and ensure job security. Confrontations between workers and government became a regular occurrence (for example, the air traffic controllers' strike in the US; the hospital porters' industrial action in the UK which reduced the NHS merely to being a provider of emergency medical care).

By the 1980s, combating inflation through constraining the growth of public sector spending while seeking to re-inject an orientation of delivering an adequate level of services to the general public became a priority issue on the political agenda of many Western governments. The identified solution, popularised by Margaret Thatcher in the UK, was to seek ways of opening up the public sector to competition. This philosophy was based upon the view that organisations operating as monopolies or whose prices are guaranteed by some form of state intervention, face minimal pressure to act in a more entrepreneurial way to develop new, more innovative products, improve levels of customer service or introduce revised internal processes capable of reducing operating costs.

REMOVING STATE PROTECTION

New Zealand is a country that provides an excellent example of what happens when governments intervene in a free market economy. Up until the 1960s, New Zealand agriculture had a reputation for being highly entrepreneurial. The industry was then hit by a number of blows – such as the invention of nylon, that had an impact on the demand for wool and led to a severe reduction in the volume of sales to the UK following the UK's entry into the European Common Market (Walker 1989). In 1976, the Livestock Incentive Scheme was introduced which offered loan concessions through the Rural Bank to stimulate sheep production. As world market prices declined for wool, the government introduced supplementary minimum prices (SMPs), which resulted in farmers receiving payments from the government when market prices fell below a minimum guaranteed price. By the early 1980s, the way to succeed in New Zealand agriculture had nothing to do with the effective management of farm marketing operations. Instead, the accepted strategy was to buy more sheep in order to receive additional SMPs. Huge agricultural surpluses were created, and when a trade board such as the New Zealand Meat Board failed to find overseas markets for output, the surplus meat was rendered down into fertiliser.

The Minister of Finance, Roger Douglas, in the face of pressure from the International Monetary Fund (IMF) and the declining value of the country's currency, was forced to introduce a number of unconventional actions to rebuild the New Zealand economy. Price supports, tax incentives and cheap loans to farmers were scrapped. The industry went through a very difficult period and, in order to survive, began to develop new, more entrepreneurial business practices. By the 1990s, by revising farming practices, introducing new approaches to processing and developing new overseas markets, the sector has again become an economically viable, entrepreneurial sector of the New Zealand economy.

A similar outcome also occurred in the New Zealand forestry industry. In the 1980s, the Forest Service owned 55 per cent of all New Zealand's forests and sold output at low prices to assist the building industry. To encourage private sector planting also, the organisation offered private sector companies a 45 per cent grant towards operating costs. The concept of entrepreneurial exploitation of the country's prolific natural resources was apparently not an issue that concerned the Forest Service. As part of Roger Douglas's economic policy changes, the organisation was forced to open up the forests it owned and offer cutting rights to the private sector. This action immediately attracted both domestic and overseas entrepreneurs to the industry. These individuals recognised that opportunities existed in overseas markets not from trees, but from the finished products which could be made from the timber. New timber mills were built, along with board plants and factories producing wood veneer. By the mid-1990s, the revitalised industry was employing 28,000 people and the annual value of exports had risen to almost NZ$2 billion.

PRIVATISATION

Returning major state monopolies such as steel or telecommunications to the private sector has a number of appealing features to governments. First, they are no longer required to underwrite operating losses or fund new capital investments. Second, the sale of assets will provide an inflow to the exchequer and, third, if the operation continues to be poorly managed, the new management, not government, is to blame. What cannot be guaranteed is that privatisation will be accompanied by the emergence of an entrepreneurial spirit within the newly created organisations orientated to meeting the needs of the customer. On the evidence to date, it would appear that an entrepreneurial, customer-focused orientation will only develop where the privatised organisation faces competition from other private sector firms. Thus, for example, the privatisation of British Airways under the guidance of Lord King eventually led to the creation of an airline that, through innovative moves in areas such as upgrading all aspects of service quality, has become en extremely successful global player in the world's airline industry. A similar success story occurred in the case of British Steel, that moved a lumbering, commodity orientated steel producer to a market orientated firm that now leads the world in the application of innovative manufacturing processes to produce certain types of specialist steel products.

Another example is provided by the New Zealand Tourist Hotel Corporation (THC) which, at the time of privatisation, was reporting a loss of almost NZ$9 million. Over many years the Corporation had acquired hotels and built up an impressive array of resorts on prime sites around the country. By the 1980s, the hotels owned by the THC had a reputation for being run-down, providing poor service and offering somewhat mediocre meals. In 1990, the government therefore decided to privatise the THC. The operation was sold in its entirety to the Southern Pacific Hotel Corporation, an Australian and American-based hotel management group. The new owners implemented the dual strategy of investing in upgrading the physical assets of that part of their hotel portfolio which they wished to retain, while selling off the sites they felt were incompatible with their overall strategy. Buyers were selected on their capability to invest and upgrade the properties they wished to purchase. In only a few years, virtually every hotel formerly owned by the THC is now commercially successful and is contributing to New Zealand's growing image in the world travel market as a top tourist location.

However, success stories about the emergence of innovative, entrepreneurial firms following privatisation of utilities in various countries around the world are much rarer. It would appear that in virtually every case a key reason for no fundamental change in organisational behaviour is that, because of either legislation or the nature of sectoral structure, the monopoly powers these organisations enjoyed when part of the public sector have been retained in the years following privatisation. Under these circumstances the organisations are not really bothered about embedding a new, entrepreneurial spirit capable of delivering an adequate level of customer satisfaction.

A possible prime example of this scenario in the UK is provided by the water industry. After privatisation, many of these organisations appeared to adopt the conventional attitude of other poorly managed industrial conglomerates: seeking to maximise returns to shareholders and improving the salaries of senior management. Certainly their domestic customers have been provided with very little evidence of innovative behaviour in relation to the launch of new products or the development of innovative practices capable of reducing the cost of services. Thus, the only tangible outcome from privatisation has been that of water bills rising at a rate significantly higher than inflation.

The various regulators appointed by the UK government to oversee the activities of the privatised utilities have recognised that the retention of a monopoly market following privatisation does act as a potential barrier to stimulating entrepreneurial behaviour by the utilities. In recent years, therefore, they have persuaded governments to seek ways of introducing competition into these industries. Legislation has been passed in the gas industry, for example, which permits new firms offering gas supplies to enter the market using the same pipelines that were previously the sole preserve of the regional, privatised gas companies. The impact has been dramatic as the regional gas companies have been forced to introduce new, innovative internal organisational practices and to significantly upgrade the level of customer service in order to be in a position to counter the lower prices being offered by the new competition.

BARRIERS TO ENTREPRENEURIAL CHANGE

The efforts of governments to engender a more entrepreneurial spirit into those organisations that have remained within the public sector have not been very successful. The UK Conservative government, for example, attempted to engender a more competitive attitude into the NHS through the creation of an 'internal market' that was supposed to result in the emergence of a higher quality of care as providers competed for patients on the basis of their excellence in the delivery of medical services. Unfortunately, the consequent new structures that emerged to deliver this promise appeared merely to have created additional, more complex administrative systems which many would claim have been funded by diverting monies away from the actual delivery of health care services.

When one examines the financial implications of funding an equitable health care system in the face of factors such as the exponentially increasing costs of modern medicine and the ageing of populations, it is clear that answers will have to be found. If this does not occur, then many nations will enter the twenty-first century facing the scenario that (a) their entire public sector budget will be consumed in providing medical services to those in the population who cannot afford medical insurance, and (b) service quality will be perceived to have no relevance among the senior managers responsible for crafting the organisational strategy of matching minimal resources to ever-increasing demand. Should this outcome not be averted, financial crises will be triggered in other aspects of welfare provision such as education, unemployment benefit and education, as their resources are diverted into the provision of medical services. Thus, to quote Drucker (1985, p. 171), 'to build entrepreneurial management into existing public service institutions may thus be the foremost political task of this generation'.

Drucker's comment is a reflection of the fact that there exists some very fundamental obstacles that act as an effective barrier preventing politicians from being successful when trying to inject an entrepreneurial, market orientated philosophy into public sector institutions. These obstacles include:

- limited managerial vision
- an unwillingness to change structure
- financial inflexibility
- potential conflicting demands of stakeholders
- the influence of 'professionals' within the workforce
- the social role motivation of staff.

The obstacle of sustaining structure

The primary objective of any public sector institution is to spend the allocated annual budget rather than be seen to be achieving results. As a consequence, what drives these organisations is their ability to utilise all available funds, because this then permits them to argue for an ever-larger budget in future financial years. The implications of this scenario can be illustrated by the example provided by the New York public (that is, state-run) school system (Ravitch and Viteritti 1997). This sector, with nearly 120,000 employees and an $8 billion budget, is the largest government agency in the US located outside of Washington DC. At the top of this massive structure is a seven-member Board of Education appointed by the mayor and the city's five Borough Presidents. Responsibility for all aspects of the operation of New York's public schools rests with this organisation, including personnel, budgeting, building construction and maintenance, purchasing of supplies, delivery of in-school catering services, school safety and student transportation.

Various investigations over the years have revealed numerous examples of the inefficiencies of this bureaucracy which seems to exist to ensure its own survival rather to deliver high-quality education. In 1995, a special investigator found gross mismanagement within the catering operation. Out-dated and rancid food was being served to schoolchildren (for example, two-year-old turkeys and twenty-month-old beans). In the case of school supplies, most head teachers believed they could purchase supplies at much lower prices than those charged by the centralised procurement operation. In 1996, the

Manhattan District Attorney launched an investigation into building maintenance activities, having discovered that a $12 million lease agreement had been negotiated by an employee who then resigned from the board to work for the landlord who won the contract. Possibly the most telling evidence of poor management is reflected in a 1997 report by a Commissioner of Education that revealed a dramatic performance gap between New York schools and those in the rest of the state, even after taking into account the differences between the socio-economic characteristics of the students. For example, 89 per cent of all elementary schools in the city failed to meet the state's requirement that 90 per cent of a school's students achieve a minimum standard for basic reading skills.

Financial inflexibility

The solution of many social problems often requires a market response involving inputs from a multiplicity of public sector organisations (for example, the problem of truancy that will normally demand inputs from an education authority, schools, social services and the police to be resolved). Unfortunately, if each of these agencies perceives different priorities for how they allocate their funding against assigned tasks, then problems can arise because not all parties are willing to assign any of their budget to the resolution of a problem that requires a multi-agency, market orientated response. Further inflexibility can arise because the statutory controls or audit guidelines put into place to avoid abuses in the use of public sector monies often result in funds under one budget heading not being able to be utilised for an alternative, more appropriate form of expenditure (for example, a surplus in the annual budget for medical supplies not being permitted to be transferred across to fund a health education marketing campaign that over time could reduce the demand for medical services).

MULTIPLICITY OF STAKEHOLDERS

Whenever a policy maker or a manager within the public sector is considering implementing any form of change, it is always necessary to recognise that a diverse range of stakeholders exhibit different needs concerning the delivery of services to the market, and will expect to have their opinions heard in the debate that must occur prior to any decision being reached. These stakeholders will be drawn from the users, the service provider employees, the funding providers, the statutory bodies responsible for delivering current legislation, the politicians and, in many cases, the taxpayer. Thus, as illustrated by Figure

11.1, even a simple matter – such as a decision to reduce the number of courses being offered by a school in the face of falling enrolments – is likely to attract a diversity of stakeholders, all of whom feel that their opinions on serving future market needs must be heard before the portfolio of courses offered by the school can be revised.

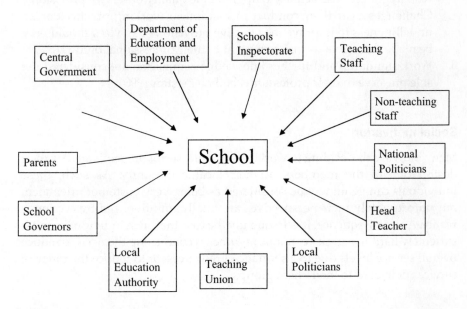

Figure 11.1 Stakeholders with an interest in acceptability of change within a school

The professionals

The term 'professional' is somewhat ambiguous, but in the main refers to individuals who are members of a professional body that sets minimum educational standards for membership. Although found in both private and public sector organisations, it tends to be the latter situation in which these individuals are rarely entrepreneurial and, in many cases, certainly do not perceive their primary role as including the responsibility for crafting strategies to meet the needs of their organisation's external customers more effectively. Consequently, these individuals often hold the following opinions that can act as an obstacle to change.

1. Their professional body should have a dominant influence on deciding what activities are considered acceptable working practices.

2. Further developing the technical skills of professionals should be placed ahead of any employer objectives concerning the provision of training that could lead to improved productivity or enhanced service delivery.
3. Other members of their profession are much more important and should receive stronger support than fellow employees from other professions who might propose actions to upgrade the quality of service provision.
4. Challenges over their conduct in relation to working practices or an unwillingness to improve the effective provision of services should only be made through a formal complaint to their professional body.
5. Work standards and further knowledge acquisition are considered the sole preserve of their professional body (Chaston 1993).

Social motivation

Many individuals deciding to work in the public sector are motivated by their desire to help the members of their local community. As such, these individuals can genuinely be considered as being very customer orientated, but unfortunately their perspectives are totally uninfluenced by economic reality. As a consequence, it is frequently the case that such individuals find it extremely hard to accept economic arguments concerning the need to reduce overall service levels due to a shortage of resources, or to reduce the range of services delivered to their client groups.

REVITALISING PUBLIC SECTOR SERVICES

As described earlier in this text, the most successful private sector companies are those which change and adapt to changing market circumstances. Regretfully, many public sector institutions do the reverse. They hold on to ways of doing things even when these are clearly out-dated or obsolete, and only accept the need for change in their approach to the marketing of services when confronted by a massive crisis. Even then the first reaction is typically the defensive one of seeking to retain out-moded conventions and create barriers to obstruct the implementation of actions to revise service provision portfolios or restructure working practices as a route by which to improve the quality of service delivery.

For most governments, there are few additional gains to be achieved by sustaining the 1980s ethos of seeking to introduce further fundamental rationalisations, restructuring the operation of entire sectors of service or privatising any more public sector bodies. Thus, if public sector organisations are to be revitalised in order that a viable, customer orientated welfare state can be sustained in a rapidly changing world where financial resources can be expect to remain severely constrained, then policy makers and managers must acquire the ability to act more entrepreneurially. In most cases, this objective cannot be achieved by importing conventional business practices from the private sector. It is usually the case that these practices are totally inappropriate for the problems confronting public sector organisations. Instead, the public sector service providers need to evolve their own style of entrepreneurship suited to the management of the obstacles and circumstances confronting their organisations.

One facet of public sector entrepreneurship relates to the issue of reviewing the current validity of the aims and visions of the organisation, because these may no longer be appropriate for effectively guiding the future provision of customer orientated services. Additionally, because of the multiplicity of stakeholders, the public sector entrepreneur will need to have the ability to bring people together, many of whom will initially hold conflicting opinions about the validity of a specific action. Thus, the public sector entrepreneur endeavouring to implement changes in marketing practices will usually have to to work willing in partnership with numerous other individuals and organisations. In many cases, this will mean working outside the boundaries of their own institutions and being able to persuade these other organisations of the advantages of sharing scarce resources. Associated with this adoption of a more collaborative attitude will be the need to be able to reject the conventional perspective that appropriate service delivery skills exist only in the public sector and to accept instead that properly guided and socially responsible private sector organisations may be able to provide a more effective solution in the future provision of services.

To achieve such goals, public sector organisations often have to be willing to accept revisions to internal structures. The poor innovators in the public sector tend to be those organisations that are hierarchical, departmentalised and unwilling to delegate authority to the actual service provider working at the supplier–customer interface. In order to implement a more entrepreneurial approach to service provision effectively, these organisations must delayer management, break down barriers between departments, introduce decentralisation as a mechanism to relocate services nearer to the location of the customer, and delegate much greater authority to the staff responsible for the actual delivery of services.

DELIVERING AN ENTREPRENEURIAL SERVICE VISION

When Norma Redfearn became Headmistress of West Walker Primary School in 1986, pupil numbers were falling and only six of the eighteen classrooms were still in use. The school is located in an area of urban deprivation with high unemployment rates, and many of the local population are in receipt of state benefits. Norma Redfearn's entrepreneurial vision was that the school should become the focal point for urban renewal by acting as a centre for delivering initiatives to improve health, housing, the environment and the employment prospects of the local population. Clearly, her perspective of a school was not the conventional one of a building used to house children during term time, but a resource that exists for, and should be used by, the entire local community (Leadbetter and Goss 1997).

Her starting point was to begin talking with the parents to gain their views on what they wanted from the school, and at the same time to gain their support for upgrading facilities such as the rundown, desolate playground. One of the first actions stimulated by these discussions was that the parents became actively involved in the conversion of the playground from an unattractive, muddy area into an all-weather playpark. Once created, this was then made available to children on a year-round basis, not just between 9 a.m. and 4 p.m. during term time.

At an away-day, school staff and parents discussed how the school facilities might be utilised for the wider benefit of the entire community. One idea was to convert the empty classrooms into a 'community wing' that would allow parents to participate in further education. However, this plan immediately encountered resistance from the conventionally minded local education authority, that felt that adult education could not be delivered in a primary school; if parents wanted such classes they should travel to the local community college. Only by the intervention of local politicians and the willingness of another department in the local authority – the leisure department – to make funds available, was Norma Redfearn able to fulfil her unconventional vision of changing her school into a family learning centre.

The school now offers a wide range of facilities and services to the local community. A cafe has been created that is open to both parents and children, and it offers a breakfast club for the more socially deprived children who arrive at school without having had breakfast. Funding has been achieved by attracting sponsorship from local firms. Again, the conventionalists in the council refused to help on the grounds that the scheme did not fulfil the criteria of being a genuine health care initiative.

The community wing contains an adult library, a computer room for both children and parents, and a training room that delivers classes in subjects such as assertiveness, keep fit, sewing, counselling and parenting skills. The community wing is also a means of bringing local authority services nearer to the customer. There is an urban park next to the school, and the ranger who manages the site has an office in the school – this enables the provision of nature classes to people visiting the urban park. The social services department has an office where a social worker works with single parents and families in cases involving abuse or social deprivation. Service provision effectiveness is seen to be much higher because the social worker is in the community rather than an office some miles away at the local council's headquarters. Additionally, parents receive formal training in child care. This has enabled the opening of a crèche in the community wing that offers parents somewhere safe to leave their children while they attend training courses to acquire skills to enhance their prospects of employment.

The new social skills acquired by parents have resulted in their decision to become involved in the renewal of the rundown housing stock in the area. A group of parents considering a project to create a local community garden realised that there was the added opportunity of building new houses. They approached two large housing associations with their idea, and the outcome has been the construction of a new housing development on a derelict site directly opposite the school. This in turn has created a whole new group of families with access to the community learning centre, that was once simply a poorly performing primary school.

VISIONING URBAN RENEWAL

In recent years, many major cities have faced increasing demand for social services and a concurrent downturn in tax revenues as industries have closed or moved away. This has led to problems in funding the provision of adequate transportation, education and crime prevention services, which in many cases has caused residents to relocate to less socially deprived areas outside the city.

The conventional response of many city managers has been to accept the emergence of inner-city wastelands as an inevitable and irreversible trend. Some cities, however, have adopted the view that by adopting an entrepreneurial attitude it is possible to rebuild inner cities as vibrant and socially attractive neighbourhoods (Koerner 1998). The Canadian city of Vancouver, for example, adopted the view that it must find a way of attracting families from the suburbs back into the city. Its solution was to rezone large areas of waterfront, formerly littered with railyards and derelict warehouses, for housing. New construction projects are required to include 25 per cent of units suitable for families with small children and to include the provision of day care facilities and playgrounds. Walking routes are also demanded that allow children to travel from home to school avoiding major traffic arteries. Additionally, plans involving new high-rise buildings are not looked upon with favour and developers are encouraged to create row housing and visually appealing streetscapes.

Further examples of entrepreneurial thinking are witnessed in the US. In Minneapolis, Minnesota, the secret to success has been an enlightened approach to the management of inner-city parks. Unlike other cities where the conventional trend is for parks to become rundown, crime-ridden 'no-go' areas, Minneapolis has a Park and Recreation Board that operates independently of the city government. It has the power to issue its own bonds and the budget is not under the control of local politicians. As a result, the Board has remained free from funds being diverted away into other welfare services favoured by local politicians, leaving it able to focus on investing in upgrading park facilities, which in turn has attracted private developers wishing to build new homes close to these attractive inner-city leisure areas.

Possibly an even more powerful example of entrepreneurial thinking is provided by Chattanooga, Tennessee, which in 1969 was labelled by the federal government as the dirtiest city in the US. The reason for this situation was the high level of pollution generated by local factories and steel foundries. In 1984, the city launched Vision 2000, a 20-week series of community meetings with interested citizens. This led to the foundation of the Chattanooga Neighborhood Network that forged partnerships with the private sector to clean up and revitalise the city's riverfront. This was followed by new housing developments and the creation of the world's largest fleet of eco-friendly electric buses. As a result of these actions, families are now beginning to relocate from the suburbs back to the city.

Tilburg, in the Netherlands, provides a European example of revising city management philosophies. When the steel industry collapsed in the 1970s, this was followed by massive increases in local taxes accompanied by a decline in the quality of public services. The city moved to streamline local government operations by offering early retirement to staff and semi-privatisation of the local utilities. The remaining employees were required to consider the citizens as customers and to adopt an entrepreneurial attitude in developing plans capable of achieving year-on-year actions to improve the quality of delivered services. By 1988, the city had achieved a budget surplus which was re-invested in the construction of a soccer stadium and a concert hall.

Melbourne, Australia, is another city where a 13-year entrepreneurial overhaul has completely revitalised the downtown areas. Planning rules were changed to block the further construction of high-rise buildings, which meant that speculative developers were no longer interested in building large office blocks. Additionally, the city encouraged developers to work on refurbishing the existing Victorian buildings by offering reduced land taxes and simplifying building regulations. Fortunately, the urban planners had left the trolley tracks in the downtown area intact; today, trams once again criss-cross the city, providing a cheap, clean and efficient public transport system. By the 1990s, over 50,000 residents had relocated to the residential areas of the downtown business district – a fivefold increase on the previous decade.

ENTREPRENEURIAL PARTNERING

Gone are the days when local authorities in the UK could afford to fund significant capital expenditure projects to upgrade the provision of local services by actions such as redeveloping shopping centres or providing the community with new recreational facilities. The outcome is that the more conventional councils simply accept that they cannot consider new building projects. The result is an ongoing decline in the fabric of the facilities and the quality of services are available to the local communities.

An entrepreneurial exception to this attitude of resigned acceptance to prevailing circumstances is provided by the Kirklees Metropolitan Authority (Leadbetter and Goss 1997). Its solution was to examine how, by the formation of partnerships with commercial organisations, it could continue to improve the provision of services by building new facilities for use by local residents. Its first major move was to work with the Henry Boot building company to redevelop council property for housing, retail and industrial use. One of its major projects has been the redevelopment of Huddersfield city centre. In this case, the council's reward for being involved in the scheme is that it receives a share of the profits generated by the project.

Possibly the council's most impressive achievement has been its involvement in the McAlpine Stadium, providing a new facility for Huddersfield's football and rugby clubs. Neither the football nor the rugby club was in a position to refurbish its existing facilities, because both were facing falling gate receipts from matches. The Kirklees Metropolitan Authority realised that the success of local football and rugby is important to a town's morale and economy. Working with Henry Boot, the council developed a plan to generate funds by redeveloping the Huddersfield Town Football Club grounds as a retail park. These monies provided the seedcorn capital to then raise £8 million to create a joint company, the Kirklees Stadium Development Ltd, of which 40 per cent is owned by the council, 40 per cent by the football club and 20 per cent by the rugby club. The council identified a tract of derelict land close to the city centre that would be suitable for its purposes, and the joint company designed, constructed and now manages a multi-use stadium. This facility – hosting sporting events, music concerts and exhibitions – is estimated to have had the added benefit of creating around 1,000 new jobs.

ENTREPRENEURIAL RESTRUCTURING

As illustrated in Figure 11.2, the conventional approach to the provision of welfare services is for public sector organisations to be departmentally structured and located in a single location. Local residents then have to travel a considerable distance to gain access to services, and even when they arrive at the central location, often waste hours trying to find the department responsible for the delivery of the desired service. This situation has, for example, recently been highlighted by the UK Audit Commission's analysis of the police service, in which they concluded that the majority of police stations are in the wrong location and that as a result, the general public faces severe difficulties gaining access to police services.

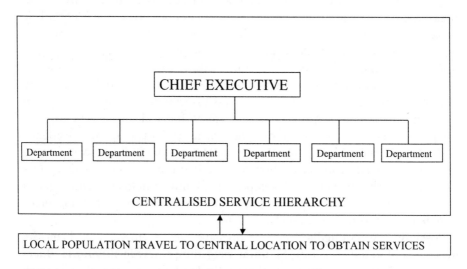

Figure 11.2   Traditional centralised local government structure

One unconventional public sector organisation that has already recognised the weaknesses associated with departmentalised, centralised structures is South Somerset District Council (Leadbetter and Goss, 1997). Its entrepreneurial decision has been to disband the traditional, hierarchical departmental structure. It also rationalised its committee structure as a mechanism for significantly reducing the amount of time the council officers spend in activities such as organising committee meetings or writing lengthy reports in response to questions by committee members. The objective of these actions was to acquire the ability to reallocate a much greater proportion of available resources to serving the needs of the local population.

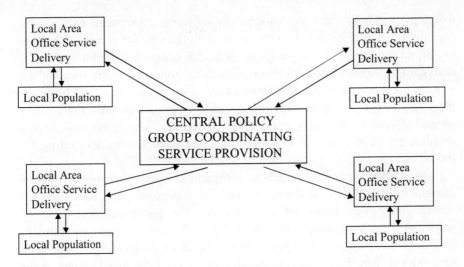

Figure 11.3 Decentralised local government structure to deliver services in required locations

In 1995, the council implemented possibly its most unconventional action by reorganising frontline staff into area teams and moving its entire service provision out into the community via the creation of four area offices (Figure 11.3). Within these local offices, environmental health officers, housing staff, benefit officers and leisure facility managers all work in close proximity to each other, thereby creating a cross-functional, team-based approach to problem resolution. The outcome is that residents now have immediate access to services in their local community and, even more importantly, council officers are encouraged to involve the residents in decisions that may impact on service provision in an area. Empowered council employees are able to initiate actions such as establishing service outlets in libraries and local shopping centres. Politicians who previously spent their time in committees have now become involved in assisting local projects and guiding consultation processes with residents on designing services that are customised to actual market need. Another important benefit that has emerged is that local residents are more willing to become involved in assisting the service provision process through actions such as managing their own building estates and being willing to manage self-building schemes.

ENTREPRENEURIAL SERVICE DELIVERY

The medical profession has always been a somewhat conventional animal, tending to focus on seeking ways of upgrading the effective delivery of existing treatments and at the same time being unprepared to consider revising the actual service delivery process. In the UK, for example, the conventional structure for the provision of health care is that 'primary care' is delivered by GPs operating local surgeries that provide treatment for standard ailments. If a patient requires specialist care or a surgical operation, he or she is referred to the local hospital which is staffed by specialist consultants. These latter individuals are seen as the 'experts' within the system and have a dominant influence of how and where medical resource are allocated within the NHS.

In the 1980s, as part of the UK government's endeavours to improve the efficiency of the NHS, GPs were offered the opportunity to acquire greater control over the allocation of resources by becoming 'fundholders' responsible for managing their own budgets. The more entrepreneurial GPs perceived this change as an opportunity to break down the demarcation lines that exist within the medical profession and to deliver locally some of the medical services that hospital clinicians had previously regarded jealously as solely their area of responsibility. Some of the fundholding GPs have sought to create a more holistic approach to medicine, and, by merging their activities with other arms of the welfare state, also a more effective delivery of a broad range of social services. In some clinics, patients thus have immediate access to social workers, specialist nurses and counsellors. GPs have also begun to offer new facilities such an on-site diagnostic services (medical tests, X-rays, and so on) and now undertake minor surgery such as cataract operations that would previously have been performed on the patient only at his or her local hospital.

Moving medical services out of hospitals and expanding the responsibilities of primary care providers is not unique to the UK. Other countries have also recognised that the move offers the dual benefits of localising service provision delivery and reducing the need for costly stays in hospital. However, one potential barrier is that most medical schools are still biased towards the medical conventions that there is greater status and career opportunities for students training as specialist clinicians. As a result, most graduates from these institutions lack the skills necessary to work in the field of primary care.

In the US, one institution that has broken with conventional educational practice is Case Western Reserve (Sanoff 1995). In recognition of the growing shortage of primary care doctors, the college has dramatically altered both syllabuses and teaching practices. Approximately one-third of students are now enrolled specifically to study primary care. The programme recognises that these individuals need to develop their abilities to work with a diverse range of patients, and that, for many patients, there is a requirement to resolve both their medical and their social problems. In their final year, instead of rotating through several medical specialties such as surgery and paediatrics, students work with the Henry Ford Health System. Case Western pairs the student with an experienced primary care provider and in this way exposes the student to the four medical areas of primary and preventive care, acute and emergency care, tertiary care and critical care. Formal studies have also been changed. Instead of concentrating on advances in medical technology, students are exposed to concepts such as maintaining the health of large populations, working in teams rather than as an individual practitioner, and developing skills in using computers to gather data on both illness and treatment patterns.

GUIDELINES FOR SUCCESSFUL ENTREPRENEURIAL ACTIONS

For the politician or public sector manager seeking to implement entrepreneurial actions capable of enhancing the delivery of affordable, high-quality welfare state services, experience gained in the marketplace has provided the basis for evolving some very clear and specific guidelines. These have been summarised extremely effectively by one of the world's most entrepreneurial political leaders, the former New Zealand Finance Minister, Roger Douglas. In his book *Unfinished Business* (1993), he tabled the following ten principles for implementing entrepreneurial reform.

1. Programmes will only succeed if led by high-quality people with the capability to act as visionary leaders.
2. Initiatives should be implemented in quantum leaps and not phased in gradually over time. In this way one avoids the opposition mobilising their defences to defeat the proposed reforms.
3. Speed is essential so that the general public can clearly perceive immediate benefit in the proposed reform.
4. Once momentum has been achieved, do not permit anybody to create obstacles that can impede progress.
5. Public sector staff must exhibit consistency and credibility if they wish to build confidence among the general public.
6. Openly publish timetables so that the general public can clearly comprehend both the final aims of a programme and the time which will be needed to achieve these aims.
7. Treat the general public with respect and involve them in honest, open debate over the issues associated with the proposed reform.

8. Be prepared to accept responsibility when projects go wrong.
9. Imposition of new regulations will rarely resolve any problem.
10. Adopt a long-term perspective and do not implement short-term actions because these appear to offer political expediency that will result in retaining the confidence of the general public.

OUTSTANDING AGENDAS

The Western world has only just begun to consider entrepreneurial actions aimed at sustaining a viable, affordable welfare state capable of maintaining the delivery of high-quality services. There are consequently a number of key agenda issues where further thought and experimentation will be demanded as the world enters the new millennium. The following are some of the more urgent issues.

1. Evolving systems whereby the socially deprived members of society can continue to be assisted in ways that (a) avoid the development of a dependency culture, and (b) can be funded without the imposition of high taxes.
2. The delivery of a much higher standard of education that both prepares children effectively for future employment and provides parents with the right to individual choice in the selection of the schooling available to their children.
3. The creation of systems to ensure that everybody enjoys an adequate level of income in retirement.
4. The provision of high-quality, affordable health care services for all members of society.

REFERENCES

Chaston, I. (1993), *Customer Focused Marketing*, McGraw-Hill, London.
Douglas, R. (1993), *Unfinished Business*, Random House, Auckland, New Zealand.
Leadbetter, C. and Goss, S. (1997), *Civic Entrepreneurship*, Demos, London.
Drucker, P.F. (1985), *Innovation and Entrepreneurship*, Butterworth-Heinemann, London.
Koerner, B.I. (1998), 'Cities that work', *US News*, 6 August, pp. 1–3.
Ravitch, D. and Viteritti, J.P. (1997), *The New Schools for a New Century*, Yale University Press, CT.
Sanoff, A.P. (1995), 'A dose of primary care', *US News*, 20 March, p. 14.
Walker, S. (1989) *Rogernomics: Reshaping New Zealand's Economy*, SP Books, Auckland.

12

LEARNING, KNOWLEDGE PLATFORMS AND NETWORKS

INTRODUCTION

During the 1970s, Sony's engineers attempted to produce a small, portable, non-aural recorder called the Pressman, designed for use by reporters for recording interviews (Nayak and Ketteringham 1986). The small size of the final design left no room for a recording system, so the engineers were left with a tape recorder that could not record. Sony's founder, Masura Ibuka, saw the product and thought that it produced an excellent sound. He suggested that if headphones were used to replace the speakers, battery life would be extended. His proposal was prompted by the fact that he was also aware that another group of engineers had developed some very small headphones.

Two machines were produced for use by Masura and the Sony Chairman, Akio Morita; both of whom carried them around to listen to music. The development engineers and company managers were resistant to the idea that the product had any commercial potential. Masura, however, exerted his influence as company founder and insisted that the machine be put into production. Sony commenced manufacture of the Walkman product – and the rest is history.

Organisational learning

In the Sony Walkman affair, the engineers and managers were exhibiting what Argyris and Schon (1978) have labelled as single-loop or 'adaptive' learning. Essentially, their orientation was focused towards incremental improvements based upon past experience. As a result there was no attempt to question fundamental assumptions (for example, 'recorders must be able to record'). Sustaining current ways of working and focusing on improving existing product forms continued to be the primary orientation of the development team. Thus when confronted by a problem, they applied prior experience and knowledge to the problem, with the consequent conclusion that their solution had no potential commercial application, as shown in Figure 12.1.

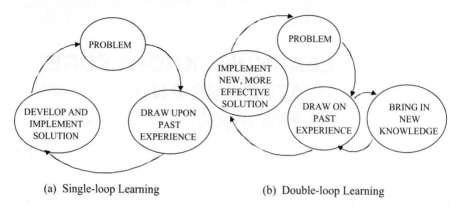

(a) Single-loop Learning   (b) Double-loop Learning

Figure 12.1   Alternative learning styles

The alternative, as demonstrated by Masura Ibuka, is to adopt a double-loop or 'generative' learning approach to problem solving. As shown in the Figure. This means that when a problem emerges, during the analysis new knowledge is sought which can be brought to the situation. This new knowledge will often be critically important in the formulation of a more effective, entrepreneurial solution.

As stressed throughout this text, world markets are changing rapidly and competitive pressures are increasing at an exponential rate. The entrepreneurial organisation is one which seeks to review structures and processes frequently in order to implement adaptive actions capable of exploiting newly emerging opportunities. This view is supported by Nystrom and Starbuck (1984) who have posited that to retain adaptability, organisations need to experiment continually with new ways of doing business. Drawing upon such perspectives, writers such as Senge (1990) have evolved the concept of 'organisational learning', which describes the processes whereby employees continually strive to acquire and exploit new knowledge as the basis for proactively responding to change, complexity and uncertainty.

The theoretical foundations of exploiting organisational learning to enhance the competences of both employees and entire organisations can be traced back to the work of Cyert and March (1963), Bateson (1972), March and Olsen (1988) and Argyris and Schon (1978). Over the last few years the literature on this topic has grown rapidly, attracting interest from a diverse range of academic perspectives. Easterby-Smith (1997), in his review of the theoretical roots from which the subject has evolved, suggests that there have been contributions from the following perspectives.

1. *Psychology/organisational development*, which focuses on the issues of the hierarchical nature of learning, adjusting individual learning to suit

organisational learning needs and recognition of the importance of cognitive maps underlying the thinking process.

2. *Management science*, where the primary concern is with the creation, utilisation and dissemination of information.

3. *Strategic management*, which is concerned with how the principles of learning can lead to competitive advantage and how the capability of firms to learn can permit new responses to changing market circumstances.

4. *Production management*, where the primary concern is with the use of productivity as a measure of learning and the impact of organisational design on the learning process.

5. *Sociology*, where the interest is directed towards the broader issues of the nature of learning, the processes which underpin it and how organisational realities such as power, politics and conflict impact on process.

6. *Cultural anthropology*, where the primary concern is the importance of values and beliefs, especially as these relate to the cultural differences that exist in different societies and the impact these may have on the learning process.

Given the increasing academic interest in organisational learning, it is perhaps not surprising that numerous definitions have been presented in the literature. Schein (1996) has concluded that as a result, there is considerable confusion about what is really meant by the term. In the context of this text, the author feels that it is appropriate to follow Schein's guidance that in discussing organisational learning, the concern is with studying how companies utilise, change and develop corporate knowledge.

Possibly the most frequently mentioned issue in the literature on organisational learning is the need to adopt an appropriate learning style. In those cases where markets are stable and customers are seeking standard products or services from suppliers, firms can be expected to exhibit 'single-loop learning', Regretfully, there is a tendency in the organisational learning literature always to condemn single-loop learning as an inappropriate learning style. However, a more reasoned and balanced case has been presented by Ayas (1996). He suggests that there is no one best way for organisations to learn, and that learning style should reflect the operational needs of the organisation. Thus, for example, a non-entrepreneurial manufacturer that has adopted a transactional marketing style would probably choose to operate in a relatively stable market, to produce standard components and to focus primarily on offering adequate quality goods at a competitive price. In such circumstances, assuming that the organisational systems are based around repetition of routine procedures, then the firm would probably be well advised to follow Fiol and Lyles's (1985) advice of focusing upon creating a single-loop learning environment as the most appropriate way for sustaining employee development aimed at optimising organisational efficiency.

In those market situations where firms face periods of significant, discontinuous change and/or there is a desire to differentiate the firm from competition through the adoption of a entrepreneurial marketing style, under these circumstances a more innovative learning orientation may be more appropriate (Nevis et al. 1995). For this type of organisation, a more appropriate learning style would be to adopt a double-loop orientation because this permits the exploitation of new knowledge to evolve new practices, perspectives and operational frameworks. Such organisations can truly be considered 'knowledge-creating' companies whose sole business is continuous innovation. Although scales to differentiate between single-loop and double-loop (or higher-order) learning can be found in many of the texts on the subject, in virtually every case it would appear that, although recommended as appropriate by the author, no real attempt is ever made to validate their application as an effective research tool. An exception to this situation was found in the case of a scale developed by Badger et al. (1998). This scale was evolved from a detailed review of the literature, and was subsequently tested extensively in both the large and small firm sectors. The authors suggest that double-loop learning is characterised by the following behaviours.

1. Constructive feedback is given to all employees on how they are doing in their task roles.
2. Employees are encouraged to undertake training and development activities.
3. Employees share training/development learning lessons with others.
4. Employees share knowledge and resources.
5. Company goals are communicated clearly to all employees.
6. Employees, suppliers and customers are all encouraged to let the firm know if anything is going wrong.
7. Employees are not afraid to voice differing opinions.
8. The company is always willing to change working practices.
9. The company is continually on the lookout for new ideas from any source (Badger et al. 1998).

Nonaka (1991) has proposed that new knowledge begins with the individual. This is then incorporated into both existing knowledge and new knowledge from other sources to provide the basis for new products and processes. He has proposed that knowledge exists in two forms: tacit and explicit. Tacit knowledge is vested within individual employees and consists of the informal, hard-to-define elements that are often referred to as 'know-how'. Explicit knowledge is the formalised and systematically collated information which is openly available to all within the organisation. In entrepreneurial, knowledge-creating companies, there exists a continuous, dynamic interaction between tacit and explicit knowledge. In many cases, during the early stages of a project, the nature of the tacit–explicit interchange is not clearly defined; but, as understanding grows, a clear vision of purpose will then emerge which is used to guide the activities of teams engaged in implementing entrepreneurial projects.

From his studies of Japanese companies, Nonaka (1991) has concluded that an important element of organisational design is to create redundancy through the overlapping of information sources, business activities and managerial responsibilities. His view is that redundancy is critical because it encourages higher levels of dialogue and communication, thus ensuring the effective exchange of tacit knowledge. This risk in this situation is that there will probably exist some degree of confusion and chaos as employees in different parts of the organisation acquire and process information from a diversity of different sources. However, the important outcome is the richness of information being accumulated; but this knowledge can only be exploited if managers are capable of orchestrating this apparently chaotic situation by conceptualising a systematic process that can lead to the development of a viable entrepreneurial idea. In many cases this is achieved through the creation of a 'conceptual umbrella'. For example, the Sharp corporation used the umbrella concept of 'optoelectrics' to combine knowledge from liquid crystal displays (LCDs) and metal oxide semiconductors to invent the first low-power electronic calculator. The firm has subsequently sustained this umbrella to develop additional entrepreneurial products, such as pocketbook organisers and LCD projection systems.

COMPETENCES AND LEARNING

Hamel and Prahalad (1994) suggest that just being a learning organisation is not sufficient. Their view is that the learning process must be translated into managerial competences which permit the firm to serve customer needs more effectively. In writings on entrepreneurial behaviour in service markets, for example, a common thread linking various streams of research on relationship marketing is that the philosophy should be perceived as being more complex than transactional marketing because it requires all employees to exhibit a higher level of competence in managing interactions with customers.

In the face of this complexity, various authors (for example, Gronroos 1997, Berry 1981, Christopher et al. 1991) have commented upon the critical importance of exploiting organisational learning in order to orchestrate the activities of all employees within an entrepreneurial organisation to ensure that the external customer receives a satisfactory service experience. In terms of optimising these internal processes, these researchers have proposed that this will require employees to become involved in learning aimed at assisting them to acquire a much broader range of competences than those demanded of their counterparts in conventional-transactional marketing organisations.

The issue of higher levels of competence has also been noted by researchers concerned with the management of customer relationships within supply chain scenarios. Kalwani and Narayandas (1995) and Moller and Wilson (1995) have suggested that entrepreneurial suppliers seeking to build closer links between themselves and key customers will need to create an intra-organisational environment in which employees are flexible, prepared to take decisions without referring back to management, self-responsible and able to communicate effectively with their counterparts in customer organisations.

Ford et al. (1997) and Buzzel and Ortmeyer (1996) have commented on the issue of organisational competence in relation to the role of information management in supporting the effective operation of organisations. They suggest that moves to form closer supplier–customer relationships are typically accompanied by the need for the creation of sophisticated information systems for the rapid and detailed interchange of data between organisations. Earlier, Huber (1991) had explicitly identified that the key role of information systems within the processes associated with organisational learning is to support organisational memory. This may be a valid perspective in an unchanging, conventional organisation, but within entrepreneurial organisations, one can usually expect the information systems also to assist in the areas of new knowledge acquisition, distributing information to both employees and customers, and the interpretation of processes such as order patterns or delivery problems.

The importance of employees exploiting new knowledge to optimise customer relationships had been noted earlier by Bell (1973). He proposed that the information and knowledge acquired by employees is now more important than the more traditional orientation of assuming that the technology contained within the firm's fixed capital assets can provide the basis for delivering products superior to competition. Woodruff (1977) also concluded that learning about the marketplace is an activity central to entre-preneurial firms seeking to offer greater customer-based value. Similar views have been expressed by Slater and Narver (1994). They believe that the skills learned by employees that are difficult to imitate provide the source of entre-preneurial competitive advantage that can permit the organisation to offer superior value by building closer relationships with customers.

LEARNING SYSTEMS

To gain further understanding of how organisations orchestrate the acquisition and exploitation of knowledge, DiBella et al. (1996) undertook an in-depth study of four different organisations: Electricité de France, Fiat, Motorola and the Mutual Investment corporation. From collected case materials, they concluded that an effective learning system consisted of seven elements, described in Figure 12.2.

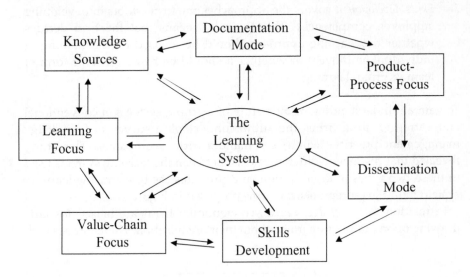

Figure 12.2 Elements supporting a learning system

1. The *knowledge source* is defined by the extent to which organisations prefer to develop new knowledge internally versus exploiting ideas from external sources.
2. The *product-process focus* describes a preference for the accumulation of knowledge related to products and services versus an orientation towards investing in knowledge to improve the processes that support internal organisational activities.
3. The *documentation mode* covers the systems whereby the organisation stores knowledge. At one extreme, knowledge may reside inside the minds of employees; and, at the other, all knowledge may be carefully documented within detailed company operating manuals.
4. The *dissemination mode* describes how the organisation manages the transfer of knowledge between employees. One possibility is to create a highly structured, formalised approach whereby insights are shared

across the entire organisation. Another approach is to adopt a more informal attitude, leaving employees to decide whether they wish to share knowledge with others who constitute the project team of which they are a part.

5. The *learning focus* describes the learning style utilised within the organisation and can be of a single-loop or double-loop variety.

6. The *value-chain focus* indicates in which areas of the value chain (marketing, manufacturing, design, logistics, and so on) the firm concentrates the majority of its learning activities.

7. *Skills development* covers the approaches the firm adopts in developing employee competences. This typically means that the firm decides whether the learning approach should be focused on the training of individual employees or whether it should be based on some form of team or group learning.

To gain an understanding of the nature of learning systems in conventional and entrepreneurial firms, the author undertook a survey of knowledge management practices within UK manufacturing companies. This study revealed that distinctive differences exist between the learning systems used in these two types of organisation, and provides the basis for the learning system found in entrepreneurial firms proposed in Figure 12.3.

In relation to *knowledge sources*, conventional firms are biased towards drawing upon information from within their organisation. This contrasts with

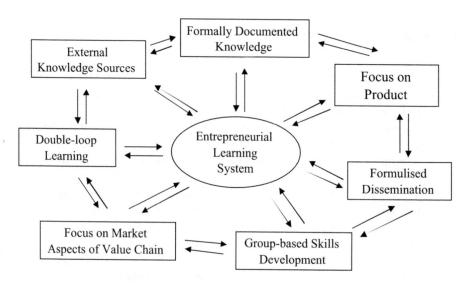

Figure 12.3 An entrepreneurial learning system

entrepreneurial firms that are biased towards exploiting knowledge sources external to the organisation. Bias in the case of entrepreneurial firms in relation to the issue of the *product–process focus* is towards ongoing development of products or customer services, whereas conventional firms usually seek ways of further upgrading internal organisational processes. On the issue of *documentation mode*, the conventional firms adopt a somewhat informal approach to knowledge storage, whereas entrepreneurial firms tend to create a formalised, central record system to act as a repository of key information critical to the effective operation of the organisation's memory system. Accompanying this latter approach to knowledge collation, entrepreneurial firms favour the creation of formal systems for their *dissemination mode* to ensure that information is shared between all employees. In contrast, conventional firms appear to adopt a somewhat informal orientation, apparently assuming that individuals will share knowledge with each other on an 'as needed' basis.

The *learning focus* of conventional firms is orientated towards single-loop learning. Similar to views expressed by other researchers, the study of UK entrepreneurial manufacturing firms revealed that their learning focus is double-loop; seeking to draw in new knowledge as the basis for enhancing the effectiveness of their problem solving activities. In relation to the *value-chain focus*, conventional firms focus their attention on activities associated with improving the efficiencies of internal organisational processes further. Entrepreneurial firms appear to be biased towards seeking to add value to those dimensions of the value chain concerned with offering greater value to customers. Management of *skills development* in entrepreneurial firms is centred on improving the competences of work teams. This is contrasted with conventional firms, where training is directed towards upgrading the capabilities of individuals within the workforce.

KNOWLEDGE PLATFORMS

Once a company decides to embrace electronic commerce, or 'e-commerce', as a path by which to exploit new, entrepreneurial opportunities, an immediate outcome is that the organisation's knowledge platform becomes much more closely linked with other knowledge sources elsewhere within the market system, such as suppliers and customers. The reason why this occurs is that once buyers and sellers become electronically linked with each other, the volume of data interchange dramatically increases as trading activities begin to occur in real time. The outcome is the emergence of highly dynamic, rapid responses by both customer and supplier to changing circumstances within the market system.

There are a number of new forms of knowledge exchange which can result from the creation of an e-commerce system. The platform permits a much fuller interchange of information between supplier and customer about the nature of product benefits and attributes being offered to the market. Furthermore, the data interchange can be interactive and customised to meet the specific knowledge needs of each customer. Hewlett-Packard, for example, has a system that helps the customer to select the best printer option by asking questions about needs (price, need for colour, speed of printing, and so on). The answers enable the system to presents a customised version of the company catalogue, recommending what the company believes to be the best solution for the customer.

Where the customer is seeking significant volumes of additional information that is hard to acquire through more traditional distribution channels, the e-commerce platform is also able to meet the customer's demands for larger volumes of additional knowledge. Virtual Vineyards, for example, is an online supplier that provides details on its winery, the type and quality of the wine, and which wine is best served with which food. As far as the supplier is concerned, an additional benefit offered by an e-commerce platform is that it provides a much more cost-effective medium through which to deliver vast quantities of knowledge when compared to more conventional channels such as mailing catalogues or communicating by telephone.

E-commerce platforms are also able to deliver instant knowledge that is especially critical in those situations where rapidly changing conditions require rapid decision making. Thus, for example, online stock market trading enables the customer instantly to acquire the data needed to determine how to act in those situations where new, emergent trends in the financial markets indicate a need to consider either the immediate purchase or sale of an investment portfolio.

In addition, by tracking and storing every aspect of a customer's search activities and purchase decision, knowledge systems allow the supplier to acquire a profile on the buying behaviour of every individual with whom the firm has had contact. Once this knowledge reaches a certain critical mass, the supplier can begin to customise future responses to meet the specific needs of each customer (for example, Amazon's online service selects and recommends new books to its regular customers). Furthermore, by linking this knowledge to an organisation's manufacturing systems, the firm may be able to provide an almost instant response to a request for a customised product or service. Motorola, for example, having obtained a customer's stated specification for a pager, can transmit this to its manufacturing plant, produce the item and deliver it to the customer the next day.

Marshall Industries

Marshall Industries is the fourth largest distributor of electronic components and production supplies in the US. The company distributes 125,000 products, manufactured by over 100 suppliers, through 38 distribution branches in North America and Europe, through an equity share in SEI. Over 75 per cent of the company's sales are semiconductor products. For many years, the distribution of electronic components has been a highly competitive business with firms seeking to exploit competences in areas such as product availability, price, customer service, technical expertise and market coverage as attributes upon which to build customer loyalty. In the 1990s, the distribution business needed to respond to a new trend: large customers acting to globalise their business and demanding that their supplies acquire a global sourcing capability. At the same time, distributors were expected to take greater responsibility for managing the inventories of their large customers as these latter organisations move towards optimising their JIT manufacturing philosophies.

In reviewing the implications of all of these trends, Marshall Industries recognised that it had become a dysfunctional organisation, relying on out-dated assumptions upon which to base internal processes. This situation was exacerbated by a tendency for their distribution branches to operate independently of the firm's overall umbrella strategy (Young et al. 1997). The conclusion of the management was that the organisation had become fixated with maximising product sales to the detriment of the more critical goal of responding to the real needs of the customer. Its revised vision, enshrined in the phrase, 'Free, Perfect, Now', is based upon the reality that customers, if given the choice, want everything: products and services at the lowest cost, highest possible quality, maximum customisation and fastest possible delivery times. To fulfil its revised vision, the company recognised that (a) every sectoral and internal operating convention would have to be challenged, and (b) there was a need to embrace totally a philosophy of integrating all aspects of internal knowledge management with the systems being operated by their customers.

Some of the changes that were implemented were based upon conventional wisdom (for example, flattening the organisation to improve response times, and replacing the reward systems based upon individual merit with a system whereby employee bonuses are linked to overall company performance.) The company also examined how entrepreneurial approaches to the use of IT could result in acquiring market leadership in an e-commerce world. To achieve this goal, the company decided against huge investments in totally new systems. Instead, it opted for exploiting the entrepreneurial skills of its own workforce to find ways of linking together existing company IT systems using low-cost, commercially available products such as groupware platforms and client-servers. In 1992, for example, Marshall Industries launched QOBRA (quality order booking and resell application) based on an IBM-DB2 platform, an Internet/electronic data interchange (EDI) front end and a Sun-Unix warehouse transaction management system.

The next stage was to link together all the knowledge contained within the organisation so that the organisation could exploit internal knowledge management capabilities as a route by which to deliver superior levels of service to its customers. All field salespersons were equipped with laptop computers that enabled them to check inventory, product specifications, data sheets and orders in process in real time. The system also allowed the sales force to communicate with other employees who had specialist knowledge that might be used by the sales force in making presentations to customers. The core element of this Intranet system is Compass, which acts as a marketing encyclopedia containing over 2,500 documents about the product lines and suppliers for whom Marshall Industries act as a distributor.

In 1994, Marshall Industries began to implement the next phase of its strategy to become a superior knowledge provider by creating an online browser that provided customers with a 24-hour, automated order-fulfilment process system. This system was complimented by an EDI automatic replenishment channel for large customers plus a fax- and telephone-based order entry system. The following year, the company launched an object-relational database that provides customers with a dynamic picture of the products that Marshall Industries can supply. Behind the system is a database containing information on almost 200,000 parts, over 100,000 data sheets and a real-time inventory system. The site allows customers to order parts and request samples. To assist customers in tracking the progress of their orders, Marshall has linked its systems with that of its logistics partner, UPS.

The system offers an extensive range of additional knowledge provision services. RealAudio broadcasts news about the electronics industry. Visitors can also talk online to Marshall engineers 24 hours a day to obtain assistance in the selection of products, troubleshooting problems and product design. The NetSeminar element of the system links together customers and suppliers to assist in the design of new products. It also offers after-sales training on new technologies. From a studio in El Monte, the firm broadcasts product information in real-time video and audio streams. Viewers and listeners can pose questions to the presenters of these programmes using a GlobalChat system. The success of NetSeminar subsequently led the company to create a separate consulting business, called the Education News and Entertainment Network. This system permits clients to hold real-time seminars over the Internet for such purposes as publicity announcements, sales training and after-sales service.

ENTREPRENEURIAL INTERMEDIATION

The Marshall Industries case demonstrates how a fundamental change in the distribution structure of an industry can be created by an entrepreneurial firm adopting e-commerce ahead of its more conventional competitors. Over the next few years it can be expected that, as more organisations come to understand the opportunities offered by e-commerce, very significant changes in the role of the intermediary will occur within in virtually every market system around the world (Bloch et al. 1996). In some cases within the new systems, firms will take over functions traditionally undertaken by intermediaries. For example, United Airlines replaced the role of the travel agent by offering an online service providing timetables, fare information and a reservation system. However, Bloch et al. conclude that a more dynamic aspect of market system change will be the emergence of entrepreneurial intermediaries who will offer more effective buying services to the customer. They point out that when a customer contacts a single supplier, the customer receives only the information that is specific to that supplier. If a new player appears in the market offering to undertake a wider search of alternative offerings, by contacting this intermediary the customer can then rapidly evaluate which is the best purchase option relative to the various offerings being made by different suppliers.

Essentially, this scenario is an example of knowledge-based competition with the winner being that organisation which offers the most comprehensive knowledge management service to the customer. Some suppliers have clearly recognised this danger and have moved to create websites that contain comprehensive information about their product offering (for example, Dell Computers). Once this trend emerges with a sector, it will usually be followed by a knowledge war as suppliers seek to offer superior customer information services. Dell, for example, is currently experimenting with the entrepreneurial idea of installing television cameras on its production line so that customers can actually observe their computer order being assembled by the company.

Some firms initially enter the world of e-commerce in order to improve their own internal operations. For example, the lighting division of the GE corporation perceived e-commerce as a process that would permit further streamlining of its procurement system (Fabris 1997). GE Lighting's existing system involved its plants electronically placing requisitions that the company's purchasing agents would use to initiate the activities associated with acquiring quotes from suppliers. In many cases, the time taken from receipt of requisition to through issuing a specification and receiving a quote was in excess of 20 days. To overcome this problem, GE Lighting created a trading partners network (TPN). This consists of an IBM mainframe ordering system linked to Autoload, a Windows-based desktop tool that automatically posts the relevant component specification drawing on to an Internet site. Suppliers can then access this site and enter bids on TPN forms. By using TPN, GE Lighting cut procurement cycles in half and reduced procurement costs by 30 per cent. As this group and other divisions of GE acquired knowledge of e-commerce, the corporation realised that this new expertise represented an entrepreneurial business opportunity: opening up its procurement system to other manufacturers that want to use the Internet for procurement but lack in-house expertise. Having observed the power of network systems to reduce procurement costs, a number of the more entrepreneurial software vendors have now also entered the market, offering firms similar systems (for example, InfoBank and Commerce One).

For the entrepreneurially minded 'techie', instead of using one's expertise to design integrated ordering and supply chain software to build systems for customers, the alternative is to use this knowledge to launch a new business. This was the approach adopted by Cliff Sharples, President of the American corporation, Garden Escape. As a former IT consultant with Coopers & Lybrand, he looked around for an appropriate entrepreneurial opportunity and discovered the gardening supplies market (Fabris 1997). This $50 billion industry is highly fragmented, but because plants are highly persishable, it is quite difficult to acquire market dominance by attempting to manage sales through establishing a conventional retail superstore chain.

Garden Escape has a website that connects gardeners with plant suppliers. The company installs an e-mail system and Netscape browser on its suppliers' PCs along with customised inventory lists and order forms. Upon receipt of a customer order for plants on the Garden Escape website, the company e-mails the order to the supplier, who then ships the required plants. The customer receives a tracking number and can link into a Federal Express page to check on the whereabouts of the shipment. When Garden Escape is running low on a specific item, the order entry system informs the customer and, assuming that the relevant supplier has provided up-to-date information on when its next batch of plants will be ready, also informs the customer of the wait time he or she can expect if he or she wishes to place an order for the item that is in short supply. The system also has the capability automatically to recontact the customer when an item is back in stock.

The firms facing probably the greatest risk in the changing world of restructured market systems are those that have come to rely on an intermediary to provide knowledge management services. In the American banking industry, Intuit has attracted over 7 million users to its personal financial management software which links customers to 37 different banks, allowing them to get statements online, transfer money between accounts and pay bills. For those banks that have decided to link into Intuit instead of developing their own electronic banking platform, the risk must be, what happens if Intuit decides to open its own banking operation? Will customers stay with their current bank, or switch to the new Intuit bank?

Another aspect of intermediation is that conventional theories of competition, based on seeking to compete by achieving superiority over other firms at the same level within a market system, are now being replaced by firms coming together in new collaborative alliances in order to provide the infrastructures required to optimise customer satisfaction. For example, when Legoland UK decided to update the website at its theme park outside London, it selected the small, Cheshire-based firm, Interactive Developments Ltd (Bray 1999). Having determined the nature of the solution required by Legoland, the Cheshire firm then brought together three other organisations to complete the client solution: Microsoft, for the Internet server; UUNet of Cambridge, for Internet services; and NetBanx, also from Cambridge, to handle the technology required to accommodate online credit-card payments.

KNOWLEDGE NETWORKS

As organisations come to appreciate the value of acquiring new knowledge as the basis for gaining competitive advantage, new intra- and interorganisational structures are beginning to emerge to provide mechanisms for delivering new, more entrepreneurial business strategies. A common denominator shared by many of these initiatives, which are seeking to embed innovative responses to changing market opportunities, is the need to break down boundaries between areas of functional management, to replace an attitude of competing for scarce resources with an orientation directed towards fostering cooperation and to ensure the effective communication of information. Because of the 'spider's web' appearance of such forms of collaboration, 'knowledge networks' and 'learning networks' are the terms that have emerged to describe these new organisational forms.

There is growing evidence to suggest that the formation of a knowledge network is possibly the most effective way for a company facing the need to implement fundamental change to achieve the aim of enhancing entrepreneurial behaviour within the organisation. Some of the earliest evidence of this concept emerged from studies of simultaneous engineering in the car industry (Clark and Fujimoto 1991). This trend in car manufacturing is based on a shift away from functional, departmental structures towards a more integrated form of working. As is usually the case, the first exemplars were provided by the Japanese car companies such as Mazda, Honda and Toyota, that were seeking to both improve and accelerate new product development processes inside their respective organisations. The following four factors are critical to the success of these knowledge networks.

1. Co-location to engender social interchange between all parties involved in the development project.
2. Formalisation of cooperation procedures to ensure that cross-functional activities are implemented effectively.
3. Basing working practices around a team culture stressing the importance of shared responsibility.
4. Ensuring that the network remains in close contact with the 'voice of the customer' at all stages in the product development process.

Ford Europe attempted to replicate the concept, but encountered the massive obstacle that the deeply embedded functional, departmentalised structure initially resulted in a failure to establish a genuinely cooperative attitude between various groups within the organisation (Starkey and McKinley, 1996). The overall driving force for change was the need for Ford to develop new exciting vehicles in order to demolish the firm's image of being a conventional car producer. Under the project banner of Ford 2000, fundamental changes in structure have been implemented involving a move towards establishing a cross-functional, team-based matrix approach. Paralleling this move, the company has sought to achieve a fundamental shift in organisational values to create a learning environment in which employees pursue cooperation and integration instead of internal competition and separation. Clearly, the scale of actions associated with the move towards a networked approach to embedding knowledge management into the organisational culture means that it will take some years before the company can genuinely claim that simultaneous engineering is the new operational philosophy driving the organisation. However, early signs of success within Ford are demonstrated over recent years by the launch of the highly innovative Ford Ka and Ford Focus products.

Another approach to building knowledge networks is for an organisation to create a hub structure by becoming the central clearing house for knowledge. As shown in Figure 12.4, the role of the central organisation in this type of hub network is to bring together knowledge exchange between market system members such as suppliers, intermediaries and customers. As exemplified by the Marshall Industries case above, the creation of hub networks has been greatly assisted by the emergence of e-commerce technology within market systems, as organisations have sought ways of processing information more rapidly as the basis for seeking entrepreneurially to exploit new opportunities. The move by firms such as Marshall Industries, which involves replacing conventional, sequential assembly-line processes and linear information flows with integrated knowledge interchange systems, has been described by Norman and Ramirez (1993) as a 'value constellation' market system. The much strengthened trading position that can result from becoming a hub organisation does mean that over the next few years, it seems extremely probable that many entrepreneurial firms will seek to exploit their knowledge management capabilities to become the hub of their respective market system universe.

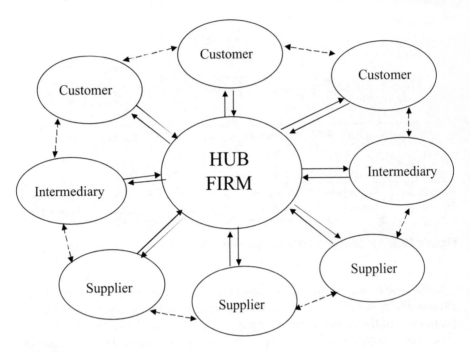

Figure 12.4   A hub knowledge network structure

A problem that faces many large OEMs is the need to become a more powerful guiding force in the development of new product forms and services. For manufacturing firms, this can only be achieved if they can find ways of reducing their involvement in component production and sub-system assembly work. Most OEMs are part of a market system that has relied heavily in the past on smaller firms to supply their needs for a diverse range of components and services. The more entrepreneurial OEMs have recognised that if they move away from adversarial, price-based procurement and act instead as a knowledge centre, this would permit them to delegate a larger proportion of the design and manufacturing of sub-assembly systems to their suppliers. This has resulted in cascading knowledge networks of the type illustrated in Figure 12.5. Within these networks, the OEM accepts the role for guiding and resourcing the learning process within its market system. This type of network has been created, for example, by aero-engine company Pratt & Whitney as a system for upgrading the ability of smaller firms on the Eastern Seaboard of the US to act as suppliers of specialist supplies to the company.

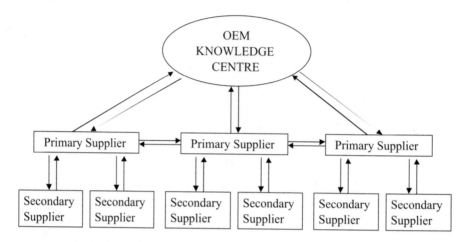

Figure 12.5   A cascade knowledge network

In the case of service firms, their aim is usually to develop new knowledge among their suppliers so that the latter are able to assume a greater proportion of the responsibility for managing additional aspects of the value chain. An example of this type of cascade network is provided by supermarket chains such as Tesco in the UK. These organisations are creating Internet sites that can be accessed by suppliers seeking knowledge on a whole range of issues, from manuals on store-level delivery policies through to examining stock movement at the individual store level. This latter information permits both the supplier and the supermarket to identify sales velocity rates and immediately to instigate actions to exploit changing consumer purchase trends.

A common constraint of small firms is that they often lack both key knowledge elements and the resources to execute entrepreneurial actions. One way to overcome this obstacle is to form a cooperative relationship with other like-minded firms to create a horizontal learning network. Examples include software firms coming together to acquire the ability to complete a systems integration project of the type described above in the Legoland case, manu-facturing firms seeking to acquire scale in the creation of a e-commerce trading system, and groups of independent retailers wishing to build an 'own brand' operation. The creation of such networks, as illustrated in Figure 12.6, is usually a four-phase process.

- Phase 1 – an idea is generated. The idea can come from a whole range of different sources, such as the firm itself, a trade association, a customer or a government agency involved in assisting the creation of small firm networks.
- Phase 2 – a series of meetings will occur as participants discuss the idea, refine their thinking and begin to evolve mutual trust and commitment. It is frequently the case during this phase that further research is needed to assist the discussions in progress.
- Phase 3 – an appropriate learning plan is crafted.
- Phase 4 – the network is formed and the agreed learning plan is implemented.

Another form of learning network is that created due to the formation of 'clusters' – geographic concentrations of firms involved in the production of goods and services for a specific industry sector. Clusters take numerous forms: some are concentrated at a single level (for example, a cluster of fish processing plants); others may consist of firms from various levels within a market system (for example, the footwear and fashion industry in Italy). These

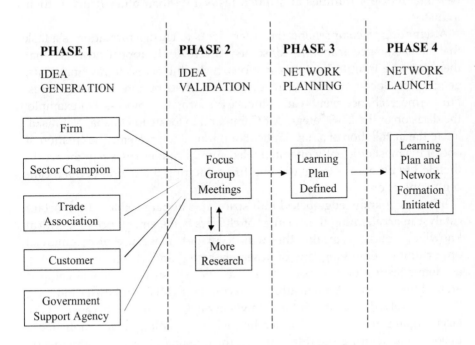

Figure 12.6 A process model for the formation of a horizontal knowledge network

structures have become of increasing interest to governments because it is now recognised that the creation and expansion of clusters can provide an effective mechanism through which to implement regional economic regeneration strategies (Porter 1996).

Much of the early writing on clusters tended to focus on the economic benefits offered, such as providing rapid, low-cost access to specialist inputs from local sources, higher productivity due to the existence of a pool of highly trained workers, and the opportunity to reduce operating costs through the sharing of common services such as distribution and marketing. However, there is now increasing evidence to suggest that one of the most powerful features of clusters is their ability to acquire and share knowledge, thereby assisting participant firms to become global leaders in innovation, able consistently to pre-empt their competitors elsewhere in the world. Cluster firms are also able to discern buyer trends faster than their more isolated competitors. Furthermore, having determined the nature of innovative opportunity, firms within the cluster have easy access to local sources of components, machinery and support services. The combined influence of these factors is the reason why, for example, IT companies based in Silicon Valley, California, and Austin, Texas, are able entrepreneurially to respond to new market opportunities at a much faster rate than other firms in their industry.

Attempting to comprehend the antecedents to cluster formation is a task that has challenged academics for some years. It would appear, however, that there can be a multitude of explanations, including access to raw materials, geographic location and well developed distribution infrastructures. Furthermore, chance events can influence the formation process. For example, the decision of the US Strategic Air Command to locate in Omaha, Nebraska, led to the installation of a fibre-optics communication system. The creation of one of the most efficiently operated telecommunications system in the world then led to numerous telemarketing firms entering the region to open call-centre operations.

In terms of knowledge-based industries, it is apparent that an important catalyst in accelerating the creation of clusters is the emergence of a critical knowledge mass. Typically, this will occur either because of commercial opportunities emerging out of research being undertaken in a leading academic institution (for example, the technology strip that has developed around the Massachusetts Institute of Technology (MIT), and the IT industry that has evolved around Stanford University in California) or because a very large organisation involved in leading-edge technology has established a major manufacturing site (for example, the opening of the Boeing plants on the West Coast of the US to build B-29 bombers in World War II) or because a new firm is created that is dramatically successful and grows into a major global player (for example, the heart pacemaker pioneer Medtronics in Minneapolis, and Microsoft in Seattle).

Some writers have suggested that the advent of the Internet and associated communication technologies will permit the emergence of virtual clusters linking together individual entrepreneurs and small entrepreneurial firms based anywhere in the world. In considering such predictions, it is necessary to note that most entrepreneurs are still social animals who find face-to-face interactions critical in terms of stimulating their thinking and causing the 'creative juices to flow'. Furthermore, it is also apparent that across different industrial sectors, entrepreneurs do appear to have lifestyle aspirations causing them to flock to certain locations (for example, the IT 'techies' love of California; yacht designers prefer to live in the South West of the UK; fashion designers are attracted to Paris or Milan). Thus, the emergence of virtual reality clusters may take somewhat longer than the time predicted by certain experts musing on the possible form the 'future world' will take.

What is certain, however, is that the Internet and associated technologies will continue to play a major role in enabling the more effective storage of information and the more rapid interchange of knowledge between interested parties within market systems. Thus, as the world moves into the twenty-first century, it can confidently be predicted that knowledge networks of various forms will become an increasingly dominant operational structure by which to ensure the effective management of entrepreneurial activities in both private and public sector organisations.

REFERENCES

Argyris, C. and Schon, D.A. (1978), *Organisational Learning: A Theory of Action Perspective*, Addison-Wesley, Reading, MA.

Ayas, K. (1996), 'Organisational learning and learning organisations for effective innovation management', Proceedings of the Symposium on Organisational Learning, Department of Management Learning, University of Lancaster, September, pp. 13–24.

Badger, B., Chaston, I. and Sadler-Smith, E. (1998), 'Developing small firms through managerial competence and organisational learning', Proceedings of the British Academy of Management Annual Conference, University of Nottingham, pp. 27–35.

Bateson, G. (1972), *Steps to an Ecology of Mind*, Ballantine Books, New York.

Bell, D. (1973), *The Coming of Post Industrial Society*, Basic Books, New York.

Berry, L.L. (1981), 'The employee as customer', *Journal of Retail Banking*, Vol. 2, pp. 25–8.

Bloch, M., Pigneur, A. and Segev, A. (1996), 'On the road to electronic commerce – a business value, framework, gaining competitive advantage and some research issues', http://www.stern.nyu.edu/-mbloch/docs/roadtoec/ec.html

Bray, P. (1999), 'Partners give on-line life', e-commerce special supplement, *Sunday Times*, p. 11.

Buzzel, R. and Ortmeyer, G. (1996), 'Channel partnerships streamline distribution', *Sloan Management Review*, Spring, pp. 41–53.

Christopher, M., Payne, A. and Ballatyne, D. (1991), *Relationship Marketing: Bringing Quality, Customer Service and Marketing Together*, Butterworth, London.

Clark, K. and Fujimoto, T. (1991), *Product Development Performance: Strategy, Organisation and Management in the World Autoindustry*, Harvard Business School Press, Boston, MA.

Cyert, R.M. and March, J.G. (1963), *A Behavioural Theory of the Firm*, Prentice Hall, Englewood Cliffs, NJ.

DiBella, A.J., Nevis, E.C. and Gould, J.M. (1996), 'Understanding organisational learning capability', *Journal of Management Studies*, Vol. 33, No. 3, pp. 361–79.

Easterby-Smith, M. (1997), 'Disciplines of organisational learning: contributions and critiques', *Human Relations*, Vol. 50, No. 9, pp. 1085–113.

Fabris, P. (1997), 'Electronic commerce', *CIO Magazine*, 15 June, pp. 23–6.

Fiol, C. and Lyles, M. (1985), 'Organisational learning', *Academy of Management Review*, Vol. 10, pp. 803–13.

Ford, D., Gadde, L., Hakansson, H., Lungren, A., Snehota, I., Turnbull, P. and Wilson, D. (1997), *Managing Business Relationships*, Wiley, Chichester.

Gronroos, C. (1997), 'Value-driven relational marketing: from products to resources and competencies', *Journal of Marketing Management*, Vol. 13, No. 5, pp. 407–20.

Hamel, G. and Prahalad, C.K. (1994), *Competing for the Future*, Harvard Business School Press, Boston, MA.

Huber, G.P. (1991), 'Organisational learning: the contributing processes and the literatures', *Organisation Science*, Vol. 2, pp. 88–115.

Kalwani, M.U. and Narayandas, N. (1995), 'Long-term supplier relationships; do they pay off for supplier firms', *Journal of Marketing*, Vol. 50, No. 1, pp. 1–16.

March, J.G. and Olsen, J.P. (1988), 'The uncertainty of the past', in March, J.G. (ed.), *Decisions and Organisations*, Blackwell, Oxford, pp. 62–74.

Moller, K. and Wilson, D. (1995), *Business Marketing: An Interaction and Network Perspectives*, Kluwer, Norwell, MA.

Nayak, P.R. and Ketteringham, J.M. (1986), *Breakthroughs!*, Rawson, New York.

Nevis, E.C., DiBella, A.J. and Gould, J.M (1995), 'Understanding organisations as learning systems', *Sloan Management Review*, Vol. 36, Winter, pp. 73–85.

Nonaka, I. (1991), 'The knowledge-creating company', *Harvard Business Review*, November–December, pp. 97–104.

Norman, R. and Ramirez, R. (1993), 'From value chain to value constellation', *Harvard Business Review*, July–August, pp. 65–77.

Nystrom, P.C. and Starbuck, W.H. (1984), 'To avoid organisational crisis, unlearn', *Organisational Dynamics*, Vol. 12, No. 4, pp. 53–66.

Porter, M. (1996), *On Competition*, Harvard Business School Press, Boston, MA.

Schein, E.H. (1996), 'Three cultures of management: the key to organisational learning', *Sloan Management Review*, Vol. 37, Fall, pp. 9–20.

Senge, P. (1990), *The Fifth Discipline: The Art and Practice of the Learning Organisation*, Doubleday, New York.

Slater, S.F. and Narver, J.C. (1994), 'Does competitive environment moderate the market orientation-performance relationship?', *Journal of Marketing*, Vol. 58, January, pp. 46–55.

Starkey, K. and McKinley, A. (1996), 'Product development in Ford of Europe', in Starkey, K. (ed.), *How Organisations Learn*, Thompson Business Press, London, pp. 214–29.

Woodruff, R.B. (1977), 'Customer value: the next source of competitive advantage', *Journal of the Academy of Marketing Science*, Vol. 25, No. 2, pp. 139–53.

Young, K.M., El Sawy, O.A., Malhotra, A. and Gosain, S. (1997), 'The relentless pursuit of "Free Perfect Now": IT enabled value innovation at Marshall Industries', 1997 SIM International Papers Award Competition, http://www.simnet.ord/public/programs/capital/97papers/paper1.html

INDEX